"Johann Hari writes like a dream. He's both a lyricist and a storyteller—but also an indefatigable investigator of one of the world's greatest problems: the systematic destruction of our attention. Read this book to save your mind."

—Susan Cain

"I don't know anyone thinking more deeply, or more holistically, about the crisis of our collective attention than Johann Hari. This book could not be more vital. Please sit with it, and focus."

—Naomi Klein

"Where other books about our relationship to technology tend to focus on personal responsibility, stressing the importance of self-control, *Stolen Focus* takes a step back and examines the ecosystem that created the problem. . . . Hari's writing is incredibly readable."

—*San Francisco Chronicle*

"Big-name websites and apps strive to distract because that's the key to profitability. When we're looking at our screens, these companies make money; when we're not, they don't. . . . It's a call to arms, to be sure, and I'm tempted to tell my Twitter followers about it—but I've deleted the app from my phone."

—*The Washington Post*

"[A] well-researched survey draw[ing] attention to important concerns while avoiding simplistic self-improvement recommendations . . . Some of the chapters are inspiring, such as the one that focuses on the concept of flow, the type of concentration that leads to an almost hypnotic state, where time melts away and thought is inhabited. Even just focusing on focus for this much time is useful, and ends up giving the reader a novel and worthwhile way of measuring our quality of attention."

—*The New York Times Book Review*

"Set to be a surefire hit, fans of Hari's new book include Stephen Fry, Naomi Klein, and Hillary Clinton."

—Insider

"If your New Year's resolution was to be more focused this year, then this is the book for you."

—Inc.

"A gripping analysis of why we've lost the capacity to concentrate, and how we might find it again. . . . *Stolen Focus* won't just capture your attention—it will keep you thinking and rethinking long after you've finished it. Johann Hari is one of the most insightful critics of our modern malaise, and he's written the book the world needs in order to win the war on distraction."

—Adam Grant

"Superb . . . *Stolen Focus* is a beautifully researched and argued exploration of the breakdown of humankind's ability to pay attention, told with the pace, sparkle, and energy of the best kind of thriller."

—Stephen Fry

"If you want to get your attention and focus back, you need to read this remarkable book. Johann Hari has cracked the code of why we're in this crisis, and how to get out of it. We all need to hear this message."

—Arianna Huffington

"In his unique voice, Johann Hari tackles the profound dangers facing humanity from information technology and rings the alarm bell for what all of us must do to protect ourselves, our children, and our democracies."

—Hillary Clinton

"A visionary, systemic, revolutionary, and practical guide for creating the new world . . . Through his tireless research and genius insight, Johann Hari certainly snapped me to attention. This is a life-changing book."

—Eve Ensler

"A necessary book, a miracle of clarity and depth, and a resonant, deeply researched warning, followed by a truly inspiring clarion call to action . . . Read it and weep, then dry your eyes and join in."

—Emma Thompson

"[A] provocative study . . . a comprehensive and chilling lay of the land."

—*Publishers Weekly*

BY JOHANN HARI

FOCUS **STOLEN FOCUS** STOLEN

CROWN
NEW YORK

STOLEN FOCUS

WHY YOU CAN'T PAY ATTENTION—
AND HOW TO THINK DEEPLY AGAIN

JOHANN HARI

Published in the United States by Crown, an imprint of Random House,
a division of Penguin Random House LLC, New York.

CROWN and the Crown colophon are registered trademarks of
Penguin Random House LLC.

Originally published in hardcover in Great Britain by Bloomsbury Publishing Plc,
London, and subsequently in the United States by Crown, an imprint of
Random House, a division of Penguin Random House LLC, in 2022.

Library of Congress Cataloging-in-Publication Data
Names: Hari, Johann, author.
Title: Stolen focus / Johann Hari.
Description: First edition. | New York: Crown, 2022 | Includes bibliographical
references and index.
Identifiers: LCCN 2021040207 (print) | LCCN 2021040208 (ebook) |
ISBN 9780593138533 (paperback) | ISBN 9780593138526 (ebook)
Subjects: LCSH: Attention. | Distraction (Psychology)
Classification: LCC BF321 .H287 2021 (print) | LCC BF321 (ebook) |
DDC 153.7/33—dc23
LC record available at https://lccn.loc.gov/2021040207

Printed in the United States of America on acid-free paper

crownpublishing.com

9

Book design by Susan Turner

For my grandmothers, Amy McRae and Lydia Hari

I have posted audio clips of all the people I quote in this book on its website, so as you read this book, you can listen along to our conversations. Go to stolenfocusbook.com/audio.

CONTENTS

FOCUS **STOLEN FOCUS** STOLEN

Walking in Memphis

When he was nine years old, my godson developed a brief but freakishly intense obsession with Elvis Presley. He took to singing "Jailhouse Rock" at the top of his voice, with all the low crooning and pelvis-jiggling of the King himself. He didn't know this style had become a joke, so he offered it with all the heart-catching sincerity of a preteen who believes he is being cool. In the brief pauses before he started singing it all over again, he demanded to know everything ("Everything! Everything!") about Elvis, and so I jabbered out the rough outline of that inspiring, sad, stupid story.

Elvis was born in one of the poorest towns in Mississippi— a place far, far away, I said. He arrived in the world alongside his twin brother, who died a few minutes later. As he grew up, his mother told him that if he sang to the moon every night, his brother could hear his voice, so he sang and sang. He began to perform in public just as television was taking off—so in a sudden swoosh, he became more famous than anyone had ever been before. Everywhere Elvis went, people would scream, until his world became a chamber of screams. He retreated into a cocoon of his own construction, where he gloried in his possessions in place of his lost freedom. For his mother he bought a palace and named it Graceland.

I skimmed through the rest—the descent into addiction, the sweating, girning stage-jammering in Vegas, the death at the age of forty-two. Whenever my godson, who I'll call Adam—I've changed some details here to avoid identifying him—asked questions about how the story ended, I got him to duet "Blue Moon" with me instead. "You saw me standing alone," he sang in his little voice, "without a dream in my heart. Without a love of my own."

One day, Adam looked at me very earnestly and asked: "Johann, will you take me to Graceland one day?" Without really thinking, I agreed. "Do you promise? Do you really promise?" I said I did. And I never gave it another thought, until everything had gone wrong.

∾

Ten years later, Adam was lost. He had dropped out of school when he was fifteen, and he spent literally almost all his waking hours at home alternating blankly between screens—his phone, an infinite scroll of WhatsApp and Facebook messages, and his iPad, on which he watched a blur of YouTube and porn. At moments, I could still see in him traces of the joyful little boy who sang "Viva Las Vegas," but it was like that person had broken into smaller, disconnected fragments. He struggled to stay with a topic of conversation for more than a few minutes without jerking back to a screen or abruptly switching to another topic. He seemed to be whirring at the speed of Snapchat, somewhere where nothing still or serious could reach him. He was intelligent, decent, kind—but it was like nothing could gain any traction in his mind.

During the decade in which Adam had become a man, this fracturing seemed to be happening—to some degree—to many of us. The sensation of being alive in the early twenty-first century consisted of the sense that our ability to pay attention—to focus—was cracking and breaking. I could feel it happen to me—I would buy piles of books, and I would glimpse them guiltily from the corner of my eye as I sent, I told myself, just *one* more tweet. I still read a lot, but with each year that passed, it felt more and more like running up a down escalator. I had just turned forty, and wherever my generation gathered, we would lament our lost capacity for concentration, as if it was a friend who had vanished one day at sea and never been seen since.

Then one evening, as we lay on a large sofa, each staring at our own ceaselessly shrieking screens, I looked at Adam and felt a low dread. We can't live like this, I said to myself.

"Adam," I said softly. "Let's go to Graceland."

"What?"

I reminded him of the promise I had made to him so many years before. He couldn't even remember those "Blue Moon" days, nor my pledge to him, but I could see that the idea of breaking this numbing routine ignited something in him. He looked up at me and asked if I was serious. "I am," I said, "but there's one condition. I'll pay for us to go four thousand miles. We'll go to Memphis, and New Orleans— we'll go all over the South, anywhere you want. But I can't do it if, when we get there, all you're going to do is stare at your phone. You have to promise to leave it switched off except at night. We have to return to reality. We have to reconnect with something that matters to us." He swore he would, and a few weeks later, we lifted off from London Heathrow, toward the land of the Delta blues.

⁓

When you arrive at the gates of Graceland, there is no longer a human being whose job is to show you around. You are handed an iPad, and you put in little earbuds, and the iPad tells you what to do—turn left; turn right; walk forward. In each room, the iPad, in the voice of some forgotten actor, tells you about the room you are in, and a photograph of it appears on the screen. So we walked around Graceland alone, staring at the iPad. We were surrounded by Canadians and Koreans and a whole United Nations of blank-faced people, looking down, seeing nothing around them. Nobody was looking for long at anything but their screens. I watched them as we walked, feeling more and more tense. Occasionally somebody would look away from the iPad and I felt a flicker of hope, and I would try to make eye contact with them, to shrug, to say, Hey, we're the only ones looking around, we're the ones who traveled thousands of miles and decided to actually see the things in front of us—but every time this happened, I realized they had broken contact with the iPad only to take out their phones and snap a selfie.

When we got to the Jungle Room—Elvis's favorite place in the mansion—the iPad was chattering away when a middle-aged man standing next to me turned to say something to his wife. In front of us, I could see the large fake plants that Elvis had bought to turn this room into his own artificial jungle. The fake plants were still there, sagging sadly. "Honey," he said, "this is amazing. Look." He waved the iPad in her direction, and then began to move his finger across it. "If you swipe left, you can see the Jungle Room to the left. And if you swipe right, you can see the Jungle Room to the right." His wife stared, smiled, and began to swipe at her own iPad.

I watched them. They swiped back and forth, looking at the different dimensions of the room. I leaned forward. "But, sir," I said, "there's an old-fashioned form of swiping you can do. It's called turning your head. Because we're here. We're in the Jungle Room. You don't have to see it on your screen. You can see it unmediated. Here. Look." I waved my hand at it, and the fake green leaves rustled a little.

The man and his wife backed away from me a few inches. "Look!" I said, in a louder voice than I intended. "Don't you see? We're *there*. We're *actually there*. There's no need for your screen. *We are in the Jungle Room.*" They hurried out of the room, glancing back at me with a who's-that-loon shake of the head, and I could feel my heart beating fast. I turned to Adam, ready to laugh, to share the irony with him, to release my anger—but he was in a corner, holding his phone under his jacket, flicking through Snapchat.

At every stage in this trip, he had broken his promise. When the plane first touched down in New Orleans two weeks before, he immediately took out his phone, while we were still in our seats. "You promised not to use it," I said. He replied: "I meant I wouldn't make phone calls. I can't not use Snapchat and texting, obviously." He said this with baffled honesty, as if I had asked him to hold his breath for ten days. I watched him scrolling through his phone in the Jungle Room silently. Milling past him was a stream of people also staring at their screens. I felt as alone as if I had been standing in an empty Iowa cornfield, miles from another human. I strode up to Adam and snatched his phone from his grasp.

"We can't live like this!" I said. "You don't know how to be present! You are missing your life! You're afraid of missing out—that's why you are checking your screen all the time! By doing that, you are *guaranteeing* you are missing out! You are missing your one and only life! You can't see the things that are *right in front of you,* the things you have been longing to see since you were a little boy! None of these people can! *Look at them!*"

I was talking loudly, but in their iPad iSolation, most people around us didn't even notice. Adam snatched his phone back from me, told me (not without some justification) that I was acting like a freak, and stomped away, out past Elvis's grave, and into the Memphis morning.

I spent hours walking listlessly between Elvis's various Rolls-Royces, which are displayed in the adjoining museum, and finally I found Adam again as night fell in the Heartbreak Hotel across the street, where we were staying. He was sitting next to the swimming pool, which was shaped like a giant guitar, and as Elvis sang in a 24/7 loop over this scene, he looked sad. I realized as I sat with him that, like all the most volcanic anger, my rage toward him—which had been spitting out throughout this trip—was really anger toward myself. His inability to focus, his constant distraction, the inability of the people at Graceland to see the place to which they had traveled, was something I felt rising within myself. I was fracturing like they were fracturing. I was losing my ability to be present too. And I hated it.

"I know something's wrong," Adam said to me softly, holding his phone tightly in his hand. "But I have no idea how to fix it." Then he went back to texting.

$\backsim$

I took Adam away to escape our inability to focus—and what I found was that there was no escape, because this problem was everywhere. I traveled all over the world to research this book, and there was almost no respite. Even when I took time out from my research to go to see some of the world's most famously chill and tranquil places, I found it waiting for me.

One afternoon, I sat in the Blue Lagoon in Iceland, a vast and infinitely calm lake of geothermal water that bubbles up at the temperature of a hot bathtub even as snow falls all around you. As I watched the falling snowflakes gently dissolve into the rising steam, I realized I was surrounded by people wielding selfie sticks. They had put their phones into waterproof casings, and they were frantically posing and posting. Several of them were livestreaming to Instagram. I wondered if the motto for our era should be: I tried to live, but I got distracted. This thought was interrupted by a ripped German, who looked like an influencer, bellowing into his camera phone: "Here I am in the Blue Lagoon, living my best life!"

Another time, I went to see the *Mona Lisa* in Paris, only to find she is now permanently hidden behind a rugby scrum of people from everywhere on earth, all jostling their way to the front, only for them to immediately turn their backs on her, snap a selfie, and fight their way out again. On the day I was there, I watched the crowd from the side for more than an hour. Nobody—not one person—looked at the *Mona Lisa* for more than a few seconds. Her smile no longer seems like an enigma. It appears as though she is looking at us from her perch in sixteenth-century Italy and asking us: Why won't you just look at me like you used to?

~

This seemed to fit with a much wider sense that had been settling on me for several years—one that went well beyond bad tourist habits. It felt like our civilization had been covered with itching powder, and we spent our time twitching and twerking our minds, unable to simply give attention to things that matter. Activities that require longer forms of focus—like reading a book—have been in free fall for years. After my trip with Adam, I read the work of the leading scientific specialist on willpower in the world, a man named Professor Roy Baumeister, who is based at the University of Queensland in Australia, and then I went to interview him. He had been studying the science of willpower and self-discipline for more than thirty years, and he is responsible for some of the most famous experiments ever carried out in the social sciences. As I sat down opposite the sixty-six-year-old, I explained I was thinking of writing a book about why we seem to have lost our sense of focus, and how we can get it back. I looked to him hopefully.

It was curious, he said, that I should bring up this topic with him. "I'm feeling like my control over my attention is weaker than it used to be," he said. He used to be able to sit for hours, reading and writing, but now "it seems like my mind jumps around a lot more." He explained that he had realized recently that "when I start to feel bad, I'd play a video game on my phone, and then that got to be fun." I pictured him turning away from his enormous body of scientific achievement to play Candy Crush Saga. He said: "I can see that I am not sustaining concentration in perhaps the way I used to." He added: "I'm just sort of giving in to it, and will start to feel bad."

Roy Baumeister is literally the author of a book named *Willpower,* and he has studied this subject more than anyone else alive. If even he is losing some of his ability to focus, I thought, who isn't it happening to?

∽

For a long time I reassured myself by saying this crisis was really just an illusion. Previous generations felt their attention and focus were getting worse too—you can read medieval monks nearly a millennium ago complaining that they were suffering from attention problems of their own. As human beings get older, they can focus less, and they become convinced that this is a problem with the world and with the next generation, rather than with their own failing minds.

The best way to know for sure would be if scientists, starting years ago, had done something simple. They could have given attention tests to random members of the public, and continued doing the same test for years and decades to track any changes that took place. But nobody did that. That long-term information was never gathered. There is, however, a different way I think we can reach a reasonable conclusion about this. As I researched this book, I learned that there are all sorts of factors that have been scientifically proven to reduce people's ability to pay attention. There is strong evidence that many of these factors have been rising in the past few decades— sometimes dramatically. Against this, there's only one trend I could find that might have been improving our attention. That's why I came to believe that this is a real crisis, and an urgent one.

I also learned that the evidence about where these trends are taking us is stark. For example, a small study investigated how often an average American college student actually pays attention to anything, so the scientists involved put tracking software on their computers and monitored what they did in a typical day. They discovered that, on average, a student would switch tasks once every sixty-five seconds. The median amount of time they focused on any one thing was just nineteen seconds. If you're an adult and tempted to feel superior, hold off. A different study by Gloria Mark, professor of informatics at the University of California, Irvine—who I interviewed—observed how long on average an adult working in an office stays on one task. It was three minutes.

So I went on a 30,000-mile journey to find out how we can get our focus and attention back. In Denmark I interviewed the first scientist who has, with his team, shown that our collective ability to pay attention really is rapidly shrinking. Then I met with scientists all over the world who have discovered why. In the end, I interviewed over 250 experts—from Miami to Moscow, from Montreal to Melbourne. My quest for answers took me to a crazy mixture of places, from a favela in Rio de Janeiro, where attention had shattered in a particularly disastrous way, to a remote office in a small town in New Zealand, where they had found a way to radically restore focus.

I came to believe that we have profoundly misunderstood what is actually happening to our attention. For years, whenever I couldn't focus, I would angrily blame myself. I would say: You're lazy, you're undisciplined, you need to pull yourself together. Or I would blame my phone, and rage against it, and wish it had never been invented. Most of the people I know respond the same way. But I learned that in fact something much deeper than personal failure, or a single new invention, is happening here.

I first began to glimpse this when I went to Portland, Oregon, to interview Professor Joel Nigg, who is one of the leading experts in the world on children's attention problems. He said it might help me grasp what's happening if we compare our rising attention problems to our rising obesity rates. Fifty years ago there was very little obesity, but today it is endemic in the Western world. This is not because we suddenly became greedy or self-indulgent. He said: "Obesity is not a medical epidemic—it's a social epidemic. We have bad food, for example, and so people are getting fat." The way we live changed dramatically—our food supply changed, and we built cities that are hard to walk or bike around—and those changes in our environment led to changes in our bodies. Something similar, he said, may be happening with the changes in our attention and focus.

He told me that after studying this topic for decades, he believes we need to ask if we are now developing "an attentional pathogenic culture"—an environment in which sustained and deep focus is extremely hard for all of us, and you have to swim upstream to achieve it. There's scientific evidence for many factors in poor attention, he said, and for some people there are some causes that lie in their biology, but he told me what we may also need to figure out: Is "our society driving people to this point so often, because we have an epidemic [that's being] caused by specific things that are dysfunctional in our society?"

Later I asked him—if I put you in charge of the world, and you *wanted* to ruin people's ability to pay attention, what would you do? He thought about it for a moment, and said: "Probably about what our society is doing."

I found strong evidence that our collapsing ability to pay attention is not primarily a personal failing on my part, or your part, or your kid's part. This is being done to us all. It is being done by very powerful forces. Those forces include Big Tech, but they also go way beyond them. This is a systemic problem. The truth is that you are living in a system that is pouring acid on your attention every day, and then you are being told to blame yourself and to fiddle with your own habits while the world's attention burns. I realized, when I learned all this, that there is a hole in all the existing books I had read about how to improve your focus. It was huge. They have, on the whole, neglected to talk about the actual causes of our attention crisis— which lie mainly in these larger forces. Based on what I learned, I have concluded there are twelve deep forces at work that are damaging our attention. I came to believe we can only solve this problem in the long term if we understand them—and then, together, we stop them from continuing to do this to us.

There are real steps you can take as an isolated individual to reduce this problem for yourself, and throughout this book you'll learn how to carry them out. I am strongly in favor of you seizing personal responsibility in this way. But I have to be honest with you, in a way that I fear previous books on this topic were not. Those changes will only get you so far. They will solve a slice of the problem. They are valuable. I do them myself. But unless you are very lucky, they won't allow you to escape the attention crisis. Systemic problems require systemic solutions. We have to take individual responsibility for this problem, for sure, but at the same time, together, we have to take collective responsibility for dealing with these deeper factors. There is a real solution—one that will actually make it possible for us to start to heal our attention. It requires us to radically reframe the problem, and then to take action. I believe I have figured out how we might start to do that.

∿

There are, I think, three crucial reasons why it is worth coming on this journey with me. The first is that a life full of distractions is, at an individual level, diminished. When you are unable to pay sustained attention, you can't achieve the things you want to achieve. You want to read a book, but you are pulled away by the pings and paranoias of social media. You want to spend a few uninterrupted hours with your child, but you keep anxiously checking your email to see if your boss is messaging you. You want to set up a business, but your life dissolves instead into a blur of Facebook posts that only make you feel envious and anxious. Through no fault of your own, there never seems to be enough stillness—enough cool, clear space—for you to stop and think. A study by Professor Michael Posner at the University of Oregon found that if you are focusing on something and you get interrupted, on average it will take twenty-three minutes for you to get back to the same state of focus. A different study of office workers in the U.S. found most of them *never* get an hour of uninterrupted work in a typical day. If this goes on for months and years, it scrambles your ability to figure out who you are and what you want. You become lost in your own life.

When I went to Moscow to interview the most important philosopher of attention in the world today, Dr. James Williams—who works on the philosophy and ethics of technology at Oxford University—he told me: "If we want to do what matters in any domain—any context in life—we have to be able to give attention to the right things. . . .

If we can't do that, it's really hard to do anything." He said that if we want to understand the situation we are in at the moment, it helps to picture something. Imagine you are driving a car, but somebody has thrown a big bucket of mud all over the windshield. You're going to face a lot of problems in that moment—you are at risk of knocking off your rearview mirror, or getting lost, or arriving at your destination late. But the first thing you need to do—before you worry about any of those problems—is clean your windshield. Until you do that, you don't even know where you are. We need to deal with our attention problems before we try to achieve any other sustained goal.

The second reason we need to think about this subject is that this fracturing of attention isn't just causing problems for us as individuals—it's causing crises in our whole society. As a species, we are facing a slew of unprecedented tripwires and trapdoors—like the climate crisis—and, unlike previous generations, we are mostly not rising to solve our biggest challenges. Why? Part of the reason, I think, is that when attention breaks down, problem-solving breaks down. Solving big problems requires the sustained focus of many people over many years. Democracy requires the ability of a population to pay attention long enough to identify real problems, distinguish them from fantasies, come up with solutions, and hold their leaders accountable if they fail to deliver them. If we lose that, we lose our ability to have a fully functioning society. I don't think it's a coincidence that this crisis in paying attention has taken place at the same time as the worst crisis of democracy since the 1930s. People who can't focus will be more drawn to simplistic authoritarian solutions—and less likely to see clearly when they fail. A world full of attention-deprived citizens alternating between Twitter and Snapchat will be a world of cascading crises where we can't get a handle on any of them.

The third reason we need to think deeply about focus is, for me, the most hopeful. If we understand what's happening, we can begin to change it. The writer James Baldwin—the man who is, for my money, the greatest writer of the twentieth century—said: "Not everything that is faced can be changed, but nothing can be changed until it is faced." This crisis is human-made, and it can be unmade by us too. I want to tell you right at the start how I gathered the evidence I'm going to present to you in this book, and why I selected it. In my research, I read a very large number of scientific studies, and then I went to interview the scientists who I thought had gathered the most important evidence. Several different kinds of scientists have studied attention and focus. One group is neuroscientists, and you'll hear from them. But the people who have done the most work on why it is changing are social scientists, who analyze how changes in the way we live affect us, both as individuals and as groups. I studied social and political sciences at Cambridge University, where I got a rigorous training in how to read the studies these scientists publish, how to assess the evidence they put forward, and—I hope—how to ask probing questions about it.

These scientists often disagree with each other about what is happening and why. This isn't because the science is rickety but because humans are extremely complex, and it's really hard to measure something as complicated as what affects our ability to pay attention. This obviously presented a challenge to me as I wrote this book. If we wait for perfect evidence, we will be waiting forever. I had to proceed, doing my best, on the basis of the best information we have—while always being conscious that this science is fallible and fragile and needs to be handled with care.

So I have tried, at every stage in this book, to give you a sense of how controversial the evidence I am offering is. On some of the topics, the subject has been studied by hundreds of scientists, and they have achieved a broad consensus that the points I am going to put forward are correct. That's obviously the ideal, and wherever it was possible, I sought out scientists who represent a consensus in their field and built my conclusions on the solid rocks of their knowledge. But there are some other areas where only a handful of scientists have studied the question I wanted to understand, and so the evidence I can draw on is thinner. There are a few other topics where different reputable scientists strongly disagree about what's really going on. In those cases, I am going to tell you up front, and try to represent a range of perspectives on the question. At every stage I have tried to build my conclusions on the strongest evidence I could find.

I have tried to always approach this process with humility. I'm not an expert on any of these questions. I'm a journalist, approaching experts, and testing and explaining their knowledge as best I can. If you want more detail on these debates, I delve much deeper into the evidence in the more than 400 endnotes I have put on the book's website, discussing the more than 250 scientific studies I have drawn on in this book. I have also sometimes used my own experiences to help explain what I learned. My individual anecdotes obviously aren't scientific evidence. They tell you something simpler: why I wanted to know the answers to these questions so badly.

∽

When I came back from my trip to Memphis with Adam, I was appalled at myself. One day, I spent three hours reading the same first few pages of a novel, getting lost in distracted thoughts every time, almost as though I was stoned, and I thought—I can't continue like this. Reading fiction had always been one of my greatest pleasures, and losing it would be like losing a limb. I announced to my friends that I was going to do something drastic.

I thought this was happening to me because I wasn't disciplined enough as an individual, and because I had been taken over by my phone. So at the time, I thought the solution was obvious: be more disciplined and banish your phone. I went online and booked myself a little room by the beach in Provincetown, at the tip of Cape Cod. I am going to be there for three months, I announced triumphantly to everyone, with no smartphone, and no computer that can get online. I'm done. I'm through. For the first time in twenty years, I'm going offline. I talked to my friends about the double meaning of the word "wired." It means both being in a manic, hyper mental state, and

being online. They seemed to me to be tied together, these twin defi-
nitions. I was tired of being wired. I needed to clear my head. And
so I did it. I quit. I set up an auto-reply saying I would be unreach-
able for the next three months. I abandoned the buzz in which I had
vibrated for twenty years.

I tried to go into this extreme digital detox without any illusions. I
knew this ditching of the entire internet couldn't be a long-term solution for me—I wasn't going to join the Amish and abandon technology forever. Even more than that, I knew this approach couldn't even
be a short-term solution for most people. I come from a working-
class family—my grandmother, who raised me, cleaned toilets; my
dad was a bus driver—and saying to them that the solution to their
attention problems would be to quit their jobs and go and live in a
shack by the sea would be a spiteful insult: they literally couldn't
do it.

I did it because I thought that if I didn't, I might lose some crucial aspects of my ability to think deeply. I did it in desperation. And
I did it because I felt that if I stripped everything back for a time,
I might start to be able to glimpse the changes we could all make
in a more sustainable way. This drastic digital detox taught me a
lot of important things—including, as you'll see, the limits of digital
detoxes.

It began on a morning in May when I set off for Provincetown,
with the glare of the screens of Graceland haunting me. I thought
the problem was in my own distractible nature and in our tech, and
I was about to give my devices away—freedom, oh freedom!—for a
long, long time.

CHAPTER ONE

Cause One: The Increase in Speed, Switching, and Filtering

don't understand what you're asking for," the man in Target in Boston kept saying to me. "These are the cheapest phones we got. They have super-slow internet. That's what you want, right?" No, I said. I want a phone that can't access the internet at all. He studied the back of the box, looking confused. "This would be really slow. You could probably get your email but you wouldn't—" Email is still the internet, I said. I am going away for three months, specifically so I can be totally offline.

My friend Imtiaz had already given me his old, broken laptop, one that had lost the ability to get online years before. It looked like it came from the set of the original *Star Trek*, a remnant from some aborted vision of the future. I was going to use it, I had resolved, to finally write the novel I had been planning for years. Now what I needed was a phone where I could be called in emergencies by the six people I was going to give the number to. I needed it to have no internet option of any kind, so that if I woke up at 3 a.m. and my resolve cracked and I tried to get online, I wouldn't be able to do it, no matter how hard I tried.

When I explained to people what I was planning, I would get one of three responses. The first was just like that of this man in Target: they couldn't seem to process what I was saying; they thought I was saying that I was going to cut back on my internet use. The idea of going offline completely seemed to them so bizarre that I had to explain it again and again. "So you want a phone that can't go online *at all?*" he said. "Why would you want that?"

The second response—which this man offered next—was a kind of low-level panic on my behalf. "What will you do in an emergency?" he asked. "It doesn't seem right." I asked: What emergency will require me to get online? What's going to happen? I'm not the president of the United States—I don't have to issue orders if Russia invades Ukraine. "Anything," he said. "Anything could happen." I kept explaining to the people my age—I was thirty-nine at the time—that we had spent half our lives without phones, so it shouldn't be so hard to picture returning to the way we had lived for so long. Nobody seemed to find this persuasive.

And the third response was envy. People began to fantasize about what they would do with all the time they spent on their phones if it was all suddenly freed up. They started by listing the number of hours that Apple's Screen Time option told them they spent on their phones every day. For the average American, it's three hours and fifteen minutes. We touch our phones 2,617 times every twenty-four hours. Sometimes they would wistfully mention something they loved and had abandoned—playing the piano, say—and stare off into the distance.

Target had nothing for me. Ironically, I had to go online to order what seemed to be the last remaining cellphone in the United States that can't access the web. It's called the Jitterbug. It's designed for extremely old people, and it doubles as a medical emergency device. I opened the box and smiled at its giant buttons and told myself that there's an added bonus: if I fall over, it will automatically connect me to the nearest hospital.

I laid out on the hotel bed everything I was taking with me. I had gone through all the routine things I normally use my iPhone for, and bought objects to replace each one. So for the first time since I was a teenager, I bought a watch. I got an alarm clock. I dug out my old iPod and loaded it with audiobooks and podcasts, and I ran my finger along its screen, thinking about how futuristic this gadget seemed to me when I bought it twelve years ago; now it looked like something that Noah might have carried onto the Ark. I had Imtiaz's broken laptop—now rendered, effectively, into a 1990s-style word processor—and next to it I had a pile of classic novels I had been meaning to read for decades, with *War and Peace* at the top.

I took an Uber so I could hand over my iPhone and my MacBook to a friend who lived in Boston. I hesitated before putting them on the table in her house. Quickly, I pushed a button on my phone to summon a car to take me to the ferry terminal, and then I switched it off and walked away from it fast, like it might come running after me. I felt a twinge of panic. I'm not ready for this, I thought. Then somewhere, from the back of my mind, I remembered something the Spanish writer José Ortega y Gasset said: "We cannot put off living until we are ready. . . . Life is fired at us point-blank." If you don't do this now, I told myself, you'll never do it, and you'll be lying on your deathbed seeing how many likes you got on Instagram. I climbed into the car and refused to look back.

I had learned years before from social scientists that when it comes to beating any kind of destructive habit, one of the most effective tools we have is called "pre-commitment." It's right there in one of the oldest surviving human stories, Homer's *Odyssey*. Homer tells of how there was once a patch of sea that sailors would always die in, for a strange reason: living in the ocean, there were two sirens— a uniquely hot blend of woman and fish—who would sing to the sailors to join them in the ocean. Then, when they clambered in for some sexy fish-based action, they'd drown. But then, one day, the hero of the story—Ulysses—figured out how to beat these tempt-resses. Before the ship approached the sirens' stretch of sea, he got his crew members to tie him to the mast, hard, hand and foot. He couldn't move. When he heard the sirens, no matter how much Ulysses yearned to dive in, he couldn't.

I had used this technique before when I was trying to lose weight. I used to buy loads of carbs and tell myself I would be strong enough to eat them slowly and in moderation, but then I would guzzle them at 2 a.m. So I stopped buying them. At 2 a.m., I wasn't going to haul myself to a store to buy Pringles. The you that exists in the present—right now—wants to pursue your deeper goals, and wants to be a better person. But you know you're fallible and likely to crack in the face of temptation. So you bind the future version of you. You narrow your choices. You tie yourself to the mast.

There has been a small range of scientific experiments to see if this really works, at least in the short term. For example, in 2013 a professor of psychology named Molly Crockett—who I interviewed at Yale—got a bunch of men into a lab and split them into two groups. All of them were going to face a challenge. They were told that they could see a slightly sexy picture right away if they wanted to, but if they were able to wait and do nothing for a little while, they would get to see a super-sexy picture. The first group was told to use their willpower, and discipline themselves in the moment. But the second group was given a chance, before they went into the lab, to "pre-commit"—to resolve, out loud, that they were going to stop and wait so they could see the sexier picture. The scientists wanted to know—would the men who made a pre-commitment hold out more often, and longer, than the men who didn't? It turned out pre-commitment was strikingly successful—resolving clearly to do something, and making a pledge that they'd stick to it, made the men significantly better at holding out. In the years since, scientists have shown the same effect in a broad range of experiments.

My trip to Provincetown was an extreme form of pre-commitment, and like Ulysses's victory, it also began on a boat. As the ferry to

Provincetown pulled out, I looked back at Boston Harbor, where the May light was reflecting on the water. I stood toward the back of the ship, next to a wet and flapping Stars and Stripes, and watched the foam of the ocean spraying behind us. After about forty minutes, Provincetown slowly appeared on the horizon when I saw the thin spike of the Pilgrim Monument come into view.

Provincetown is a long, lush strip of sand where the United States juts into the Atlantic Ocean. It is the last stop in the Americas, the end of the road. You can stand there, the writer Henry David Thoreau said, and feel the whole of the United States at your back. I felt a giddy sense of lightness, and as beach appeared through the foam, I began to laugh, though I didn't know why. I was almost drunk with exhaustion. I was thirty-nine, and I had been working nonstop since I was twenty-one. I had taken almost no holidays. I fattened myself with information every waking hour to make myself a more productive writer, and I had started to think that the way I lived was a bit like the process where, in a factory farm, a foie gras goose is force-fed gross amounts in order to turn its liver into pâté. In the previous five years, I had traveled over 80,000 miles, researching, writing, and talking about two books. All day, every day, I tried to inhale more information, interview more people, learn more, talk more, and I was now manically skipping between topics, like a record that has been scratched from overuse, and I was finding it hard to retain anything. I had felt tired for so long that all I knew was how to outrun it.

As people began to disembark, I heard the ping of an incoming text message somewhere on the ferry and reached instinctively for my pocket. I felt a panic—where's my phone?—and then remembered, and laughed even more.

I found myself thinking, at that moment, about the first time I had ever seen a cellphone. I was around fourteen or fifteen—so this was 1993 or 1994—and I was on the top deck of the 340 bus in London, coming home from school. A man in a suit was talking loudly into an object that in my memory is the size of a small cow. All of us on that top deck turned and looked at him. He seemed to be enjoying us looking, and he talked louder. This continued for some time, until another passenger said to him: "Mate?" "Yes?" "You're a wanker." And the people on the bus broke the first rule of public transport in London. We looked at each other, and we smiled. These small rebellions were happening all over London, I recall, at the birth of mobile phones. We saw them as an absurd invasion.

I sent my first email about five years later, when I went to university. I was nineteen years old. I wrote a few sentences, and clicked send, and waited to feel something. No surge of excitement came. I wondered why there was such a fuss about this new email thing. If you had told me then that within twenty years a combination of these two technologies—that seemed initially either repellent or yawnsome—would come to dominate my life to the point where I would have to get on a boat and flee, I would have thought you had lost your mind.

I tugged my bag off the boat and pulled out the map I had printed from the internet. I hadn't navigated anywhere without Google Maps in years, but fortunately, Provincetown consists of one long street, so there are literally only two directions you can give—go left, or go right. I had to go right, to the real estate agent I had rented my sliver of a beach house from. Commercial Street runs through the middle of Provincetown, and I walked past the neat New England stores selling lobsters and sex toys (these are not the same shops, obviously—that's a niche even Provincetown would shun). I remembered that I chose this place for a few reasons. A year before, I had come over for a day from Boston to visit my friend Andrew, who lives there every summer. Provincetown is like a cross between a quaint Cape Cod village in the old New England style, and a sex dungeon. For a long time, it was a working-class fishing town populated by Portuguese immigrants and their kids. Then artists started to move in, and it became a bohemian enclave. Then it became a gay destination. Today it is a place where, in old fishermen's cottages, there now live men whose full-time job is to dress as Ursula, the villain from

The Little Mermaid, and sing songs about cunnilingus to the tourists who dominate the town in summer.

I chose Provincetown because I found it charming but not complex—I felt (slightly arrogantly) that I had figured out its essential dynamics in my first twenty-four hours there. I was determined to go to a place that would not trigger my journalistic curiosity too much. If I had chosen (say) Bali, I know that I would have soon started trying to figure out how Balinese society worked, and begun interviewing people, and soon I would be back to my manic information-sucking. I wanted a pretty purgatory where I could decompress, and nothing more.

The real estate agent, Pat, drove me out to the beach house. It was close to the sea, a forty-minute walk from the center of Provincetown—almost in the neighboring town of Truro, in fact. It was a plain wooden house, split into four different apartments. Mine was to the bottom left. I asked Pat to remove the modem—in case, in some fit of madness, I went and bought an internet-connected device—and to cut off all the cable packages on the television. I had two rooms. Beyond the house, there was a short gravel path, and at the end of it, waiting for me, was the ocean, vast and open and warm. Pat bid me good luck, and I was alone.

I unpacked my books and began to flick through them. I couldn't get any traction with the one I picked up. I left it aside and walked over toward the ocean. It was early in the Provincetown season, and there were only around six other people that I could see in any direction stretching for miles. I felt then a sudden certainty—you only get these feelings a few times in a lifetime—that I had done absolutely the right thing. For so long I had been fixing my gaze on things that were very fast and very temporary, like a Twitter feed. When you fix your gaze on the speedy, you feel pensive, amped-up, liable to be washed away if you don't move, wave, shout. Now I found myself staring at something very old and very permanent. This ocean was here long before you, I thought, and it will be here long after your small concerns are forgotten. Twitter makes you feel that the whole world is obsessed with you and your little ego—it loves you, it hates you, it's talking about you *right now.* The ocean makes you feel like the world is greeting you with a soft, wet, welcoming indifference. It's never going to argue back, no matter how loud you yell.

I stood there for a long time. There was something shocking to me about being so still—to be not scrolling, but static. I tried to remember the last time I had felt like this. I walked down toward Provincetown through the ocean with my jeans rolled up. The water was warm and my feet sank a little into the sand. Little fish swam past and around my pasty white legs. I watched crabs burrow into the sand ahead of me. Then, after about fifteen minutes, I saw something so strange that I kept staring at it, and the more I stared, the more confused I became. There was a man standing on the water, out in the middle of the ocean. He was not on a boat, or on any floating device I could see. But he was far out at sea, and he was standing tall and firm. I wondered if, in my exhaustion, I had somehow begun to hallucinate. I waved to him; he waved back; and then he turned away, and stood with his palms out, facing the water. He stood there for a long time, and I stood there just as long, watching him. Then he began to walk toward me, seemingly on top of the ocean.

He saw my puzzled expression and explained to me that when the tide comes in in Provincetown, it covers the beach—but what you can't see is that the sand beneath the water is uneven. Beneath its surface there are sandbars and islands of raised sand—and if you walk along them, it gives the peculiar impression to anyone watching that you are walking on water. I would see this man often after that, as the weeks and months passed, standing out in the Atlantic, his palms facing outward, still and unmoving for hours. That, I thought to myself, is the opposite of Facebook—standing perfectly still, looking out toward the ocean, with your palms open.

Eventually I came to my friend Andrew's house. One of his dogs ran to greet me. We strolled down to have dinner together.

Andrew had been on a long silent retreat the year before—no phone, no talking—and he told me to enjoy this sense of bliss, because it wouldn't last long. It's when you set aside your distractions, he said, that you begin to see what you were distracting yourself from. Oh, Andrew, you're such a drama queen, I said, and we both laughed.

Later, I walked down Commercial Street, past the library, and the town hall, and the AIDS monument, and the cupcake store, and the drag queens handing out flyers for their shows that night, until I heard some singing. In a pub, the Crown & Anchor, people were gathered around a piano, singing show tunes. I went in. Together with these strangers, we covered most of the soundtrack of *Evita* and *Rent*. I was struck again by a big difference—between standing in a group of strangers singing with them, and interacting with groups of strangers through screens. The first dissolves your sense of ego; the second jabs and pokes at it. The last song we sang was "A Whole New World."

I walked back to the beach house alone at 2 a.m. I thought about the difference between the glowing blue light I had spent so much of my life staring at, which keeps you always alert, and the natural light that had faded all around me, which seemed to say: The day is over; rest now. The beach house was empty. There were no texts or voice messages or emails waiting for me—or, if there were, I wouldn't know for three months. I climbed into bed, and I fell into the deepest sleep I could remember. I didn't wake up until fifteen hours later.

⌐◦

I spent a week in this haze of decompression, feeling almost stoned with a mixture of exhaustion and stillness. I sat in cafés and talked to strangers. I wandered around Provincetown's library and its three bookstores, picking out yet more books I was going to read. I ate enough lobsters that, if that species ever evolves consciousness, I will be remembered as their Stalin figure, destroying them on an industrial scale. I walked all the way out to the spot where the Pilgrims first arrived on American soil, four hundred years before. (They wandered around, couldn't find much, and sailed farther down, landing on Plymouth Rock.)

Strange things started to bubble up into my consciousness. I kept hearing in my head the opening lines of songs from the 1980s and 1990s, when I was a kid, ones I hadn't thought about for years—"Cat Among the Pigeons" by Bros, or "The Day We Caught the Train" by Ocean Colour Scene. Without Spotify, I had no way to listen to the songs in full, so I sang them to myself as I walked down the beach. Every few hours, I would feel an unfamiliar sensation gurgling inside me and I would ask myself: What is that? Ah, yes. Calm. But all you've done is leave two lumps of metal behind; why does this feel so different? It felt like I had spent years holding two screaming, colicky babies, and now the babies had been handed over to a babysitter, and their yelling and vomiting had vanished from view.

Everything slowed down for me. Normally I follow the news every hour or so, getting a constant drip-feed of anxiety-provoking factoids and trying to smush it together into some kind of sense. In Provincetown, I could no longer do this. Every morning, I would buy three newspapers and sit down to read them—and then I wouldn't know what happened in the news until the next day. Instead of a constant blast running all through my waking life, I got one in-depth, curated guide to what happened, and then I could turn my attention to other things. One day, not long after I arrived, a gunman went into a newspaper office in Maryland and murdered five journalists. As a journalist myself, that's obviously close to my heart, and in my normal life, I would have received texts from my friends as soon as it happened, and then followed it for hours on social media, absorbing garbled accounts, gradually assembling a picture. In Provincetown, the day after the massacre, I knew within ten minutes all the clear, tragic details I needed to know, from a dead tree. Suddenly, physical newspapers—the very thing this gunman had targeted—seemed to me like an extraordinarily modern invention, and one we all needed.

My normal mode of consuming news, I realized, induced panic; this new style induced perspective.

I felt like something was happening in that first week that was slowly opening my receptors a little—to more attention, to more connection. But what was it? I only began to understand those first two weeks in Provincetown—and why I felt the way I did—later, when I went to Copenhagen.

∿

Sune Lehmann's sons jumped into his bed, and he knew—with a lurch in his gut—that there was something wrong. Every morning, his two boys would leap all over him and his wife, excitedly shrieking, glad to be awake for another day. It's the kind of scene you picture longingly when you imagine becoming a parent, and Sune adored his sons. He knew he should be thrilled by their joy at being awake and alive—but each morning, whenever they appeared, he would instinctively stretch out his hand, not for them, but for something colder. "I would reach over and grab my phone to check my email," he told me, "even though these amazing, wonderful, sweet creatures are crawling around my bed."

Every time he thought about it, he felt ashamed. Sune had trained as a physicist, but after a while, he figured he was going to have to investigate—at the Technical University of Denmark, where he is a professor in the Department of Applied Mathematics and Computer Science—what was happening not just in physics, but in himself. "I had been obsessed with how I was losing my own ability to focus," he told me. "I was realizing that, somehow, I was not able to control my own use of the internet." He found himself mindlessly following the small details of events like the U.S. presidential election on social media, hour after hour, achieving nothing. This wasn't just affecting him as a parent, but as a scientist. He said: "I came to this realization that my job in a way is to think something that is different from everyone else—but I was in an environment where I was just getting all the same information as everyone else, and I was just thinking the same things as everyone else."

He had a sense that the deterioration he was experiencing in his focus was happening to a lot of the people around him—but he also knew that at many points in history, people have thought they were experiencing some kind of disastrous social decline, when in fact, they were merely aging. It's always tempting to mistake your personal decline for the decline of the human species. Sune—who was in his late thirties at the time—asked himself: Am I a grumpy old man, or is the world really changing? So with scientists across Europe, he launched the largest scientific study yet conducted to answer a key question—is our collective attention span really shrinking?

As a first step they drew up a list of sources of information that they could analyze. The first and most obvious was Twitter. The site had launched in 2006 and Sune began this work in 2014—so there was eight years of data to draw on. On Twitter, you can track what topics people are talking about and how long they discuss them for. The team began to do a massive analysis of the data. How long do people talk about a topic on Twitter for? Has the length of time they focus, collectively, on any one thing changed? Do people talk about the topics that obsess them—the trending hashtags—for more or less time now, compared to in the recent past? What they found is that in 2013 a topic would remain in the top fifty most-discussed subjects for 17.5 hours. By 2016 that had dropped to 11.9 hours. This suggested that together, on that site, we were focusing on any one thing for ever-shorter periods of time.

Okay, they thought, that's striking, but maybe this was a quirk of Twitter. So they started to look at a whole range of other data sets. They looked at what people search for on Google—what's the rate of churn in that? They analyzed movie-ticket sales—how long did people carry on going to the cinema to watch a movie after it became a hit? They studied Reddit—how long did topics last there? All the data suggested that, as time passed, we were focusing less on any one individual topic. (The one exception, intriguingly, was

Wikipedia, where the level of attention on topics has held steady.) With almost every data set they looked at, the pattern was the same. Sune said: "We looked at a lot of different systems . . . and we see that in every system, there is an accelerating trend." It is "faster to reach peak popularity," and then there is "a faster drop again."

The scientists wanted to know how long this has been happening for—and that's when they made a really eye-opening discovery. They turned to Google Books, which has scanned the full text of millions of books. Sune and his team decided to analyze books that were written between the 1880s and the present day using a mathematical technique—the scientific term for it is "detecting n-grams"—that can spot the rise and fall of new phrases and topics in the text. It's the equivalent of finding hashtags from the past. The computers could detect new phrases as they appear—think of, say, "the Harlem Renaissance," or "no-deal Brexit"—and they could see how long they were discussed for, and how quickly they faded from discussion. It was a way of finding out how long the people who came before us talked about a fresh topic. How many weeks and months did it take for them to get bored and move on to the next thing? When they looked at the data, they found that the graph looked remarkably similar to Twitter's. With each decade that passed, for more than 130 years, topics have come and gone faster and faster.

When he saw the results, Sune told me, he thought: "Goddammit, it really is true. . . . Something is changing. It's not just the same-old, same-old." This was the first proof gathered anywhere in the world that our collective attention spans have been shrinking. Crucially, this has been happening not just since the birth of the web, but for the whole of my life, my parents' lives, and my grandparents' lives. Yes, the internet had rapidly accelerated the trend—but, crucially, this scientific team had discovered it was not the sole cause.

Sune and his colleagues wanted to understand what has been driving this change, so they built a complex mathematical model to try to figure it out. It's a bit like the systems that climate scientists construct to successfully predict changes in the weather. (The full technical details of how they did it, if you're interested, are in their published research.) It was designed to see what you could do to data to make it rise and fall at faster and faster rates in ways that resembled the decline in collective attention they had been documenting. What they discovered is there is one mechanism that can make this happen every time. You just have to flood the system with more information. The more information you pump in, the less time people can focus on any individual piece of it.

"It's a fascinating explanation of why this acceleration is happening," Sune told me. Today, "there's just more information in the system. So if you think about one hundred years ago, literally it would take time for news to travel. If there was some kind of huge catastrophe in a Norwegian fjord, they would have to get up from the fjord down to Oslo, someone would have to write it up," and it would slowly wend its way across the globe. Compare that with the 2019 massacre in New Zealand, when a depraved racist began to murder Muslims in a mosque and it was "literally streaming live," so anyone could watch it, anywhere.

One way of thinking about this, Sune said, is that at the moment, it is like we're "drinking from a fire hose—there's too much coming at us." We are soaked in information. The raw figures on this have been analyzed by two other scientists, Dr. Martin Hilbert at the University of Southern California and Dr. Priscilla López at the Open University of Catalonia. Picture reading an eighty-five-page newspaper. In 1986, if you added up all the information being blasted at the average human being—TV, radio, reading—it amounted to 40 newspapers' worth of information every day. By 2007, they found it had risen to the equivalent of 174 newspapers per day. (I'd be amazed if it hasn't gone up even more since then.) The increase in the volume of information is what creates the sensation of the world speeding up.

How is this change affecting us? Sune smiled when I asked. "There's this thing about speed that feels great. . . . Part of why we feel absorbed in this is that it's awesome, right? You get to feel that you are connected to the whole world, and you feel that anything that happens on the topic, you can find out about it and learn about it." But we told ourselves we could have a massive expansion in the amount of information we are exposed to, and the speed at which it hits us, with no costs. This is a delusion: "It becomes exhausting." More importantly, Sune said, "what we are sacrificing is depth in all sorts of dimensions. . . . Depth takes time. And depth takes reflection. If you have to keep up with everything and send emails all the time, there's no time to reach depth. Depth connected to your work in relationships also takes time. It takes energy. It takes long time spans. And it takes commitment. It takes attention, right? All of these things that require depth are suffering. It's pulling us more and more up onto the surface."

There was a phrase in Sune's scientific paper, summarizing his findings, that kept rattling around in my head. It said that we are, collectively, experiencing "a more rapid exhaustion of attention resources." When I read this, I realized what I had experienced in Provincetown. I was—for the first time in my life—living within the limits of my attention's resources. I was absorbing as much information as I could actually process, think about, and contemplate—and no more. The fire hose of information was turned off. Instead, I was sipping water at the pace I chose.

Sune is a smiling, affable Dane, but when I asked him about how these trends will develop in the future, his body stiffened, and his smile turned to a tight pucker. "We've been accelerating for a very long time, and for sure, we're getting closer and closer to whatever limits we have," he said. This acceleration, he said, "can't continue indefinitely. There's some physical limit to how fast things can move. It must stop at some point. But I don't see any slowing down right now."

Shortly before I met with him, Sune had seen a photograph of Mark Zuckerberg, the founder of Facebook, standing in front of a room of people who were all wearing virtual reality headsets. He was the only person standing in actual reality, looking at them, smiling, pacing proudly around. When he saw it, Sune said, "I was like—holy shit, this is a metaphor for the future." If we don't change course, he fears we are headed toward a world where "there's going to be an upper class of people that are very aware" of the risks to their attention and find ways to live within their limits, and then there will be the rest of the society with "fewer resources to resist the manipulation, and they're going to be living more and more inside their computers, being manipulated more and more."

Once he had learned all this, Sune deeply changed his own life. He stopped using all social media, except Twitter, which he checks only once a week, on Sundays. He stopped watching TV. He stopped getting his news from social media, and instead took out a newspaper subscription. He read many more books instead. "As you know, everything with self-discipline is not like it's a thing you fix and then it's fixed forever," he said. "I think the first thing you have to realize is it's an ongoing battle." But he told me it had helped to trigger a philosophical shift in how he approached life. "In general, we want to take the easy way out, but what makes us happy is doing the thing that's a little bit difficult. What's happening with our cellphones is that we put a thing in our pocket that's with us all the time that always offers an easy thing to do, rather than the important thing." He looked at me and smiled. "I wanted to give myself a chance at choosing something that's more difficult."

Sune's study is pioneering, so it only provides us with a small base of evidence—but, as I dug deeper, I found two related areas of scientific investigation that helped me to understand this more. The first comes, intriguingly, from studies investigating if we can really learn how to speed-read. Several teams of scientists have spent years figuring out: Can you make humans read things really, really fast? They found that you can—but it always comes at a cost. These teams took ordinary people and got them to read much faster than they ordinarily would; with training, and with practice, it sort of works. They can run their eyes over the words quickly and retain something of what they are seeing. But if you then test them on what they read, you'll discover that the faster you make them go, the less they will understand. More speed means less comprehension. Scientists then studied professional speed-readers—and they discovered that even though they are obviously better at it than the rest of us, the same thing happens. This showed there's just a maximum limit for how quickly humans can absorb information, and trying to bust through that barrier simply busts your brain's ability to understand it instead.

The scientists investigating this also discovered that if you make people read quickly, they are much less likely to grapple with complex or challenging material. They start to prefer simplistic statements. After I read this, I looked again at my own habits. When I read a physical newspaper, I'll often be drawn to the stories that I don't understand yet—why, say, is there an uprising in Chile? But when I read the same newspaper online, I usually skim those stories, and click on the simpler, more scannable stories related to the stuff I already know. After I noticed this, I wondered if in some ways we are increasingly speed-reading life, skimming hurriedly from one thing to another, absorbing less and less.

One day, in my webless summer, after slowly reading a book, slowly eating a meal, and slowly wandering around town, I wondered if, in my normal life, I suffer from a kind of mental jet lag. When you fly into a distant time zone, you feel like you've moved too fast and now you are out of sync with the world around you. The British writer Robert Colville says we are living through "the Great Acceleration," and like Sune, he argues it's not simply our tech that's getting faster—it's almost everything. There's evidence that a broad range of important factors in our lives really are speeding up: people talk significantly faster now than they did in the 1950s, and in just twenty years, people have started to walk 10 percent faster in cities.

Usually, this acceleration is sold to us in a spirit of celebration—the original BlackBerry advertising slogan was "Anything worth doing is worth doing faster." Internally, at Google, the unofficial motto among the staff is "If you're not fast, you're fucked."

But there's a second way in which scientists have learned how this societal slamming on the accelerator is affecting our attention. It comes from studying what happens to focus not when we speed up, but when we deliberately slow down. One of the leading experts on this topic is Guy Claxton, professor of learning sciences at the University of Winchester, who I went to interview in Sussex, in England. He has analyzed what happens to a person's focus if they engage in deliberately slow practices, like yoga, or tai chi, or meditation, as discovered in a broad range of scientific studies, and he has shown they improve your ability to pay attention by a significant amount. I asked him why. He said that "we have to shrink the world to fit our cognitive bandwidth." If you go too fast, you overload your abilities, and they degrade. But when you practice moving at a speed that is compatible with human nature—and you build that into your daily life—you begin to train your attention and focus. "That's why those disciplines make you smarter. It's not about humming or wearing orange robes." Slowness, he explained, nurtures attention, and speed shatters it.

At some level, in Provincetown, I sensed this was true—so I decided to try these slow practices. The first time I went to see my yoga teacher, Stefan Piscitelli, I said to him: "This is going to be like teaching yoga to Stephen Hawking. After his death." I explained that I was an immobilized lump of flesh designed only to read, write, and occasionally walk. He laughed and said: "We'll see what we can do." And so every day, for an hour, under his guidance, I slowly moved my body in ways I had never done before. At first I found it extraordinarily boring, and I tried to draw Stefan into arguing about politics or philosophy. He would always gently guide me back to trying to move into some weird pretzel shape I had never tried before. By the end of the summer, I was able to be silent for an hour, and to stand on my head. Afterward, sometimes with Stefan's guidance, I would meditate for twenty minutes—a practice I had tried at various points in my life but always let lapse. I felt a kind of slowness spreading through my body. I felt my heartbeat slow down, and my shoulders—which are normally in a kind of permanent hunch—relax gently.

But even when I felt the physical relief from this slowness, it was always followed by a kind of bubbling guilt. I thought, How can I explain this to my sped-up, stressed-out friends back home? How can we all change our lives so we feel more like this? How do you slow down in a world that is speeding up?

~

I started to ask myself an obvious question: If life has accelerated, and we have become overwhelmed by information to the point that we are less and less able to focus on any of it, why has there been so little pushback? Why haven't we tried to slow things down to a pace where we can think clearly? I was able to find the first part of an answer to this—and it's only the first part—when I went to interview Professor Earl Miller. He has won some of the top awards in neuroscience in the world, and he was working at the cutting edge of brain research when I went to see him in his office at the Massachusetts Institute of Technology (MIT). He told me bluntly that instead of acknowledging our limitations and trying to live within them, we have—en masse—fallen for an enormous delusion.

There's one key fact, he said, that every human being needs to understand—and everything else he was going to explain flows from that. "Your brain can only produce one or two thoughts" in your conscious mind at once. That's it. "We're very, very single-minded." We have "very limited cognitive capacity." This is because of the "fundamental structure of the brain," and it's not going to change. But rather than acknowledge this, Earl told me, we invented a myth. The myth is that we can actually think about three, five, ten things at the same time. To pretend this was the case, we took a term that was never meant to be applied to human beings at all. In the 1960s, computer scientists invented machines with more than one processor, so they really could do two things (or more) simultaneously. They called this machine-power "multitasking." Then we took the concept and applied it to ourselves.

When I first learned about Earl's claim that our ability to think about several things at once is a delusion, I bristled—he couldn't be right, I thought, because I have done several things at the same time myself. In fact, I do it often. Here's the first example that came to mind: I have checked my email while thinking about the next draft of my book and planning out an interview I was going to do later that day. I did them all from the same toilet seat. (I apologize for putting this image in your head.) Where's the fantasy in that?

Some scientists used to side with my initial gut instinct—they believed it was possible for people to do several complex tasks at once. So they started to get people into labs, and they told them to do lots of things at the same time, and they monitored how well it went. What the scientists discovered is that, in fact, when people think they're doing several things at once, they're actually—as Earl explained—"juggling. They're switching back and forth. They don't notice the switching because their brain sort of papers it over, to give a seamless experience of consciousness, but what they're actually doing is switching and reconfiguring their brain moment to moment, task to task—[and] that comes with a cost."

There are three ways, he explained, in which this constant switching degrades your ability to focus. The first is called the "switch cost effect." There is broad scientific evidence for this. Imagine you are doing your tax return and you receive a text, and you look at it—it's only a glance, taking five seconds—and then you go back to your tax return. In that moment, "your brain has to reconfigure, when it goes from one task to another," he said. You have to remember what you were doing before, and you have to remember what you thought about it, "and that takes a little bit of time." When this happens, the evidence shows that "your performance drops. You're slower. All as a result of the switching."

So if you check your texts often while trying to work, you aren't only losing the little bursts of time you spend looking at the texts—you are also losing the time it takes to refocus afterward, which can be much longer. He said: "If you're spending a lot of your time not really thinking, but wasting it on switching, that's just wasted brain-processing time." This means that if your Screen Time shows you are using your phone four hours a day, you are losing much more time than that in lost focus.

When Earl said this, I thought, yes, but it must be a small effect, a tiny drag on your attention. But when I went and read the relevant research, I learned there is some science suggesting the effect can be surprisingly large. For example, a small study commissioned by Hewlett-Packard looked at the IQ of some of their workers in two situations. At first they tested their IQ when they were not being distracted or interrupted. Then they tested their IQ when they were receiving emails and phone calls. The study found that "technological distraction"—just getting emails and calls—caused a drop in the workers' IQ by an average of ten points. To give you a sense of how big that is: in the short term, that's twice the knock to your IQ that you get when you smoke cannabis. So this suggests, in terms of being able to get your work done, you'd be better off getting stoned at your desk than checking your texts and Facebook messages a lot.

From there, the research shows, it gets worse. The second way switching harms your attention is what we might call the "screw-up effect." When you switch between tasks, errors that wouldn't have happened otherwise start to creep in, because—Earl explained—"your brain is error-prone. When you switch from task to task, your brain has to backtrack a little bit and pick up and figure out where it left off"—and it can't do that perfectly. Glitches start to occur. "Instead of spending critical time really doing deep thinking, your thinking is more superficial, because you're spending a lot of time correcting errors and backtracking."

Then there's a third cost to believing you can multitask, one that you'll only notice in the medium or longer term—which we might call the "creativity drain." You're likely to be significantly less creative. Why? "Because where do new thoughts [and] innovation come from?" Earl asked. They come from your brain shaping new connections out of what you've seen and heard and learned. Your mind, given free undistracted time, will automatically think back over everything it absorbed, and it will start to draw links between them in new ways. This all takes place beneath the level of your conscious mind, but this process is how "new ideas pop together, and suddenly, two thoughts that you didn't think had a relationship suddenly have a relationship." A new idea is born. But if you "spend a lot of this brain-processing time switching and error-correcting," Earl explained, you are simply giving your brain less opportunity to "follow your associative links down to new places and really [have] truly original and creative thoughts."

I later learned about a fourth consequence, based on a smaller amount of evidence—which we might call the "diminished memory effect." A team at UCLA got people to do two tasks at once, and tracked them to see the effects. It turned out that afterward they couldn't remember what they had done as well as people who did just one thing at a time. This seems to be because it takes mental space and energy to convert your experiences into memories, and if you are spending your energy instead on switching very fast, you'll remember and learn less.

So if you spend your time switching a lot, then the evidence suggests you will be slower, you'll make more mistakes, you'll be less creative, and you'll remember less of what you do. I wanted to know: How often are most of us engaging in switching like this? Professor Gloria Mark, at the Department of Informatics at the University of California, Irvine, who I interviewed, has discovered that the average American worker is distracted roughly once every three minutes. Several other studies have shown a large chunk of Americans are almost constantly being interrupted and switching between tasks. The average office worker now spends 40 percent of their work time wrongly believing they are "multitasking"—which means they are incurring all these costs for their attention and focus. In fact, uninterrupted time is becoming rare. One study found that most of us working in offices never get a whole hour uninterrupted in a normal day. I had to look again at that figure several times before I really absorbed it: most office workers *never* get an hour to themselves without being interrupted. This is happening at every level of businesses—the average CEO of a Fortune 500 company, for example, gets just twenty-eight uninterrupted minutes a day.

Whenever this problem is talked about in the media, it's described as "multitasking"—but I think using this old computing term is a mistake. When I picture multitasking, I picture a 1990s single mother trying to feed a baby while also taking a work call and preventing the food she's cooking from catching fire. (I watched a lot of bad sitcoms in the 1990s.) I don't picture somebody taking a work call while also checking their text messages. We now use our phones so habitually that I don't think we consider doing a task and checking our phones at the same time as multitasking, any more than we think scratching your butt during a work call is multitasking. But it is. Simply having your phone switched on and receiving texts every ten minutes while you try to work is itself a form of switching—and these costs start to kick in for you too. One study at Carnegie Mellon University's Human Computer Interaction Lab took 136 students and got them to take a test. Some of them had to have their phones switched off, and others had their phones on and received intermittent text messages. The students who received messages performed, on average, 20 percent worse. Other studies in similar scenarios have found even worse outcomes of 30 percent. It seems to me that almost all of us with a smartphone are losing that 20 to 30 percent, almost all the time. That's a lot of brainpower for a species to lose.

If you want to understand how much harm this does, Earl told me, just look at one of the fastest-rising causes of death in the world: distracted driving. The cognitive neuroscientist Dr. David Strayer at the University of Utah conducted detailed research where he got people to use driving simulators and tracked how safe their driving was when they were distracted by technology—something as simple as their phone receiving texts. It turned out their level of impairment was "very similar" to if they were drunk. It's worth dwelling on that. Persistent distractions have as bad an effect on your attention on the road as consuming so much alcohol that you got drunk. The distraction all around us isn't just annoying, it's deadly: around one in five car accidents is now due to a distracted driver.

The evidence is clear, Earl told me: there's no alternative, if you want to do things well, to focusing carefully on one thing at a time. As I learned all this, I realized that my desire to absorb a tsunami of information without losing my ability to focus was like my desire to eat at McDonald's every day and stay trim—an impossible dream. The size and capacity of the human brain hasn't significantly changed in 40,000 years, Earl explained, and it isn't going to upgrade anytime soon. Yet we are deluded about this fact. Dr. Larry Rosen, a professor of psychology at California State University, discovered that the average teen and young adult genuinely believes they can follow six or seven forms of media at once. We are not machines. We cannot live by the logic of machines. We are humans, and we work differently.

When I learned all this, I realized another crucial reason why I had felt so good—and so mentally restored—in Provincetown. For the first time in a long time, I was allowing myself to focus on one thing at a time for long stretches. It felt like I had had an enormous boost in my mental capacity—because I was respecting my mind's limitations. I asked Earl if, given what we know about the brain, it was fair to conclude that attention problems today really are worse than at some points in the past. He replied: "Absolutely." We have, he believes, created in our culture "a perfect storm of cognitive degradation, as a result of distraction."

This was hard to take on board. It's one thing to have a hunch that there's a crisis. It's another thing to hear one of the leading neuroscientists in the world tell you we are living in a "perfect storm" that's degrading your capacity to think. "The best we can do now," Earl told me, is "try to get rid of the distractions as much as possible." At one point in our conversation, he sounded quite optimistic, suggesting that we can all achieve progress on this, starting today. He said: "The brain is like a muscle. The more you use certain things, the stronger the connection's getting, and the better things work." If you are struggling to focus, he said, just try monotasking for ten minutes, and then allow yourself to be distracted for a minute, then monotask for another ten minutes, and so on. "As you do it, it becomes more familiar, your brain gets better and better at it, because you're strengthening the [neural] connections involved in that behavior. And pretty soon you can do it for fifteen minutes, twenty minutes, half an hour, you know? . . . Just do it. Practice at it. . . . Start slow, but practice, and you'll get there."

To achieve this, he said you have to separate yourself—for increasing periods of time—from the sources of your distraction. It's a mistake, he said, to "try to monotask by force of will—because it's too hard to resist that informational tap on the shoulder." When I asked him about how, as a society, we could find a way to do this, he told me that he's not a sociologist, and I'd have to look elsewhere for answers to that.

~

Our brains are not only overloaded now with switching—I learned they are also overloaded with something else. Adam Gazzaley, who is a professor of neurology, physiology, and psychiatry at the University of California, helped me to understand it when I sat down with him in a coffee shop in San Francisco. He explained that you should think of your brain as like a nightclub where, standing at the front of that club, there's a bouncer. The bouncer's job is to filter out most of the stimuli that are hitting you at any given moment—the traffic noise, the couple having an argument across the street, the cellphone ringing in the pocket of the person next to you—so that you can think coherently about one thing at a time. The bouncer is essential. This ability to filter out irrelevant information is crucial if you are going to be able to attend to your goals. And that bouncer in your head is strong and ripped: he can fight off two, four, maybe even six people trying to barge into your brain at a time. He can do a lot. The part of your brain doing this is known as the prefrontal cortex.

But today, Adam believes, the bouncer is besieged in an unprecedented way. In addition to switching tasks like never before, our brains are also being forced to filter more frantically than at any point in our past. Think about something as simple as noise. There's broad scientific evidence that if you are sitting in a noisy room, your ability to pay attention deteriorates, and your work gets worse. For example, children in noisy classrooms have worse attention than kids in quiet classrooms. Yet many of us are surrounded by high levels of noise, working in open-plan offices, sleeping in crowded cities, and tapping away on our laps in crammed coffee shops like the one we were sitting in at that moment. Rising noise pollution is just one example—we live surrounded by shrieking distractions calling for our attention, and the attention of others. That's why, Adam said, the bouncer has to work "way harder" to keep out distractions. He's exhausted. And so a lot more is fighting its way past him, into your mind—interfering with the flow of your thoughts.

As a result, a lot of the time, he can't filter like he used to. The bouncer is overwhelmed, and the nightclub becomes full of rowdy assholes disrupting the normal dancing. "We have fundamental limitations," Adam added. "We could ignore them, and pretend we're capable of everything we would wish—or we can acknowledge them, and live our lives in a better way."

～

In my first two weeks in Provincetown, I felt I had finally stepped out of the madness. I had gone to live in a monotasking world that wasn't forcing on me the mental pressure of switching and filtering. This is how my summer is going to be, I thought to myself. An oasis of calm. An example of how to live differently. I ate cupcakes and laughed with strangers. I felt light, and free.

And then something happened that I didn't expect. On the

fourteenth day I woke up, and my hand reached immediately for the nightstand to grab my iPhone, as it had done every morning since I arrived. It found only my dumb-phone, on which there were no messages, only the option to tell the nearest hospital I had fallen over. I could hear the ocean whispering in the distance. I turned and saw all the books I had been longing to read, waiting for me. And I felt an intense sensation—something I couldn't quite place. And at that moment, the worst week I had experienced in years began.

CHAPTER TWO

Cause Two: The Crippling of Our Flow States

On the first day of my mental free fall, I walked down the beach and saw the same thing that had been scratching at me since Memphis. Almost everyone was staring at their screens. People seemed to be using Provincetown simply as a backdrop for selfies, rarely looking up, at the ocean, or each other. Except this time, the itch I felt wasn't to yell: You're wasting your lives, put the damn phone down. It was to yell: Give *me* that phone! *Mine!*

Every time I switched on my iPod to listen to an audiobook or some music, I also had to switch on my noise-canceling headphones, and they would say: "Searching for Johann's iPhone. Searching for Johann's iPhone." The Bluetooth was trying to connect, but it couldn't, so then it would say sadly: "Connection cannot be made." That was how it felt. The French philosopher Simone de Beauvoir said that when she became an atheist, it felt like the world had fallen silent. When my phone was taken away, I felt like a large part of the world had vanished. As that first week ended, its absence flooded me with an angry panic. I wanted my phone. I wanted my email. And I wanted them at once. Every time I left the beach house, I instinctively patted my pocket to make sure my phone was there, and I always felt a lurch when I realized it was missing. It was like I had lost part of my own body. I turned to my piles of books, thinking idly of how, all through my teens and twenties, I would spend days on end lying in bed, doing nothing but reading in one great gulp. But in Provincetown up to that point, I had been reading in a rushed, hyperactive way—I was scanning Charles Dickens the way you might scan a blog for vital information. My reading was manic and extractive: Okay, I've got it, he's an orphan. What's your point? I could see this was foolish, but I couldn't stop. I couldn't slow my mind in the way that yoga slowed my body.

At a loss, I took to taking out my comically large medical-device phone and stabbing at its massive buttons. I stared at it helplessly. An image came into my head of a wildlife documentary I had seen as a kid, of a penguin whose baby died. She kept nudging it with her beak for hours, hoping it would come to life. But no matter how much I prodded it, my chunky Jitterbug could not access the web.

All around me, I could see reminders of why I had cast aside my phone in the first place. I sat in Café Heaven, a lovely little place in the West End of Provincetown, and ate an eggs Benedict. Next to me there were two men in, I guess, their mid-twenties. I shamelessly eavesdropped on their conversation while pretending to read *David Copperfield*. It was clear they had met on an app, and this was the first time they had seen each other in person. Something about their conversation seemed odd to me, and I couldn't place it at first. Then I realized they weren't, in fact, having a conversation at all. What would happen is the first one, who was blond, would talk about himself for ten minutes or so. Then the second one, who was dark-haired, would talk about himself for ten minutes. And they alternated in this way, interrupting each other. I sat next to them for two hours, and at no point did either of them ask the other person a question. At one point, the dark-haired man mentioned that his brother had died a month before. The blond didn't even offer a cursory "I'm so sorry to hear that"; he simply went back to talking about himself. I realized that if they had met up simply to read out their own Facebook status updates to each other in turn, there would have been absolutely no difference.

I felt like everywhere I went, I was surrounded by people who were broadcasting but not receiving. Narcissism, it occurred to me, is a corruption of attention—it's where your attention becomes turned in only on yourself and your own ego. I don't say this with any sense of superiority. I am embarrassed to describe what I realized in that week that I missed most about the web. Every day in my normal life—sometimes several times a day—I would look at Twitter and Instagram to see how many followers I had. I didn't look at the feed, the news, the buzz—just my own stats. If the figure had gone up, I felt glad—like a money-obsessed miser checking the state of his personal stocks and finding he was slightly richer than yesterday. It was as if I was saying to myself, See? More people are following you. You matter. I didn't miss the content of what they said. I just missed the raw numbers, and the sense that they were growing.

I found that I had started to panic about irrational things. I kept wondering how, when I left Provincetown and took the boat back to Boston, I was going to get to my friend's house to retrieve my phone and laptop. What if there were no taxis at the dock? Would I be stranded? Would I never get to my phone? I have been around a lot of addiction in my life, and I knew what I was feeling—the addicted person's craving for the thing that numbs their nagging sense of hollowness.

One day, I lay on the beach, using puffy dried seaweed as a pillow, trying to read, and I started to angrily reproach myself for not being relaxed, for not being focused, for not starting to write the novel I had been planning for so long. Here you are in paradise, I kept saying to myself; you ditched the phone; now focus. Focus, damn you. I thought back to this moment when, over a year later, I interviewed Professor Gloria Mark, who has spent years studying the science of interruptions. She explained to me that if you have spent long enough being interrupted in your daily life, you will start to interrupt yourself even when you are set free from all these external interruptions. I kept looking at things and imagining how I would describe them in a tweet, and then imagining what people would say in response.

I realized I had, for over twenty years now, been sending out and receiving signals with large numbers of people all throughout the day. Texts, Facebook messages, phone calls—they were all little ways in which the world seemed to say: I see you. I hear you. We need you. Signal back. Signal more. Now the signals were gone, and it felt like the world was saying: You don't matter. The absence of these insistent signals seemed to suggest an absence of meaning. I would start conversations with people—on the beach, in bookstores, in cafés—and they were often friendly, but the conversations seemed to have a low social temperature compared to the web-based ones I had lost. No stranger is going to flood you with hearts and tell you you're great. For years I had derived a large part of my meaning in life from the thin, insistent signals of the web. Now they were gone, and I could see how paltry and lacking in substance they were. But, still, I missed them.

I now faced a choice. I told myself: By leaving that world behind, you've created a vacuum. If you're going to stay away from it, now you need to fill the vacuum with something. It was only in the third week—after feeling wretched—that I began to find a way to do this. I found a way out of my funk by returning to the research of a remarkable man who opened up a whole new field of psychology in the 1960s, and whose work I had studied over the years. He made a breakthrough—this man identified a way human beings can access their own powers of focus, in a way that makes it possible to concentrate for long periods without it feeling like a huge effort.

To understand how it works, I think it helps to first hear the story of how he made this discovery. I learned a lot of this story from him directly, later, when I went to visit him in Claremont, California. It

begins with him as an eight-year-old boy, fleeing Nazi bombs at the
height of the Second World War, in a city on the coast of Italy, alone.

∽

Mihaly had to run, but he had no idea where to go. The air-raid siren
was making a familiar shrieking sound, warning the townspeople
that soon there would be Nazi planes overhead. These planes were
flying from Germany to Africa, and everybody in the town—even
a kid like Mihaly—knew that if the planes couldn't make it across
because of bad weather, they had a plan B. It was to drop their bombs
right here, onto this small town. Mihaly tried to get into the nearest air-raid shelter, but it was full. Go next door, he thought, to the
butcher's shop—you could hide in there. Its shutters were down. A
few grown-ups managed to find the key, and they all hurried inside.

In the darkness, it became clear something was dangling from the
ceiling. It was hanging meat. But they saw this wasn't an animal—it
was the wrong shape. As their eyes refocused, they realized it was
the bodies of two men. They recognized them as the butchers themselves, sagging from their own meat hooks. Mihaly ran again, deeper
into the shop—only to run into the hanging body of a third man.
They had been suspected of being collaborators with the fascists,
so they had been killed. The air-raid siren was still sounding, and
Mihaly hid there, close to the corpses.

It had seemed to the boy for some time that the adult world had
lost its mind. Mihaly Csikszentmihalyi (pronounced cheek-sent-me-
high-ee) was born in 1934 in Fiume, an Italian town close to the
Yugoslavian border. His father was a diplomat there for the Hungar-
ian government, so Mihaly grew up on a street where people routinely spoke three or four languages. It was a family where people
came up with big, sometimes mad projects; one of his big brothers
was the first person ever to hang glide from Russia to Austria. But
when Mihaly was six, the war began, and "the collapse happened,"
he told me. He was not allowed to play outside on the street, so
he invented worlds of play within his own home. He would stage

elaborate battles with toy soldiers that went on for weeks, planning out every move in this fantasy war. He spent a lot of his nights in chilly bomb shelters, sitting under blankets, terrified. "You never knew what was actually happening," he recalled. When the all clear sounded in the morning, people would leave politely and go to work.

Italy was getting too dangerous, so his family took him to a seaside town across the border named Opatija—but before long, the town was besieged from all sides. Partisans would come down and kill anyone suspected of collaborating with the invaders, while the Nazis bombarded from the air. "Now, nothing was getting safe," Mihaly told me. "I never found a stable world in which I [could] live." By the time the war ended, Europe was in ruins, and his family had lost everything. They got word that one of his brothers had been killed in the fighting, and another, Moricz, had been taken by Stalin to a Siberian concentration camp. "By the time I was ten years old," he remembered years later, "I was convinced that grown-ups didn't know how to live a good life."

After the war, he and his parents ended up in a refugee camp, which he found squalid, and lacking in hope. One day, in these ruins of a life, Mihaly was told that he was going to join a Scout troop for boys in the camp, and he started going out into the wilderness with them. He discovered that he felt most alive when he was doing something difficult, like navigating a steep ascent, or finding his way through a ravine. He thinks this experience saved him.

When he was thirteen, he quit school, because he couldn't see how all this adult wisdom was going to help him when it had driven European civilization off a cliff. He found his own way to Rome, and he started working as a translator in that trashed, half-starved city. He wanted to get back out into the mountains, so he saved up for a long time to go to Switzerland. When he was fifteen, he was finally able to take the train to Zurich, and while he was waiting around for the transport to the Alps, he saw an advertisement for a psychology lecture. The lecturer was Carl Jung, the legendary Swiss psychoanalyst, and while Mihaly wasn't drawn to the content of Jung's ideas, he was thrilled by the notion of looking at how the human mind works in a scientific way. He decided to become a psychologist, but it turned out there were no psychology degrees in Europe. He learned, though, that the subject existed in a distant country he had only seen in the movies: the United States.

Finally, after years of saving, he made it there—only to get a nasty shock when he arrived. American psychology was dominated by one big idea, epitomized by a famous scientist. A Harvard professor named B. F. Skinner had become an intellectual celebrity by discovering something strange. You can take an animal that seems to be freely making up its own mind about what to pay attention to— like a pigeon, or a rat, or a pig—and you can get it to pay attention to whatever you choose for it. You can control its focus, as surely as if it was a robot and you had created it to obey your whims. Here's an example of how Skinner did it that you can try for yourself. Take a pigeon. Put it in a cage. Keep it until it is hungry. Then introduce a bird feeder that releases seed into the cage when you push a button. Pigeons move around a lot—so wait until the pigeon makes a random movement that you have chosen in advance (like, say, jerking its head up high, or sticking out its left wing), and at that precise moment, release some pellets. Then wait for it to make the same random movement again, and give it more pellets.

If you do this a few times, the pigeon will quickly learn that if it wants pellets, it should carry out the random gesture you have chosen—and it will start to do it a lot. If you manipulate it correctly, its focus will come to be dominated by the twitch that you chose to reward. It will come to jerk up its head or stick out its left wing obsessively. When Skinner discovered this, he wanted to figure out how far you could take this. How elaborately can you program an animal using these reinforcements? He discovered you can take it really far. You can teach a pigeon to play ping-pong. You can teach a rabbit to pick up coins and put them into piggy banks. You can teach a pig to vacuum. Many animals will focus on very complex—and, to them, meaningless—things, if you reward them right.

Skinner became convinced that this principle explained human behavior almost in its entirety. You believe that you are free, and that you make choices, and you have a complex human mind that is selecting what to pay attention to—but it's all a myth. You and your sense of focus are simply the sum total of all the reinforcements you have experienced in your life. Human beings, he believed, have no minds—not in the sense that you are a person with free will making your own choices. You can be reprogrammed in any way that a clever designer wants. Years later, the designers of Instagram asked: If we reinforce our users for taking selfies—if we give them hearts and likes—will they start to do it obsessively, just like the pigeon will obsessively hold out its left wing to get extra seed? They took Skinner's core techniques, and applied them to a billion people.

Mihaly learned that these ideas ruled American psychology, and they were hugely influential in American society too. Skinner was a star, featured on the front page of *Time* magazine. He was so famous that by 1981, 82 percent of the American college-educated public could identify who he was.

To Mihaly, this seemed like a bleak and limited view of human psychology. It clearly yielded some results, but he believed it was missing most of what it means to be human. He decided he wanted to explore the aspects of human psychology that were positive, and nourishing, and generated something more than hollow mechanical responses. But there weren't many people in American psychology that thought like this. To begin, he decided to study something that seemed to him to be one of the great achievements of human beings—the making of art. He had seen destruction; now it was time to study creation. So, in Chicago, he persuaded a group of painters to let him witness their process over many months, so he could try to figure out the underlying psychological processes that were driving the unusual kind of focus they had chosen to dedicate their lives to. He watched one artist after another focusing on a single image and attending to it with great care.

Mihaly was struck by one thing above all else—for the artist, when they were in the process of creation, time seemed to fall away. They almost appeared to be in a hypnotic trance. It was a deep form of attention that you rarely see elsewhere.

Then he noticed something puzzling. After investing all this time in creating their paintings, when they were finished, the artists didn't triumphantly gaze at what they had made and show it off and seek out praise for it. Almost all of them simply put the painting away and started working on another one. If Skinner was right—that human beings do things just to gain rewards and avoid punishments—this made no sense. You'd done the work; now here's the reward, right in front of you, for you to enjoy. But creative people seemed mostly uninterested in rewards; even money didn't interest most of them. "When they finished," Mihaly said to an interviewer later, "the object, the outcome was not important."

He wanted to understand what was actually driving them. What made it possible for them to focus on just one thing for so long? It became clear to Mihaly that "what was so enthralling about painting was" something about "the process of painting itself." But what? To try to understand this better, Mihaly started to study adults who engaged in other activities—people who were long-distance swimmers, or rock climbers, or chess players. He only looked at first at nonprofessionals. Often they were doing things that were physically uncomfortable, exhausting, and even dangerous, for no obvious reward—yet they loved it. He talked to them about how they felt when they were doing the thing that drew this extraordinary focus out of them. He noticed that although these activities were very different, the way the people described how they felt had striking similarities. One word kept cropping up again and again. They kept saying things like: "I was carried on by the flow."

One rock climber told him later: "The mystique of rock-climbing is climbing; you get to the top of a rock glad it's over but really wish it could go on forever. The justification of climbing is climbing, like the justification of poetry is writing. You don't conquer anything except things in yourself. . . . The act of writing justifies poetry. Climbing is the same: recognizing you are a flow. The purpose of flow is to keep on flowing, not looking for a peak or utopia but staying in the flow. It is not a moving up but a continuous flowing; you move up to keep the flow going."

Mihaly began to wonder if these people were in fact describing a fundamental human instinct that had not been studied by scientists before. He called it a "flow state." This is when you are so absorbed in what you are doing that you lose all sense of yourself, and time seems to fall away, and you are flowing into the experience itself. It is the deepest form of focus and attention that we know of. When he began to explain to people what a flow state is and asked if they had ever experienced something like it, 85 percent of them recognized and remembered at least one time they'd felt this way—and they often said these moments were the highlights of their lives. It didn't matter if they got there by performing brain surgery or strumming the guitar or making great bagels—they described their flow states with wonder. He found himself thinking back to being a child on the floor of a war-smashed city, planning elaborate battles with his toy soldiers, and then of himself at the age of thirteen, exploring the hills and mountains around his refugee camp.

He was discovering that if human beings drill down in the right way, we can hit a gusher of focus inside ourselves—a long surge of attention that will flow forth and carry us through difficult tasks in a way that feels painless, and in fact pleasurable. So the obvious questions are: Where do we drill to get it? How can we bring about flow states? At first, most people assume they will achieve flow simply by relaxing into it—you picture yourself lying by the pool in Vegas sipping a cocktail. But when he studied it, he found that in fact, relaxing rarely gets you into a flow state. You have to get there by a different route.

Mihaly's studies identified many aspects of flow, but it seemed to me—as I read over them in detail—that if you want to get there, what you need to know boils down to three core components. The first thing you need to do is to choose a clearly defined goal. I want to paint this canvas; I want to run up this hill; I want to teach my child how to swim. You have to resolve to pursue it, and to set aside your other goals while you do. Flow can only come when you are monotasking—when you choose to set aside everything else and do one thing. Mihaly found that distraction and multitasking kill flow, and nobody will reach flow if they are trying to do two or more things at the same time. Flow requires all of your brainpower, deployed toward one mission.

Second, you have to be doing something that is meaningful to you. This is part of a basic truth about attention: we evolved to pay attention to things that are meaningful to us. As Roy Baumeister, the leading expert on willpower I quoted in the introduction, put it to me: "A frog will look at a fly it can eat much more than a stone it can't eat." To a frog, a fly is meaningful and a stone is not—so it easily pays attention to a fly, and rarely pays attention to a stone. This, he said, "goes back to the design of the brain. . . . It's designed to pay attention to the stuff that matters to you." After all, "the frog who sat around all day looking at stones would have starved." In any situation, it will be easier to pay attention to things that are meaningful to you, and harder to pay attention to things that seem meaningless. When you are trying to make yourself do something that lacks meaning, your attention will often slip and slide off it.

Third, it will help if you are doing something that is at the edge of your abilities, but not beyond them. If the goal you choose is too easy, you'll go into autopilot—but if it's too hard, you'll start to feel anxious and off-kilter and you won't flow either. Picture a rock climber who has medium-ranking experience and talent. If she clambers up any old brick wall at the back of a garden, she's not going to get into flow because it's too easy. If she's suddenly told to climb Mount Kilimanjaro, she won't get into flow either because she'll freak out. What she needs is a hill or mountain that is, ideally, slightly higher and harder than the one she did last time.

So, to find flow, you need to choose one single goal; make sure your goal is meaningful to you; and try to push yourself to the edge of your abilities. Once you have created these conditions, and you hit flow, you can recognize it because it's a distinctive mental state. You feel you are purely present in the moment. You experience a loss of self-consciousness. In this state it's like your ego has vanished and you have merged with the task—like you are the rock you are climbing.

By the time I met him, Mihaly was eighty-seven, and he had spent more than five decades studying flow states. He—along with scientists all over the world—had built up a broad and robust body of scientific evidence to show flow states are a real and deep form of human attention. They have also shown that the more flow you experience, the better you feel. Until his research, professional psychology in the U.S. had been focused either on when things go wrong—when you're mentally distressed—or on the manipulative vision of B. F. Skinner. Mihaly made the case for "positive psychology": that we should primarily focus on the things that make life worth living, and find ways to boost them.

This disagreement seemed to me to lay the groundwork for one of the defining conflicts in the world today. We now live in a world dominated by technologies based on B. F. Skinner's vision of how the human mind works. His insight—that you can train living creatures to desperately crave arbitrary rewards—has come to dominate our environment. Many of us are like those birds in cages being made to perform a bizarre dance to get rewards, and all the while we imagine we are choosing it for ourselves—the men I saw in Provincetown obsessively posting selfies to Instagram started to look to me like Skinner's pigeons with a six-pack and a piña colada. In a culture where our focus is stolen by these surface-level stimuli, Mihaly's deeper insight has been forgotten: that we have within us a force that makes it possible to focus for long stretches and enjoy it, and it will make us happier and healthier, if only we create the right circumstances to let it flow.

Once I knew this, I understood why, when I felt constantly distracted, I didn't just feel irritated—I felt diminished. We know, at

some level, that when we are not focusing, we are not using one of
our greatest capacities. Starved of flow, we become stumps of ourselves, sensing somewhere what we might have been.

∽

As an old man, something strange happened to Mihaly. After the
Second World War was over, his older brother, Moricz, had been
taken to a Stalinist concentration camp in Russia, and people who
vanished into these gulags were often never heard from again—but
after many years of silence, in which everyone assumed he was dead,
Moricz reappeared. Released at last into a thawing Soviet Union, he
struggled to find work; survivors of the gulags were marked as inher-
ently suspect. Eventually he found employment as a stoker on the
railways, even though he had advanced degrees from Switzerland.
He didn't complain.

When Moricz was in his eighties, Mihaly went to Budapest, in
Hungary, to be reunited with him. Moricz's ability to find flow had
been cut off in the most brutal ways, but Mihaly discovered that,
very late in his life, his brother was able, for the first time, to pursue
something he had always loved. He was fascinated by crystals. He
began to collect these sparkling rocks, and he gathered examples
from every continent. He went to meet dealers, he attended con-
ventions, he read magazines about them. When Mihaly went to his
home, it looked like a museum of crystals running from the ceiling to
the floor, with special lighting fitted to show off their sparkle. Moricz
handed Mihaly a crystal the size of a child's fist and said: "I was looking at this thing just yesterday. It was nine in the morning when I put
it under the microscope. Outside, it was sunny, just like today. I kept
turning the rock around, looking at all the fissures, the intrusions,
the dozen or so different crystal formations inside and around . . .
then I looked up, and thought that a storm must be coming, because
it had gotten so dark . . . then I realized it was not overcast, but the
sun had been setting—it was seven in the evening." Mihaly thought
the crystal was gorgeous, but wondered—ten hours?

Then he realized. Moricz had learned how to read the rocks—to see where they came from, and their chemical composition. It was a chance for him to use his skills. For him, this triggered a flow state. All his life Mihaly had been learning how flow states can save us. Now he saw it in the face of his own gulag-starved brother, as they stared together into a shimmering crystal.

The more he studied flow states, the more Mihaly noticed something else crucial about them. They are extraordinarily fragile and easily disrupted. He wrote: "Many forces, both within ourselves and in the environment, stand in the way" of flow. In the late 1980s, he discovered that staring at a screen is one of the activities we take part in that on average provides the lowest amount of flow. (He warned that "surrounded by an astonishing panoply of recreational gadgets . . . most of us go on being bored and vaguely frustrated.") But as I reflected on this in Provincetown, I realized that even though I had set aside my screens, I was still making a basic mistake. "To have a good life, it is not enough to remove what is wrong with it," Mihaly has explained. "We also need a positive goal; otherwise why keep going?"

In our normal lives, many of us try to seek relief from distraction simply by crashing—we try to recover from a day of overload by collapsing in front of the TV. But if you only break away from distraction into rest—if you don't replace it with a positive goal you are striving toward—you will always be pulled back to distraction sooner or later. The more powerful path out of distraction is to find your flow.

So at the end of that third week in Provincetown, I asked myself: Why did you come here? It wasn't just to get away from the phone and the Skinnerian reinforcements of constant likes and retweets and shares. You came here to write. Writing and reading have always been the primary sources of flow in my life. I had been nurturing an idea for a novel for a long time, and I told myself I would get around to it one day, when I had the time. Well, I thought, here is the time. Drill there. See if it brings you flow. This seemed to fit perfectly into

Mihaly's model for how to create flow states—it required me to set aside my other goals; it was something meaningful to me; and it was something at the edge of my comfort zone, but not, I hoped, beyond it. So on the first day of my third week, in my panicked funk, I sat on the sofa in my little corner of the beach house. I nervously opened the broken old laptop my friend Imtiaz had loaned me, and I wrote the first line of my novel. And I wrote the second line. And it became a paragraph, then a page. It was hard. I didn't particularly enjoy it. But the next day, conscious that I had to retrain my habits, I made myself do the same. And so it went on, day after day. I struggled. I disciplined myself.

By the end of the fourth week, the flow states started to come. And so it ran, into the fifth and sixth weeks—and soon, I was hurrying to my laptop, hungry to do it. Everything Mihaly had described was there—the loss of ego; the loss of time; the sense that I was growing into something bigger than I had been before. Flow was carrying me through the difficult patches, the frustrations. It had unlocked my focus.

I noticed that if I spent a day where I experienced three hours of flow early on, for the rest of the day, I felt relaxed and open and able to engage—to walk along the beach, or start chatting to people, or read a book, without feeling cramped, or irritable, or phone-hungry. It was like the flow was relaxing my body and opening my mind—perhaps because I knew I had done my best. I felt myself falling into a different rhythm. I realized then that to recover from our loss of attention, it is not enough to strip out our distractions. That will just create a void. We need to strip out our distractions and to replace them with sources of flow.

After three months in Provincetown, I had written 92,000 words of my novel. They might be terrible, but in one sense, I didn't care. The reason why became clear to me when one day, shortly before I left Provincetown, I placed my deck chair in the ocean so the sea was lapping at my feet and I finished the third volume of *War and*

Peace. As I closed its last page, I realized I had been sitting there for most of the day. I had been reading like this, day after day, for weeks. And I thought suddenly: It came back! My brain came back! I feared my brain had been broken, and this experiment might just reveal I was a permanently degenerated blob. But I could see now that healing was possible. I cried with relief.

I thought to myself, I never want to go back to email. I never want to go back to my phone. What a waste of time! What a waste of life! I felt this as strongly as I have ever felt anything. It might seem odd to describe something as immaterial as the internet as heavy, but that's how it felt to me in that moment—like there had been a vast weight on my back, and I had sloughed it off.

And then I immediately felt uncomfortable with all these thoughts, and guilty. How will this sound, I wondered, when I describe it to people back home? It won't sound like a liberation to them. It will sound like a taunt. Yes, I managed to get away and find flow in a blissful way, but my situation in Provincetown was so radically different from the lives of anyone I knew—so wildly privileged—that I wondered for a while if it had anything to teach anyone else. I realized that this experience would only be meaningful if we could all find ways to integrate these experiences into our everyday lives. Later, in a very different place, I learned how this could be done.

～

When I said goodbye to Mihaly, it was clear he was unwell. His eyes were heavy, and he told me he had been sick lately. At one point in our conversation, a little stream of ants began to crawl across his desk, and he stopped and stared at them for a while. He was in his late eighties, and it seemed likely he was approaching the end of his life. But his eyes lit up when he told me: "The best experiences in life that I had, when I thought back on it, came from times when I had been in the mountains climbing . . . climbing and doing something really kind of difficult and dangerous—but within the scope of what I could do." When you are approaching death, I thought, you won't think about your reinforcements—the likes and retweets—you'll think about your moments of flow.

I felt in that moment that we all have a choice now between two profound forces—fragmentation, or flow. Fragmentation makes you smaller, shallower, angrier. Flow makes you bigger, deeper, calmer. Fragmentation shrinks us. Flow expands us. I asked myself: Do you want to be one of Skinner's pigeons, atrophying your attention on dancing for crude rewards, or Mihaly's painters, able to concentrate because you have found something that really matters?

CHAPTER THREE

Cause Three: The Rise of Physical and Mental Exhaustion

The first thing I heard when I opened my eyes was the sound of the ocean lapping in the distance. Then I felt the sun flooding my bed, bathing me in light. Every morning in Provincetown, when this happened, I felt something strange in my body. It took me more than a month to realize what it was.

Ever since I went through puberty, I'd thought of sleep as something I wrestled myself into and fought my way out of. I would go to bed sometime between one and three in the morning and immediately bunch up the pillows so they supported my hunched shoulders. Then I would try to stop my mind jangling as it ran through all the things that had happened that day, and all the things I would need to do when I woke up, and all the things to worry about in the world. To take my mind off this internal electrical storm, I'd usually watch a noisy TV show on my laptop. Sometimes that would lull me to sleep, but more often, it would awaken a new wave of anxious energy, and I would start emailing or researching again for another few hours.

Finally, on most nights, I would power down by taking a few melato-nin gummies, and finally pass out.

Once I was in Zimbabwe and I spoke to some rangers who—as part of their jobs—had to knock out rhinos in order to give them medical treatment. They explained that they did it by darting them with a very powerful tranquilizer. As they described how the rhinos would stagger about in a panicked funk and then crash to the ground, I thought, hey, that's my sleep routine too.

After my chemical crash, I would be woken up six or seven hours later by a tag team of loud alarms. First, a radio alarm playing the BBC World Service would jolt me with the horrors of the day's news; then ten minutes later my phone would play a loud clanging alert; ten minutes after that another alarm clock would howl. When my ability to out-sleep all three finally wore off, I would stagger to my feet and immediately douse myself with enough caffeine to kill a small herd of cows. I lived on the permanent cliff-edge of exhaustion.

In Provincetown, when night fell, I would return to my little rooms to find there was no noise to rouse me and no portal to let in the wider world. I would go to lie in my bedroom, where the only source of light was a small reading lamp next to a pile of books. I would lie there reading and feel the paroxysms of the day slowly wend their way out of my body as I gently eased out of conscious-ness. I realized I had left my melatonin unused in the bathroom cabinet.

One day I woke up without any alarms after sleeping for nine hours and realized that I didn't want any coffee. This was such an alien sensation that it made me stop for a moment and stand there in my boxer shorts in the kitchen in front of the unboiling kettle, staring at it. Then it finally occurred to me what I was feeling—I had awo-ken from my sleep feeling fully refreshed. My body didn't feel heavy. I was alert. As the weeks passed, I realized that I felt like this every day now. The last time I remembered feeling like this was when I was a child.

For a long time, I had been trying to live by the rhythms of machines—going endlessly, day or night, until finally the battery conked out. Now I was living by the rhythm of the sun. As the sky went dark, I gradually wound down and finally rested, and when the sun came up, I woke naturally.

This was making something shift in my understanding of my body. I could see now it craved far more sleep than I normally allowed it, and when sleep came without any chemical nudging, my dreams were more vivid. It was as though my body and my mind were unclenching, and then replenishing.

I wondered if this was playing a role in why I was able to think more clearly, and for much longer stretches, than I had for years. I decided to explore the best scientific evidence about how the mysterious long stretches of unconsciousness our bodies crave—and that we so often deny them—might affect our ability to pay attention.

⌒

In 1981, in a lab in Boston, a young research scientist was keeping people awake all through the night and all through the following day, in long, yawn-strewn stretches. His job was to make sure they stayed conscious and, as he did it, to give them tasks to carry out. They had to add up numbers, and then sort cards into different groups, and then take part in memory tests. For example, he would show them a picture, then take it away, and ask: What color was the car in the picture I just showed you? Charles Czeisler—a tall, long-limbed man with wire-framed glasses and a deep voice—had, until this moment, never been interested in studying sleep. He had been taught in his medical training that when you are asleep, you are mentally "switched off." This is how lots of us see sleep—as a purely passive process, a mental dead zone in which nothing of consequence happens. Who, he shrugged, would want to study switched-off people? He was researching something he thought was much more important—it was a technical investigation of what time of day certain specific hormones are released in the human body. This required keeping people awake.

But as the days and nights went on, Charles couldn't help but notice something. When people are kept awake, "one of the first things to go is the ability to focus our attention," he told me, in a teaching room at Harvard. He had been giving his test subjects really basic tasks, but with each hour that passed, they were losing their ability to carry them out. They couldn't remember things he'd just told them or focus enough to play very simple card games. He told me: "I was just stunned by how performance would deteriorate. It's one thing to say that the average performance on a memory task would be twenty percent worse, or thirty percent worse. But it's another thing to say that your brain is so sluggish that it takes ten times longer for your brain to reply to something." As people stayed awake, it seemed their ability to focus fell off a cliff. In fact, if you stay awake for nineteen hours straight, you become as cognitively impaired—as unable to focus and think clearly—as if you had gotten drunk. He found that when they were kept awake for one whole night and continued walking about the next day, instead of taking a quarter of a second to respond to a prompt, the participants in his experiment were taking four, five, or six seconds. "It's kind of amazing," he said.

Charles was intrigued. Why would this be? He switched to studying sleep, and over the next forty years he would go on to become one of the leading figures in the world on this question, making several key breakthroughs. He runs the unit on sleep problems at one of the major hospitals in Boston, teaches at Harvard Medical School, and advises everyone from the Boston Red Sox to the U.S. Secret Service. He came to believe that, as a society, we are currently getting sleep all wrong—and it is ruining our focus.

With each passing year, he warned, this has become more urgent. Today 40 percent of Americans are chronically sleep-deprived, getting less than the necessary minimum of seven hours a night. In Britain, an incredible 23 percent are getting less than five hours a night. Only 15 percent of us wake up from our sleep feeling refreshed. This is new. Since 1942, the average amount of time a person sleeps has been slashed by an hour a night. Over the past century, the average child has lost eighty-five minutes of sleep every night. There's a scientific debate about the precise scale of our sleep loss, but the National Sleep Foundation has calculated that the amount of sleep we get has dropped by 20 percent in just a hundred years.

One day Charles had an idea. He wondered if, when you are tired, you begin to experience what he called "attentional blinks." This is where, initially for just a fraction of a second, you lose your ability to pay attention. To see if this is true, he started to study both alert and tired people using sophisticated technology that can track their eyes to see what they are focusing on—and at the same time, it can also scan your brain, to see what is happening there. He discovered something remarkable. As you become tired, your attention will indeed blink out, for a simple reason. People think you're either awake or asleep, he told me, but he found that even if your eyes are open and you are looking around you, you can lapse—without knowing it—into a state called "local sleep." This is where "part of the brain is awake, and part of the brain is asleep." (It's called local sleep because the sleep is local to one part of the brain.) In this state, you believe you are alert and mentally competent—but you aren't. You are sitting at your desk and you look awake, but parts of your brain are asleep, and you are not able to think in a sustained way. When he studied people in this state, he found "amazingly, sometimes their eyes were open, but they couldn't see what was in front of them."

The effects of sleep deprivation, Charles found, are especially terrible for children. Adults usually respond by becoming drowsy, but kids usually respond by becoming hyperactive. He said: "We're chronically sleep-depriving them, so it's no shock they're exhibiting all the symptoms of sleep deficiency—the first and foremost of which is the [in]ability to pay attention."

There has now been a lot of scientific investigation into this, and there's a broad scientific consensus that if you sleep less, your attention will likely suffer. I went to the University of Minneapolis to interview professor of neuroscience and psychology Roxanne Prichard, who has produced some cutting-edge work on these questions.

When she started teaching college students full-time in 2004, the first thing that struck her, she told me, was "how just exhausted young adults were." They would often fall asleep the moment the lecture-theater lights were dimmed, and they were visibly struggling to stay awake and focused on anything. She began to study how much sleep they were getting. She discovered that on average, a typical student has the same sleep quality as an active-duty soldier or a parent of a newborn baby. As a result, the majority of them were "constantly fighting off this drive to sleep. . . . They're not able to access their neural resources."

She decided to teach them the science of why their bodies need sleep—but she found herself in a strange position. The students knew they were bone-tired, but "the problem is—they've been accustomed to that since puberty, basically." They have seen their parents and grandparents chronically sleep-depriving themselves too. "They've grown up being accustomed to being exhausted and trying to medicate that away [with caffeine or other stimulants] as a state of normal. So I'm fighting against a current that says it's normal to be exhausted all the time." She started to show them some experiments. You can test the time it takes for a person to react to something—a picture that changes on a screen, say, or a ball that's thrown to them. "The people with the quickest reaction times are the ones sleeping the most," she shows them—and the less they sleep, the less they see or react. This is just one way, of many, that shows that "you are more efficient when you are rested—that it takes you less time to do things. That you don't need to have six screens or tabs open when you're doing your homework just to keep yourself awake."

At first, when I talked with Charles and Roxanne and other sleep experts, I thought, yes, this is bad, but they are talking about really exhausted people, an outlying group of the truly knackered. But they kept explaining to me that it only takes a small amount of sleep loss for these negative effects to kick in. Roxanne showed me that if you stay awake for eighteen hours—so you woke up at 6 a.m. and went to sleep at midnight—by the end of the day, your reactions are equivalent to if you had 0.05 percent blood alcohol. She said: "Stay up another three hours, and you're [the equivalent of being] legally drunk." Charles explained: "Many people say, 'Well, I don't stay up all night, so I'm fine,' but in fact, if you miss a couple of hours of sleep every night and you do this night after night, within a week or two, you're at the same level of performance and impairment as you would be staying up all night. Everybody falls apart with two nights of missed sleep—or you can get to that same point by sleeping four or five hours a night and going for a couple of weeks." As he said this, I remembered: 40 percent of us live on the brink of that.

"If you're not sleeping well, your body interprets that as an emergency," Roxanne said. "You can deprive yourself of sleep and live. We could never raise children if we couldn't drop down on our sleep, right? We'd never survive hurricanes. You can do that—but it comes at a cost. The cost is [that] your body shifts into the sympathetic nervous system zone—so your body is like, 'Uh-oh, you're depriving yourself of sleep, must be an emergency, so I'm going to make all these physiological changes to prepare yourself for that emergency. Raise your blood pressure. I'm going to make you want more fast food, I'm going to make you want more sugar for quick energy. I'm going to make your heart-rate [rise].' . . . So it's like all this shifts, to say—I'm ready." Your body doesn't know why it's staying awake. "Your brain doesn't know you're sleep-deprived because you're goofing off and watching *Schitt's Creek*, right? It doesn't know why you're not sleeping—but the net effect is a physiological sort of alarm bell."

In this bodily emergency, your brain doesn't just cut back on immediate short-term focus. It cuts off resources to other longer-term forms of focus too. When we sleep, our minds start to identify connections and patterns from what we've experienced during the day. This is one of the key sources of our creativity—it's why narcoleptic people, who sleep a lot, are significantly more creative. Sleep deprivation damages memory as well. When you go to bed tonight, your mind will start to transfer the things you have learned during the day into your long-term memory. Xavier Castellanos, who

I interviewed at New York University, where he is a professor of child and adolescent psychiatry, explained to me that you can get rats to learn a maze, and that night, you can monitor what happens in their brains as they sleep. What you find is that they are retracing their steps in the maze, one by one, encoding them into their long-term memory. The less you sleep, the less this happens, and the less you will be able to recall.

These effects are especially powerful for children. If you deprive kids of sleep, they begin to show attention problems rapidly, and often go into a manic state.

～

For years I believed I could cheat my way into getting all the benefits of proper sleep through technical fixes. The most obvious is caffeine. I once heard an almost certainly apocryphal story about Elvis—that in the last years of his life, his doctor would wake him up by inject-ing caffeine directly into his veins. When I heard this, I didn't think: How awful. I thought: Where's that doctor been all my life? For years I reasoned—okay, I don't sleep enough, but I make up for it with cof-fee, Coke Zero, and Red Bull. But Roxanne explained to me what I was really doing when I drank all this. Throughout the day, in your brain, a chemical called adenosine is building up, and it signals to you when you are sleepy. Caffeine blocks the receptor that picks up on the level of adenosine. "I liken it to putting a Post-it note over your fuel-gauge indicator. You're not giving yourself more energy—you're just not realizing how empty you are. When the caffeine wears off, you're doubly exhausted."

The less you sleep, the more the world blurs in every way—in your immediate focus, in your ability to think deeply and make con-nections, and in your memory. Charles told me that even if nothing else were changing in our society, this decline in how much we sleep is on its own enough to prove that our crisis in focusing and paying attention is real. "It's very sad to watch this play out and not be able to stop this," he said. "It's like watching a crash that's happening."

Every expert I spoke to said this transformation explains, in part, our declining attention. Dr. Sandra Kooij is one of the leading experts on adult ADHD in Europe, and when I went to interview her in The Hague, she told me bluntly: "Our Western society is a bit ADHD-ish because we're all sleep-deprived. . . . It's huge. And it means something for us. So we're all in a hurry, we're all impulsive, we're easily irritated in traffic. You see it everywhere around you. . . . This has been studied and proven in laboratories: you think you're thinking clearly, but you're not. You're much less clear than you could be." She added that "when we sleep better, a lot of problems get less— like mood disorders, like obesity, like concentration problems. . . . It repairs a lot of damage."

$\backsim$

As I learned all this, I had some obvious questions. The first was— why does our lack of sleep damage our ability to focus so much? Surprisingly, this is a relatively new research question. Roxanne told me: "In 1998, when I chose [the subject of sleep] to focus on for my dissertation, there wasn't a lot of research on what sleep was for. We knew what it was and we all do it . . . and it's kind of mysterious. You're spending a third of your life unconscious, not engaging with the world. . . . It was just this mystery—it seems like a waste of resources."

Charles had been told when he was a young man there was no point studying sleep because it's a passive process—but in fact, he learned, sleep is an incredibly active process. When you go to sleep, all sorts of activities take place in your brain and body—and these are necessary for you to be able to function and focus. One of the things that happens is that during sleep, your brain cleans itself of waste that has accumulated during the day. "During slow-wave sleep, your cerebral spinal fluid channels open up more and remove metabolic waste from your brain," Roxanne explained to me. Every night, when you go to sleep, your brain is rinsed with a watery fluid. This cerebrospinal fluid washes through your brain, flushing out toxic proteins and carrying them down to your liver to get rid of them. "So when I'm talking to college students, I call this brain-cell poop. If you can't focus well, it might be you have too much brain-cell poop circulating." That can explain why, when you are tired, "you get a hung-over sort of feeling"—you are literally clogged up with toxins.

This positive kind of brainwashing can only happen when you are asleep. Dr. Maiken Nedergaard, at the University of Rochester, told one interviewer: "The brain only has limited energy at its disposal, and it appears that it must choose between two different functional states—awake and aware, or asleep and cleaning up. You can think of it as like having a house party. You can either entertain the guests or clean up the house, but you can't really do both at the same time." A brain that hasn't been through this necessary cleaning process becomes more clogged and less able to concentrate. Some scientists suspect this is why people who are under-slept are at greater risk, in the long term, of developing dementia. When you are sleeping, Roxanne says, "you're repairing."

Another thing that happens during sleep is that your energy levels are restored and replenished. Charles told me that "the prefrontal cortex is the judgment area of the brain, and that seems to be particularly sensitive to sleep loss. . . . You see that, with even one night of sleep loss, that area of the brain is just not utilizing glucose, which is the main energy source of the brain. It's sort of going stone-cold." Without renewing your sources of energy, you can't think clearly.

But for me, the most intriguing process that happens when we sleep is that we dream—and this, I learned, also performs an important function. I went to Montreal to interview Tore Nielsen, who is a professor of psychiatry there. He often tells people he has a "dream job" and asks them to guess what it is. After they've run through the list—racing-car driver? chocolate-taster?—he tells them: he runs the Dream Lab at the University of Montreal. He told me that some scientists in the field believe that "dreaming somehow helps you to adapt emotionally to waking events." When you dream, you can revisit stressful moments, but without stress hormones flooding your system. Over time, those scientists believe, this can make it easier to handle stress—which we know makes it easier to focus. Tore emphasizes that there seems to be some evidence supporting this theory and some contradicting it, and we need to know more to be sure.

But if it is correct, then we have a problem—because as a society, we are dreaming less and less. Dreams occur most during the stage known as rapid eye movement (REM) sleep. Tore told me: "The longest and most intense REM periods are the ones that occur toward the seven- or eight-hour mark of the sleep cycle. So if you're curtailing your sleep down to five or six hours, chances are good that you're not getting those long, intense REM periods." As he said this, I wondered: What does it mean to be a society and culture so frantic that we don't have time to dream?

◦

As we find ourselves wired and unable to sleep, more and more of us are turning to drugs to knock ourselves out—whether it's melatonin or alcohol or Ambien. Nine million Americans—4 percent of adults—are using prescription sleeping pills, and vastly more are using over-the-counter sleep aids, like I did for many years. But Roxanne told me bluntly: "If you chemically induce sleep, it's not the same kind of sleep." Remember—sleep is an active process, in which your brain and body do lots of things. Many of these things don't happen, or happen far less, in drugged or drunk sleep. The different ways of artificially inducing sleep can have different effects. If you take five milligrams of melatonin—which is often a standard dose that's sold over the counter in the U.S.—Roxanne said you risk "blowing out your melatonin receptors," which would make it harder to sleep without them.

Bigger effects kick in with the harder stuff. Of Ambien and the other prescribed sedatives, she warns: "Sleep is a really important balance of many, many neurotransmitters, and if you artificially . . . pump up one, it changes the balance of that sleep." You will likely have less REM sleep, and fewer dreams, and so you lose all the benefits that come from this crucial stage. You are likely to be groggy throughout the day—which is why sleeping pills increase your risk of death from all causes; you're more likely to get into a car accident, for example. "If you've ever had surgery and recovered from that, like coming off anesthesia," Roxanne said, you don't say, "Oh, I feel so refreshed." Knocking yourself out is like taking a minor anesthetic. Your body doesn't rest and clean and refresh and dream like it needs to.

Roxanne told me that there are some legitimate uses for sleeping pills—for example, taking them for a short time after you've had a traumatic bereavement might be sensible. But she warned, "It's definitely not the solution for insomnia," and that's why doctors are not supposed to prescribe them over the long term.

∽

It's a sign of how dysfunctional we have become when it comes to sleep that the people who should be warning us most about this crisis—doctors—are in fact required to become sleep-deprived to get their qualifications. As part of their medical training, doctors have to do grueling twenty-four-hour shifts on call—they nickname it "doing a Jack Bauer," after the TV show 24, where Kiefer Sutherland can't sleep because he's chasing terrorists. This endangers their patients. But we have become a culture where even the people who should know best about sleep fetishize staying sleepless beyond the point of reason, just like the rest of us.

∽

The second question I found myself asking was: Given that lack of sleep is so harmful, and at some level we all know it, why are we doing it less? Why would we give up on one of our most basic needs?

There's a big scientific debate about this, and several factors seem to be having an effect. Some are going to come up later in this book. One of them—unexpectedly—is our relationship with physical light. Charles made some of the key breakthroughs on this. Until the nineteenth century, the lives of almost all humans were shaped primarily by the rise and fall of the sun. Our natural rhythms evolved to match it—we would get a rush of energy when it got light, and we would feel sleepy after it got dark. For almost all of human history, our ability to intervene in this cycle was pretty limited—we could light fires, but that was it. As a result, humans evolved to be as sensitive to changes of light, Charles says, as algae and cockroaches. But suddenly, with the invention of the electric lightbulb, we gained the power to control the light we are exposed to—and this power has started to scramble our internal rhythms.

Here's a clear example. We evolved to get a rush of energy— a "surge of waking drive," Charles says—when the sun began to set. This was very helpful to our ancestors. Imagine you're out camping, and the sun starts to fall—it's very useful if you then feel a rush of wakefulness, because then you'll be able to set up your tent before it's too dark to do it. In the same way, our ancestors got a fresh rush of energy just as the light waned so they could safely get back to their tribe and finish the things they needed to do that day. But now we control the light. We decide when sunset happens. So if we keep bright lights switched on right until the moment we decide to go to sleep, or we watch TV on our phones in bed, when we switch them off we accidentally trigger a physical process—our bodies think this sudden waning of the light is the arrival of sunset, so they release a rush of fresh energy to help you get back to your cave.

"Now this surge of waking drive, instead of happening at three or four o'clock in the afternoon before the sun sets at six, is now happening at ten, eleven, midnight," Charles says. "You have the surge of waking energy at the time you're deciding whether to go to sleep. Now you get up in the morning; you feel like you're going to die. You swear to God that you're going to get more sleep the next day, but you're not tired the next evening," because you've watched more TV on your laptop in bed, and triggered the same process all over again. "The surge is very powerful, and so people are like, 'I'm fine,' and the morning is a blur that they've forgotten." Charles believes that—as he said to another interviewer—"every time we turn on a light, we are inadvertently taking a drug that affects how we will sleep." This goes on day after day. "That's a major contributing factor to this epidemic of sleep deficiency—because we're exposing ourselves to light later and later," he explained. Indeed, 90 percent of Americans look at a glowing electronic device in the hour before they go to bed—triggering precisely this process. We are now exposed to ten times the amount of artificial light that people were exposed to just fifty years ago.

I wondered if one of the reasons why I slept so much better on Cape Cod was because I returned to something closer to this natural rhythm. When the sun sets on Provincetown, the town gets much darker, and by my beach house there was almost no artificial light, barely even a streetlamp. The orange haze of air pollution that lights up the sky in every place I have ever lived was gone, and there was only the gentle light of the moon and the stars.

～

But Charles told me you can only really understand our crisis of sleep if you understand it in a much bigger context. At first glance, he says, what we are doing is crazy: "We wouldn't deprive children of nutrition. We wouldn't think of doing that. Why are we depriving them of sleep?" But it makes a dark kind of sense when you see it as part of a broader picture. In a society dominated by the values of consumer capitalism, "sleep is a big problem," he told me. "If you're asleep, you're not spending money, so you're not consuming anything. You're not producing any products." He explained that "during the last recession [in 2008] . . . they talked about global output going down by so many percent, and consumption going down. But if everybody were to spend [an] extra hour sleeping [as they did in the past], they wouldn't be on Amazon. They wouldn't be buying things." If we went back to sleeping a healthy amount—if everyone did what I did in Provincetown—Charles said, "it would be an earthquake for our economic system, because our economic system has

become dependent on sleep-depriving people. The attentional failures are just roadkill. That's just the cost of doing business." I only
really understood how significant this point was toward the end of
writing this book.

~

All this leads to one last big question about sleep—how do we solve
this crisis? There are several layers to the solution. The first is personal and individual. As Charles explains, you need to radically limit
your exposure to light before you go to sleep. He believes you should
have no sources of artificial light in your bedroom at all, and you
should avoid the blue light of screens for at least two hours before
you go to bed.

We also need, all the sleep experts told me, to have different
relationships with our phones. Roxanne told me that to lots of us,
"it's like your baby, right? So as a new parent, you're like—I've got to
be vigilant for this thing. I've got to pay attention. I'm not sleeping as
deeply. Or you are like a firefighter who's listening for a call." We're
constantly a little tensed to see: "Did something happen?" She says
your phone should always recharge overnight in a different room,
where you can't see or hear it. Then you need to make sure your
room is the right temperature—it should be cool, almost cold. This
is because your body needs to cool its core to send you to sleep, and
the harder that is, the longer it takes.

These are helpful (and relatively well-known) tips—but, as every
expert I spoke to acknowledged, they are not enough for most people.
We live in a culture that is constantly amping us up with stress and
stimulation. You can tell people all this, and explain the health benefits of a good long night in bed, and they will agree, and then they say,
"Do you want me to list everything I need to do in the next twenty-
four hours? And you want me to spend nine hours sleeping too?"

As I learned about several of the things we need to do to improve
our focus, I realized that we live in an apparent paradox. Many of
the things we need to do are so obvious they are banal: slow down,

do one thing at a time, sleep more. But even though at some level we all know them to be true, we are in fact moving in the opposite direction: toward more speed, more switching, less sleep. We live in a gap between what we know we should do and what we feel we can do. The key questions, then, are: What's causing that gap? Why can't we do the obvious things that would improve our attention? What forces are stopping us? I spent a large part of the rest of my journey uncovering the answers.

CHAPTER FOUR

Cause Four: The Collapse of Sustained Reading

I n the West End of Provincetown there's a gorgeous bookstore named Tim's Used Books. You walk in and you immediately inhale the tangy must that comes from having old books stacked everywhere. I went in almost every other day that summer to buy another book to read. There was a young woman who worked at the cash register who was really smart, and I took to chatting with her. I noticed that every time I went in, she was reading a different book—one day Vladimir Nabokov, another day Joseph Conrad, another day Shirley Jackson. Wow, I said, you read fast. Oh, she replied, I don't. I can only read the first chapter or two of a book. I asked: Really? Why? She said: I guess I can't focus. Here was an intelligent young woman with lots of time, surrounded by many of the best books ever written, and with a desire to read them—but she could only get through the first chapter or two, and then her attention puttered out, like a failing engine.

I have lost count of how many people I know who have told me this. When I first met him, David Ulin, who was a book critic and editor at the *Los Angeles Times* for more than thirty years, told me that he had lost his ability to read deeply over long periods, because whenever he tried to settle down, he kept being drawn back to the buzz of the online conversation. This is an incredibly smart man whose whole life had been dedicated to books. It was disconcerting.

The proportion of Americans who read books for pleasure is now at its lowest level ever recorded. The American Time Use Survey—which studies a representative sample of 26,000 Americans—found that between 2004 and 2017 the proportion of men reading for pleasure had fallen by 40 percent, while for women, it was down by 29 percent. The opinion-poll company Gallup found that the proportion of Americans who never read a book in any given year tripled between 1978 and 2014. Some 57 percent of Americans now do not read a single book in a typical year. This has escalated to the point that by 2017, the average American spent seventeen minutes a day reading books and 5.4 hours on their phone. Complex literary fiction is particularly suffering. For the first time in modern history, less than half of Americans read literature for pleasure. It's been less well studied, but there seem to be similar trends in Britain and other countries: between 2008 and 2016 the market for novels fell by 40 percent. In one single year—2011—paperback fiction sales collapsed by 26 percent.

Mihaly Csikszentmihalyi has discovered in his research that one of the simplest and most common forms of flow that people experience in their lives is reading a book—and, like other forms of flow, it is being choked off in our culture of constant distraction. I thought a lot about this. For many of us, reading a book is the deepest form of focus we experience—you dedicate many hours of your life, coolly, calmly, to one topic, and allow it to marinate in your mind. This is the medium through which most of the deepest advances in human thought over the past four hundred years have been figured out and explained. And that experience is now in free fall.

In Provincetown I noticed I wasn't just reading more—I was

reading differently. I was becoming much more deeply immersed in the books I had chosen. I got lost in them for really long stretches, sometimes whole days—and I felt like I was understanding and remembering more of what I read. It seemed like I traveled farther in that deck chair by the sea, reading book after book, than I had in the previous five years of shuttling frantically around the world. I went from fighting on the battlefields of the Napoleonic Wars, to being an enslaved person in the Deep South, to being an Israeli mother trying to avoid hearing the news that her son has been killed. As I reflected on this, I started to think again about a book I had read ten years before: *The Shallows* by Nicholas Carr—a landmark work that really alerted people to a crucial aspect of the growing attention crisis. He warned that the way we are reading seems to be changing as we migrate to the internet—so I went back to one of the key experts he drew on, to see what they have learned since.

Anne Mangen is a professor of literacy at the University of Stavanger in Norway, and she explained to me that in two decades of researching this subject, she has proved something crucial. Reading books trains us to read in a particular way—in a linear fashion, focused on one thing for a sustained period. Reading from screens, she has discovered, trains us to read in a different way—in a manic skip and jump from one thing to another. "We're more likely to scan and skim" when we read on screens, her studies have found—we run our eyes rapidly over the information to extract what we need. But after a while, if we do this long enough, she told me, "this scanning and skimming bleeds over. It also starts to color or influence how we read on paper. . . . That behavior also becomes our default, more or less." It was precisely what I had noticed when I tried to settle into Dickens when I arrived in Provincetown and found myself rushing ahead of him, as if it was a news article and I was trying to push for the key facts.

This creates a different relationship with reading. It stops being a form of pleasurable immersion in another world and becomes more like dashing around a busy supermarket to grab what you need and then get out again. When this flip takes place—when our screen-reading contaminates our book-reading—we lose some of the pleasures of reading books themselves, and they become less appealing.

It has other knock-on effects. Anne has conducted studies that split people into two groups, where one is given information in a printed book, and the other is given the same information on a screen. Everyone is then asked questions about what they just read. When you do this, you find that people understand and remember less of what they absorb on screens. There's broad scientific evidence for this now, emerging from fifty-four studies, and she explained that it's referred to as "screen inferiority." This gap in understanding between books and screens is big enough that in elementary-school children, it's the equivalent of two-thirds of a year's growth in reading comprehension.

As she spoke, I realized that the collapse in reading books is in some ways a symptom of our atrophying attention, and in some ways a cause of it. It's a spiral—as we began to move from books to screens, we started to lose some of the capacity for the deeper reading that comes from books, and that, in turn, made us less likely to read books. It's like when you gain weight, and it gets harder and harder to exercise. As a result, Anne told me, she is worried we are now losing "our ability to read long texts anymore," and we are also losing our "cognitive patience . . . [and] the stamina and the ability to deal with cognitively challenging texts." When I was at Harvard conducting interviews, one professor told me that he struggled to get his students there to read even quite short books, and he increasingly offered them podcasts and YouTube clips they could watch instead. And that's Harvard. I started to wonder what happens to a world where this form of deep focus shrinks so far and so fast. What happens when that deepest layer of thinking becomes available to fewer and fewer people, until it is a small minority interest, like opera, or volleyball?

As I wandered the streets of Provincetown contemplating some of these questions, I found myself thinking back over a famous idea that I now realized I had never really understood before—one that was also mulled, in a different way, by Nicholas Carr in his book. In the 1960s, the Canadian professor Marshall McLuhan talked a lot about how the arrival of television was transforming the way we see the world. He said these changes were so deep and so profound that it was hard to really see them. When he tried to distill this down into a phrase, he explained that "the medium is the message." What he meant, I think, was that when a new technology comes along, you think of it as like a pipe—somebody pours in information at one end, and you receive it unfiltered at the other. But it's not like that. Every time a new medium comes along—whether it's the invention of the printed book, or TV, or Twitter—and you start to use it, it's like you are putting on a new kind of goggles, with their own special colors and lenses. Each set of goggles you put on makes you see things differently.

So (for example) when you start to watch television, before you absorb the message of any particular TV show—whether it's *Wheel of Fortune* or *The Wire*—you start to see the world as being shaped like television itself. That's why McLuhan said that every time a new medium comes along—a new way for humans to communicate—it has buried in it a message. It is gently guiding us to see the world according to a new set of codes. The way information gets to you, McLuhan argued, is more important than the information itself. TV teaches you that the world is fast; that it's about surfaces and appearances; that everything in the world is happening all at once.

This made me wonder what the message is that we absorb from social media, and how it compares to the message that we absorb from printed books. I thought first of Twitter. When you log in to that site—it doesn't matter whether you are Donald Trump or Bernie Sanders or Bubba the Love Sponge—you are absorbing a message through that medium and sending it out to your followers. What is that message? First: you shouldn't focus on any one thing for long.

The world can and should be understood in short, simple statements of 280 characters. Second: the world should be interpreted
and confidently understood very quickly. Third: what matters most
is whether people immediately agree with and applaud your short,
simple, speedy statements. A successful statement is one that lots of
people immediately applaud; an unsuccessful statement is one that
people immediately ignore or condemn. When you tweet, before you
say anything else, you are saying that at some level you agree with
these three premises. You are putting on those goggles and seeing the
world through them.

How about Facebook? What's the message in that medium? It
seems to be first: your life exists to be displayed to other people, and
you should be aiming every day to show your friends edited highlights of your life. Second: what matters is whether people immediately like these edited and carefully selected highlights that you
spend your life crafting. Third: somebody is your "friend" if you regularly look at their edited highlight reels, and they look at yours—this
is what friendship means.

How about Instagram? First: what matters is how you look on the
outside. Second: what matters is how you look on the outside. Third:
what matters is how you look on the outside. Fourth: what matters is
whether people *like* how you look on the outside. (I don't mean this
glibly or sarcastically; that really is the message the site offers.)

I realized one of the key reasons why social media makes me
feel so out of joint with the world, and with myself. I think all of
these ideas—the messages implicit in these mediums—are wrong.
Let's think about Twitter. In fact, the world is complex. To reflect
that honestly, you usually need to focus on one thing for a significant amount of time, and you need space to speak at length. Very
few things worth saying can be explained in 280 characters. If your
response to an idea is immediate, unless you have built up years
of expertise on the broader topic, it's most likely going to be shal-
low and uninteresting. Whether people immediately agree with you
is no marker of whether what you are saying is true or right—you

have to think for yourself. Reality can only be understood sensibly by adopting the *opposite* messages to Twitter. The world is complex and requires steady focus to be understood; it needs to be thought about and comprehended slowly; and most important truths will be unpopular when they are first articulated. I realized that the times in my own life when I've been most successful on Twitter—in terms of followers and retweets—are the times when I have been least useful as a human being: when I've been attention-deprived, simplistic, vituperative. Of course there are occasional nuggets of insight on the site—but if this becomes your dominant mode of absorbing information, I believe the quality of your thinking will rapidly degrade.

The same goes for Instagram. I like looking at pretty people, like everyone else. But to think that life is primarily about these surfaces—getting approval for your six-pack or how you look in a bikini—is a recipe for unhappiness. And the same goes for a lot of how we interact on Facebook too. It's not friendship to pore jealously over another person's photos and boasts and complaints, and to expect them to do the same for you. In fact, that's pretty much the opposite of friendship. Being friends is about looking into each other's eyes, doing things together in the world, an endless exchange of gut laughs and bear hugs, joy and grief and dancing. These are all the things Facebook will often drain from you by dominating your time with hollow parodies of friendship.

After thinking all this, I would return to the printed books I was piling up against the wall of my beach house. What, I wondered, is the message buried in the medium of the printed book? Before the words convey their specific meaning, the medium of the book tells us several things. Firstly, life is complex, and if you want to understand it, you have to set aside a fair bit of time to think deeply about it. You need to slow down. Secondly, there is a value in leaving behind your other concerns and narrowing down your attention to one thing, sentence after sentence, page after page. Thirdly, it is worth thinking deeply about how other people live and how their minds work. They have complex inner lives just like you.

I realized that I agree with the messages in the medium of the book. I think they are true. I think they encourage the best parts of human nature—that a life with lots of episodes of deep focus is a good life. It is why reading books nourishes me. And I don't agree with the messages in the medium of social media. I think they primarily feed the uglier and shallower parts of my nature. It is why spending time on these sites—even when, by the rules of the game, I am doing well, gaining likes and followers—leaves me feeling drained and unhappy. I like the person I become when I read a lot of books. I dislike the person I become when I spend a lot of time on social media.

~

But I wondered if I was getting carried away—these were just my hunches, after all—so later, I went to York University in Toronto to interview Raymond Mar, who is a professor of psychology there. Raymond is one of the social scientists who has done most in the world to study the effects that reading books has on our consciousness, and his research has helped to open up a distinctive way of thinking about this question.

When he was a little boy, Raymond read obsessively—but it had never occurred to him to try to figure out how reading itself might affect the way in which our minds work until he was a grad student, and one day, his mentor, Professor Keith Oatley, put a thought to him. When you read a novel, you are immersing yourself in what it's like to be inside another person's head. You are simulating a social situation. You are imagining other people and their experiences in a deep and complex way. So maybe, he said, if you read a lot of novels, you will become better at actually understanding other people off the page. Perhaps fiction is a kind of empathy gym, boosting your ability to empathize with other people—which is one of the most rich and precious forms of focus we have. Together, they decided to begin to study this question scientifically.

It's a tricky thing to study. Some other scientists had developed a technique where you give somebody a passage to read, and then immediately afterward you test their empathy. But to Raymond, this was flawed. If reading affects us, it reshapes us over the longer term—it's not like taking ecstasy, where you swallow it and experience immediate effects for a few hours.

With his colleagues he came up with a clever three-stage experiment designed to see if this longer-term effect existed. If you took part in the test, you were brought into a lab and you were shown a list of names. Some were famous novelists; some were famous nonfiction writers; and some were random people who weren't writers at all. You were asked to circle the names of the novelists, and then, separately, you were asked to circle the names of the nonfiction writers. Raymond reasoned that people who had read more novels over their lifetime would be able to recognize the names of more fiction writers. He also now had an interesting comparison group—people who had read a lot of nonfiction books.

Then he gave everyone two tests. The first used a technique that's sometimes used to diagnose autism. You are shown lots of pictures of people's eye areas, and you are asked: What is this person thinking? It's a way of measuring how good you are at reading the subtle signals that reveal the emotional state of another person. In the second test, you sat down and watched several videos of real people in real situations like, for example, two men who had just played a squash game talking to each other. You had to figure out: What's going on here? Who won the game? What's the relationship between them? How do they feel? Raymond and the experimenters knew the real answers—and so they could see who, in the test, was best at reading the social signals and figuring them out.

When they got the results, they were clear. The more novels you read, the better you were at reading other people's emotions. It was a huge effect. This wasn't just a sign that you were better educated—because reading nonfiction books, by contrast, had no effect on your empathy.

I asked Raymond why. Reading, he told me, creates a "unique

form of consciousness. . . . While we're reading, we're directing attention outward toward the words on the page and, at the same time, enormous amounts of attention is going inward as we imagine and mentally simulate." It's different from if you just close your eyes and try to imagine something off the top of your head. "It's being structured—but our attention is in a very unique place, fluctuating both out toward the page, toward the words, and then inward, toward what those words represent." It's a way of combining "outwardly directed attention and inwardly directed attention." When you read fiction in particular, you imagine what it is like to be another person. You find yourself, he says, "trying to understand the different characters, their motivations, their goals, tracking those different things. It's a form of practice. We're probably using the same kinds of cognitive processes that we would use to understand our real peers in the real world." You simulate being another human so well that fiction is a far better virtual reality simulator than the machines currently marketed under that name.

Each of us can only ever experience a small sliver of what it's like to be a human being alive today, Raymond told me, but as you read fiction, you see inside other people's experiences. That doesn't vanish when you put down the novel. When you later meet a person in the real world, you'll be better able to imagine what it's like to be them. Reading a factual account may make you more knowledgeable, but it doesn't have this empathy-expanding effect.

There have now been dozens of other studies replicating the core effect that Raymond discovered. I asked Raymond what would happen if we discovered a drug that boosted empathy as much as reading fiction has been shown to in his work. "If it had no side effects," he said, "I think that it would be a very popular drug." The more I talked with him, the more I reflected that empathy is one of the most complex forms of attention we have—and the most precious. Many of the most important advances in human history have been advances in empathy—the realization by at least some white people that other ethnic groups have feelings and abilities and dreams just like them;

the realization by some men that the way they have exerted power over women was illegitimate and caused real suffering; the realization by many heterosexuals that gay love is just like straight love. Empathy makes progress possible, and every time you widen human empathy, you open the universe a little more.

But—as Raymond is the first to point out—these results can be interpreted in a very different way. It could be that reading fiction, over time, boosts your empathy. But it could also be that people who are already empathetic are simply more drawn to reading novels. This makes his research controversial, and contested. He told me that it's likely that both are true—that reading fiction boosts your empathy, and that empathetic people are more drawn to reading fiction. But there's a hint, he said, that reading fiction really does have a significant effect: one of his studies found that the more a child is read storybooks—something the parents, more than the kid, choose—the better they are at reading other people's emotions. This suggests that the experience of stories really does expand their empathy.

If we have reasons to believe that reading fiction boosts our empathy, do we know what the forms that are largely replacing it—like social media—are doing to us? Raymond said it's easy to be snobbish about social media and to fall into a moral panic, and he finds that way of thinking silly. There's a lot that is good about social media, he stressed. The effects he is describing aren't to do primarily with the printed page, he said—they are to do with being immersed in a complex narrative that simulates the social world. His studies have found that long TV series are just as effective, he said. But there's a catch. One of his studies showed that children are more empathetic if they read storybooks or watch movies, but not if they watch shorter shows. This appears to fit, it seemed to me, with what we see on social media—if you see the world through fragments, your empathy often doesn't kick in, in the way that it does when you engage with something in a sustained, focused way.

As I talked with him, I thought: We internalize the texture of the voices we're exposed to. When you expose yourself to complex stories about the inner lives of other people over long periods of time, that will repattern your consciousness. You too will become more perceptive, open, and empathetic. If, by contrast, you expose yourself for hours a day to the disconnected fragments of shrieking and fury that dominate social media, your thoughts will start to be shaped like that. Your internal voices will become cruder, louder, less able to hear more tender and gentle thoughts. Take care what technologies you use, because your consciousness will, over time, come to be shaped like those technologies.

Before I said goodbye to Raymond, I asked him why he had spent so much time studying the effects of reading fiction on human consciousness. Up to the moment when I asked this, he had been something of a data geek, explaining his methods in great detail. But as he answered, his face opened up. "We're all on the same ball of mud and water that is heading toward a catastrophic end potentially. If we are going to solve these problems, we can't do it alone," he said. "That's why I think empathy is so valuable."

CHAPTER FIVE

Cause Five: The Disruption of Mind-Wandering

For more than one hundred years, there has been one image—a metaphor—that has, above all others, dominated how experts think about attention. Picture the Hollywood Bowl, crammed with tens of thousands of people, with all the laughing and jostling and yelling that takes place as people saunter in and wait for the show. Then, suddenly, the lights go down, and on the stage, a spotlight appears. It lights up one individual: Beyoncé. Or Britney. Or Bieber. Suddenly all the chatter and clatter cease, and the focus of that room narrows to one person and their awesome power. In 1890 the founder of modern American psychology, William James, wrote—in the most influential text ever (in the Western world, at least) on this subject—that "everyone knows what attention is." Attention, he said, is a spotlight. To put it in our terms, it's the moment Beyoncé appears, alone, on the stage, and everyone else around you seems to vanish.

James himself offered other images at the time too, and

psychologists have tried other ways of thinking about it—but ever since, the study of attention has primarily been the study of the spotlight. This image, I realized when I stopped to think about it, dominated how I thought about attention too. Attention is usually defined as a person's ability to selectively attend to something in the environment. So when I said I was distracted, I meant that I couldn't narrow the spotlight of my attention down to the one thing I wanted to focus on. I wanted to read a book, but the light of my attention wouldn't fade from my phone, or from the people talking in the street outside, or from my anxieties about work. There's a lot of truth in this way of thinking about attention—but I learned that, in fact, this is only one form of attention that you need in order to function fully. It exists alongside other forms of attention that are just as essential for you to be able to think coherently—and those forms are under even greater threat right now than your spotlight.

$\backsim$

In my life before I fled to Cape Cod, I lived in a tornado of mental stimulation. I would never go for a walk without listening to a podcast or talking on the phone. I would never wait two minutes in a store without looking at my phone or reading a book. The idea of not filling every minute with stimulation panicked me, and I found it weird when I saw other people not doing it. On long train or bus journeys, whenever I would see somebody just sit there for six hours, doing nothing but stare out of the window, I would feel an urge to lean over to them and say, "I'm sorry to disturb you. It's none of my business, but I just wanted to check—you do realize that you have a limited amount of time in which to be alive, and the clock counting down toward death is constantly ticking, and you'll *never* get back these six hours you are spending doing nothing at all? And when you are dead, you'll be dead *forever*? You know that, right?" (I never did this, as you can tell from the fact I am not writing this book from a psychiatric institution, but it crossed my mind.)

So I thought that in Provincetown, stripped of distractions, I would gain one benefit—I would be able to be even more stimulated, for even longer periods, and retain even more of what I inhaled. I can listen to longer podcasts! I can read longer books! That did happen—but it occurred alongside something else, something I didn't see coming. One day I left my iPod at home, and I decided to simply go for a walk along the beach. I walked for two hours, and I let my thoughts float, without my spotlight settling on anything. I felt my mind roam—from looking at the little crabs on the beach, to memories of my childhood, to ideas for books I might write years from now, to the shapes of the men sunning themselves in Speedos. My consciousness drifted like the boats I could see bobbing on the horizon.

At first I felt guilty. You came here to focus, I said to myself, and to learn about focus. But what you are indulging in is its opposite—a mental detumescence. But I continued. Before long, I was doing this every day, and my periods of meandering started to stretch to three, four, sometimes even five hours. This would be unthinkable to me in my normal life. But in that time, I felt more creative than I had since I was a child. Ideas started spinning out of my head. When I would get home and write them down, I realized I was having more creative ideas—and making more connections—in a single three-hour walk than I usually had in a month. I started to let smaller moments of mind-wandering in too. When I finished reading a book, I would just lie there for twenty minutes, thinking about it, staring out to sea.

Weirdly, it seemed like letting my spotlight disappear entirely was improving my ability to think and to focus in some way I couldn't articulate. How could that be? I only began to understand what was happening when I learned that over the past thirty years, there has been a sudden bubbling up of research into this very topic: mind-wandering.

~

In the 1950s, in the small town of Aberdeen in Washington state, a high school chemistry teacher named Mr. Smith had a problem with one of his students, a teenage boy named Marcus Raichle. He called in the boy's parents and explained sternly that he was doing something bad. "Your son has a habit of daydreaming," he said. We all know this is one of the worst things you can do at school.

Thirty years later, their son helped to make a breakthrough on this very topic—one that Mr. Smith would not have approved of. Marcus became a prominent neuroscientist and won the Kavli Prize, a leading honor in the field. In the 1980s, a whole new way of seeing what was happening in people's brains—the PET (positron-emission tomography) scan—evolved right outside his office, where the technology was being applied for the first time, by him and his colleagues. I stood on that very spot, in the Washington School of Medicine in St. Louis, Missouri, when I went to interview him. He was one of the first scientists who was able to use this new tool, and when he switched it on with a patient inside, he was able to see into a living human brain in a way almost nobody ever had before.

Back in his medical training, Marcus had been confidently told that we know what's happening inside your head in the moments when you are not focusing. Your brain is "lying there dormant, quiet, doing nothing, like muscles do until you start to move them," he was told. But one day Marcus noticed something odd. He had some patients strapped in for a PET scan, and those patients were waiting for him to give them a task and just letting their minds wander. As he got the task ready, he glanced at the machine, and he was puzzled. Their brains, it seemed, were not inactive, as his med-school tutors had said they should be. Activity had shifted from one part of the brain to another—but the brain was still highly active. Surprised, he began to study this in detail. He named the region of the brain that becomes more active when you think you're not doing much "the default mode network"—and as he studied this more, analyzing what people's brains do when they seem to be doing nothing, he could physically see this region light up on the brain scans. As he looked at them, Marcus said, "God, there she was. The whole thing. It was just stunning."

It was a paradigm shift in what scientists thought happens inside our brains, and it triggered an explosion of scientific research into dozens of topics all over the world. One of them was a sudden surge of interest in the science of mind-wandering, asking: What happens when our thoughts float freely, without any immediate focus to anchor them? We can see something is happening—but what? As the debate developed over decades, some scientists came to think that the default mode network is the part of the brain that becomes most active during mind-wandering, and others strongly disagreed— it's an ongoing debate. But Marcus's findings led to a rush of scientific research into why our minds wander at all, and what benefits it might produce.

To understand this better, I went to Montreal in Quebec to interview Nathan Spreng, who is a professor of neurology and neurosurgery at McGill University, and to York in England to interview Jonathan Smallwood, who is a professor of psychology at the university there. They are two of the people who have studied this question in most depth. It is a relatively new field of science, so some of its basic ideas are still quite contested, and more will become clear in the coming decades. But in their dozens of scientific studies, they had discovered—it seemed to me—three crucial things that are happening during mind-wandering.

First, you are slowly making sense of the world. Jonathan gave me an example. When you read a book—as you are doing now—you obviously focus on the individual words and sentences, but there's always a little bit of your mind that is wandering. You are thinking about how these words relate to your own life. You are thinking about how these sentences relate to what I said in previous chapters. You are thinking about what I might say next. You are wondering if what I am saying is full of contradictions, or whether it will all come together in the end. Suddenly you picture a memory from your childhood, or from what you saw on TV last week. "You draw together the different parts of the book in order to make sense of the key theme," he said. This isn't a flaw in your reading. This *is* reading. If you weren't letting your mind wander a little bit right now, you wouldn't really be reading this book in a way that would make sense to you. Having enough mental space to roam is essential for you to be able to understand a book.

This isn't just true of reading. It is true of life. Some mind-wandering is essential for things to make sense. "If you couldn't do it," Jonathan told me, "so many other things would go out of the window." He has found that the more you let your mind wander, the better you are at having organized personal goals, being creative, and making patient, long-term decisions. You will be able to do these things better if you let your mind drift, and slowly, unconsciously, make sense of your life.

Second, when your mind wanders, it starts to make new connections between things—which often produces solutions to your problems. As Nathan put it to me, "I think what's happening is that, when there's unresolved issues, the brain tries to make things fit," if it's just given the space to do it. He gave me a famous example: The nineteenth-century French mathematician Henri Poincaré was wrestling with one of the hardest problems in math, and he had narrowed his spotlight down onto every squiggle of it for ages, but he was getting nowhere. Then one day when he was away on a trip, suddenly, as he was stepping onto a bus, the solution came to him in a flash. It was only when he turned off the spotlight of his focus, and let his mind wander on its own, that he could connect the pieces and finally solve the problem. In fact, when you look back over the history of science and engineering, many great breakthroughs don't happen during periods of focus—they happen during mind-wandering.

"Creativity is not [where you create] some new thing that's emerged from your brain," Nathan told me. "It's a new association between two things that were already there." Mind-wandering allows "more extended trains of thought to unfold, which allows for more associations to be made." Henri Poincaré couldn't have come up with his solution if he had remained narrowly focused on the math problem he was trying to solve, or if he had been totally distracted. It took mind-wandering to get him there.

Third, during mind-wandering, your mind will—Nathan said—engage in "mental time-travel," where it roams over the past and tries to predict the future. Freed from the pressures of thinking narrowly about what's right in front of you, your mind will start to think about what might come next—and so it will help to prepare you for it.

Up until I met these scientists, I thought that mind-wandering—what I was doing in Provincetown so much, and so pleasurably—was the opposite of attention, and that's why I felt guilty about doing it. I realized I was wrong. It is actually a different form of attention—and a necessary one. Nathan told me that when we narrow our attention down into a spotlight to focus on one thing, that takes "a certain amount of bandwidth," and when we turn off the spotlight, "we still have the same bandwidth—it's just we can allocate more of those resources" toward other ways of thinking. "So it's not like attention necessarily goes down—it just shifts," to other, crucial forms of thinking.

This, I realized, is quite challenging to the whole way I had been raised to think about productivity. I feel instinctively like I've done a good hard day of work when I have been sitting at my laptop, spotlight-focused on tapping out words—at the end of it, I feel a little Puritan rush of pride at my productivity. Our whole culture is built around this belief. Your boss wants to see you sitting at your desk every hour of the day; this is what she thinks work is. This way of thinking is implanted in us from a very young age when, like Marcus Raichle, we are told off at school for daydreaming. That's why, on the days I spent simply wandering aimlessly on the beaches of Provincetown, I didn't feel productive. I thought I was slacking, being lazy, indulging myself.

But Nathan—after studying all this—had found that to be productive, you can't aim simply to narrow your spotlight as much as possible. He said: "I try to go for a walk every day and just let my mind kind of sort things out. . . . I don't think our full conscious control of our thoughts is necessarily our most productive way of thinking. I think loose patterns of association can lead to unique insight." Marcus agreed. Focusing on what's right in front of you, he told me, gives you "some of the raw material that has to be digested, but at some point, you need to stand back from that." He warned: "If we're just frantically running around focusing on the external world exclusively, we miss the opportunity to let the brain digest what's been going on."

As he said this, I thought about the people I had looked at on the train, staring out the window for hours. I had been silently judging them for their lack of productivity—but now I realized they may have been more meaningfully productive than me, as I frantically took notes on one book after another, without taking time to sit back and digest. The kid in the class who is staring out of the window mind-wandering might be doing the most useful thinking.

I thought back over all the scientific studies I had read about how we spend our time rapidly switching between tasks, and I realized that in our current culture, most of the time we're not focusing, but we're not mind-wandering either. We're constantly skimming, in an unsatisfying whir. Nathan nodded when I asked about this, and told me he is constantly trying to figure out how to get his phone to stop sending him notifications for things he doesn't want to know. All this frenetic digital interruption is "pulling our attention away from our thoughts," and "suppressing your default mode network. . . . I think we're almost in this constant stimulus-driven, stimulus-bound environment, moving from one distraction to the next." If you don't remove yourself from that, it will "suppress whatever train of thought you had."

⁓

So we aren't just facing a crisis of lost spotlight focus—we are facing a crisis of lost mind-wandering. Together they are degrading the quality of our thinking. Without mind-wandering, we find it harder to make sense of the world—and in the jammed-up state of confusion that creates, we become even more vulnerable to the next source of distraction that comes along. When I interviewed him, Marcus Raichle—who made the breakthrough that opened up this whole area of science—had just given up playing in a symphony orchestra, at the age of eighty. He was an oboe player, and his favorite piece to perform was Dvořák's Ninth Symphony. If you want to think about thinking itself, he told me, you should see it as being like a symphony. "You've got two violin sections, violas, cellos, basses, woodwinds, brass, percussion—but it operates as a whole. It has rhythms." You need space in your life for the spotlight of focus—but alone, it would be like a solo oboe player on a bare stage, trying to play Beethoven. You need mind-wandering to activate the other instruments and to make the sweetest music. I thought I had come to Provincetown to learn to focus. I realized that, in fact, I was learning to think—and that required much more than the spotlight of focus.

On the long walks I try to go on now without any devices at all, I spend a lot of time reflecting on Marcus's metaphor. A few days ago, I wondered if it could be taken further. If thinking is like a symphony that requires all these different kinds of thought, then right now, the stage has been invaded. One of those heavy-metal bands who bite the heads off bats and spit them at the audience has charged the stage, and they are standing in front of the orchestra, screaming.

∽

And yet, as I dug deeper into the research on mind-wandering, I learned there is an exception to what I just explained—and it's a big one. In fact, it is one you have probably experienced.

In 2010 the Harvard scientists Professor Dan Gilbert and Dr. Matthew Killingsworth developed a web app to study how people feel when they do all sorts of everyday things, from commuting to watching TV to exercising. People would get random prompts from the app that would ask: "What are you doing now?" They would then be asked to rank how they felt. One of the things Dan and Matthew tracked was how often people found themselves mind-wandering—and what they discovered was surprising, given everything I had just learned. In general, when people are mind-wandering in our culture, they rank themselves as less happy than when they are doing almost any other activity. Even housework, for example, is associated with higher levels of happiness. They concluded: "A wandering mind is an unhappy mind."

I thought about this a lot. Given that mind-wandering has been shown to have so many positive effects, why does it so often make us feel bad? There is a reason for this. Mind-wandering can easily descend into rumination. Most of us have had that feeling at some point or another—if you stop focusing and let your mind drift, you become jammed up with stressful thoughts. I thought back to my life at many points before Provincetown. When I was sitting on those trains, clucking in my own mind at the people who could sit staring out of the window while I manically worked and worked and worked, what was my mental state? Often, I saw now, I was loaded with stress and anxiety. Any attempt to relax my thinking would have let those bad feelings flood in. In Provincetown, by contrast, I had no stresses, and I felt safe—so my mind-wandering could float freely and do its positive work.

In situations of low stress and safety, mind-wandering will be a gift, a pleasure, a creative force. In situations of high stress or danger, mind-wandering will be a torment.

~

On the beach in the center of Provincetown, just off the long strip of Commercial Street, there is a comically large wooden blue chair that faces the ocean. It must be eight feet tall, as if it is waiting for a giant. I would often sit on that chair, looking tiny as darkness fell, talking with people I had befriended around the town. Sometimes we would be silent, and simply watch the light change. The light in Provincetown is unlike the light anywhere else I have ever been. You are on a thin, narrow sandbar in the middle of the ocean, and as you sit on that beach, you are facing east. The sun is setting behind you in the west—but its light is flowing forward, onto the water in front of you, and reflecting back into your face. You seem to be flooded with the waning light of two sunsets. I watched it with the people I met, and I felt radically open, to them, and to the sun, and to the ocean.

⁓

One day, about ten weeks into my time in Provincetown, I was sitting alone in my friend Andrew's house with one of his dogs, Bowie, at my feet. I was reading a novel and occasionally looking out toward the ocean, when I noticed that Andrew had left his laptop on a chair, open and glowing. On its screen, there was an internet browser. It had no password. There was the World Wide Web, glowing at me. You could look at the internet now, I thought to myself. You could look at anything you want—your social media, your email, the news. The thought made me feel heavy, and I made myself leave Andrew's house.

But the clock kept running down, and before long, I realized I had only two weeks left. I knew I had to go online to book a hotel for when I went back to Boston. In the Provincetown Library, there is a small bank of six computers that are open to the public. I had walked past them many times and I always averted my gaze, as if they were a toilet stall somebody had accidentally left open. I logged on and booked the hotel in two minutes, and then opened my email. I thought I knew what was about to happen. I spend around half an hour a day dealing with email in my normal life, spread from morning to night (and sometimes it's drastically more). So I calculated that in the time I had been away, I had clocked up thirty-five hours' worth of emails that I would now have to plow through over the next few months, scrambling to catch up. (When I had gone away, I left an auto-reply saying I was totally uncontactable.) I didn't want it. I felt exhausted just thinking about it.

But then something strange happened. I opened my inbox nervously and skimmed through my emails—and there was hardly anything there. In two hours, I had seen everything. The world had accepted my absence with a shrug. I realized that email breeds email, and if you just stop, it stops. I would like to say I felt calmed and soothed by this. In truth, I felt affronted—like my ego had been poked with a knitting needle. All this mania, all these demands on my time, I realized, made me feel important. I wanted in a sudden rush to send emails in order to get emails back—to feel needed again. I clicked over to my Twitter feed. I had precisely the same number of Twitter followers that I had when I left. My absence had been entirely unnoticed. I wandered away from the library and returned to the things that had given me nourishment in Provincetown—long passages of writing flowed from me; the ocean washed over my feet; my friends sat with me and talked all night. I tried to forget the wound to my ego.

On my last day in Provincetown, I took a boat out to Long Point, which is the tip of the tip of Cape Cod, a yellow crest of sand and sea. There, I could look back over the whole of the place where I had spent my summer, stretching from the Pilgrim Monument all the way down to Hyannis. It was a peculiar feeling, to see the boundaries of my summer in one single scan of the horizon. I felt more still and centered than I ever had before in my life.

You can't just go back and live the way you used to, I told myself, sitting in the shadow of the lighthouse. It's not hard. This summer has shown you how to do it. I demonstrated pre-commitment by cutting myself off. You can show pre-commitment in your everyday life now. I already owned the tools. On my laptop, I have a program called Freedom. It's easy—you download it, and you tell it you want it to deny you access to a specific website, or to the entire internet, for an amount of time you designate, from five minutes to a week. You hit the button, and no matter what you do, your laptop won't take you to that site, or get online at all. And for my phone, I owned something called a kSafe. Again, it's simple—it's a little plastic safe that opens at the top. You put your phone in it, and you put the lid on, and you twist the top to determine how long you want to shut your phone away for. Then it's gone—locked away, so you'd have to smash the kSafe with a hammer to get the phone out. Using these two devices, I said to myself, you can re-create Provincetown wherever you are. You can use your phone and the internet part of your laptop for maybe ten or fifteen minutes a day.

That evening, I gave away the small mountain of books I had read, and boarded the ferry to Boston. I got violently seasick on the journey back, and it felt like a rude metaphor for how I felt about returning to the online world. I reclaimed my phone from my friend the next day, and I lay on my hotel bed staring at it. It seemed strangely alien now—even the Apple font looked unfamiliar. I found myself flicking between icons, looking at various programs and websites. I looked at social media and thought, I don't want this. I flicked through Twitter and felt like I had stood on a termites' nest. When I looked up, three hours had passed.

I left it behind and went to eat. When I got back, people had started replying to my emails and texts, and despite myself, I felt a little rush of affirmation. In the next few weeks, I started to post on social media—and I felt myself become cruder and meaner than I had been in the summer. I made snarky comments. The complexity and compassion I had felt in Provincetown was, I felt, being replaced by something thinner. At moments I didn't like what I was saying. And then I felt the slow rush of approval, the retweets, the likes. I want to tell you that I learned the lessons of my time in Provincetown in a linear and life-affirming way, but that would be a lie. What happened was more complex. I left Provincetown in August, and I used Freedom and the kSafe, and slowly it slipped, and by December, the Screen Time on my iPhone indicated that I was spending four hours a day on my phone. I told myself that includes using Google Maps to navigate the city, and the hours I spent listening to podcasts and the radio and audiobooks. But I felt ashamed when I thought of it. I wasn't quite back to where I had been at the start, but I had clearly slid into distraction and disruption.

I felt like a failure. I had a strong sensation that something was pulling me down. Then I told myself: You're making excuses for your-self. You are doing this, nobody else. These are *your* failings. And I felt weak. I had gained a lot of insights in Provincetown—but I felt they were fragile, and easily broken by something bigger, something I didn't quite yet understand.

I wanted to know what was preventing me from doing what I wanted, in the better part of myself, to do. I discovered that the answer is more complex than we have been led to believe, and has many facets—and I learned about the first of them when I went to Silicon Valley.

CHAPTER SIX

Cause Six: The Rise of Technology That Can Track and Manipulate You (Part One)

James Williams told me I had made a fundamental mistake in Provincetown. He was a senior Google strategist for many years, and he left, horrified, to go to Oxford University, to study human attention, and figure out what his colleagues in Silicon Valley have done to it. He told me a digital detox is "not the solution, for the same reason that wearing a gas mask for two days a week outside isn't the answer to pollution. It might, for a short period of time, keep, at an individual level, certain effects at bay. But it's not sustainable, and it doesn't address the systemic issues." He said our attention is being deeply altered by huge invasive forces in the wider society. Saying the solution is primarily to personally abstain is just "pushing it back onto the individual," he said, when "it's really the environmental changes that will really make the difference."

For a long time I didn't fully understand what this meant. What would changing our environment entail, when it came to attention, if not each of us trying to change our own personal behavior? The answer slowly became clear to me when I met with many people who had designed crucial aspects of the world in which we now live. In the hills of San Francisco and the hot, arid streets of Palo Alto, I realized that there are six ways in which our technology, as it currently works, is harming our ability to pay attention—and that these causes are united by one deeper underlying force that needs to be overcome.

One of the first people to guide me on this journey was Tristan Harris, another former Google engineer, who, after I had been interviewing him for several years, became globally famous for appearing in the viral Netflix documentary *The Social Dilemma*. That film explored a whole range of ways in which social media, as it is currently designed, can be destructive. I wanted to tease out something the film largely didn't explore—its effect on our focus. To grasp it, I think it helps to know Tristan's own story, and what he witnessed at the heart of the machine that is repatterning the world's attention.

∾

In the early 1990s, in the town of Santa Rosa, California, a little boy with a bowl haircut and a bright golden bow tie was learning magic. Tristan was seven years old when he first tried out one of the most basic tricks. He would ask you to hand him a coin, and then— poof! It was gone. After he mastered more tricks, he put on a magic show for his elementary-school class, and then—to his glee—he was selected to go to a magic camp out in the hills, where he was taught for a week by professional magicians. It seemed to him like a real-life Jedi training camp.

He discovered, at this young age, the most important fact about magic. He explained years later: "It's really about the limits of attention." The job of a magician is—at heart—to manipulate your focus. That coin didn't really vanish—but your attention was somewhere else when the magician moved it, so when your focus comes back to the original spot, you're amazed. To learn magic is to learn to manipulate someone's attention without them even realizing it—and once the magician controls their focus, Tristan realized, he can do what he wants. One of the things that he was taught at camp is that a person's susceptibility to magic has nothing to do with their intelligence. "It's about something more subtle," he said later. It's "about the weaknesses, or the limits, or the blind spots, or the biases that we're all trapped inside of."

Magic, in other words, is the study of the limits of the human mind. You think you control your attention; you think that if somebody messes with it, you will know, and you'll be able to spot and resist it right away, but, in reality, we are fallible sacks of meat, and we are fallible in predictable ways that can be figured out by magicians and messed with.

As he got to know better and better magicians—eventually befriending one of the best in the world, Derren Brown—Tristan learned something he found both remarkable and disconcerting. It is possible to manipulate your attention to such a degree that a magician can, in many cases, turn you into his puppet. He can make you choose whatever he wants you to choose, while all along you think you're simply using your own free will. When Tristan first said this to me, I thought he was overstating his case, so he introduced me to another magician friend, James Brown. Tristan told me James would show me what it meant. I'll give you one example. When we sat together, James showed me a standard pack of cards. He said: See? Some of them are red, and some of them are black, and they are all mixed up together. Then he turned the cards so the colors were facing toward him, and I couldn't see them anymore. He told me he was going to get me to sort them neatly into two piles—one black, one red—without me ever getting to look at the color of the cards for myself. It was, obviously, impossible. How could I sort cards I couldn't see?

He told me to look into his eyes, and—entirely using my own free will—to tell him whether to put the next card into a pile on the left, or a pile on the right. So I gave him my orders—left, left, right, and so on—according to what I was confident were my own random whims. At the end, he lifted up the piles of cards and showed them to me. The red cards were neatly in one pile; the black cards were in the other.

I was baffled. How did he do it? He eventually told me he had been subtly guiding my choices. He said he would do it again, a little more crudely this time, to see if I could spot it. Finally—and he had to be pretty blatant—I saw it. When he told me to pick the next card, he indicated very slightly with his eyes to the left or to the right—and I always chose in the way he unconsciously guided me to. Everyone always does, he told me. Later, Tristan explained to me that this is a core insight of magic—you can manipulate people and they don't even know it's happening. They will swear to you that they made their own free choices—as I would have about those cards.

One morning, in his office in San Francisco, Tristan leaned forward and said to me: "How does a magician do their work? It works because they don't have to know your strengths—they just have to know your weaknesses. How well do you know your weaknesses?" I wanted to believe I understood my weaknesses very well, but Tristan shook his head gently. "If people did know their weaknesses," he said, "then magic wouldn't work."

Magicians play on these weaknesses to delight and entertain us. As Tristan grew up, he became part of another group of people who were figuring out our weaknesses to manipulate us—but they had very different goals.

⁓

It was in his first year at Stanford University, in 2002, that Tristan first heard whispers of a mysterious-sounding research facility known as the Persuasive Technology Lab. It was, the rumors went, a place where a leading scientist was figuring out how to design technology that could change your behavior in unprecedented ways. In his teens Tristan had become obsessed with coding, and he had already been an intern at Apple after his freshman year at Stanford, designing a piece of code that is still used in many of your devices today.

This much-discussed course, he learned, was about taking a huge amount of what scientists had discovered over the twentieth century about how to change other people's behavior, and enabling students to understand how these classic influence techniques could be used in tech products.

The course was taught by a warm, upbeat behavioral scientist in his forties named Professor B. J. Fogg. At the start of each day, he would take out a stuffed frog and a cuddly monkey and introduce them to the class, and then he would play on his ukulele. Whenever he wanted the group to break or wrap up, he would tap on a toy xylophone. B.J. explained to students that computers had the potential to be far more persuasive than people. They could, he believed, "be more persistent than human beings, offer greater anonymity," and "go where humans cannot go or may not be welcome." Soon, he was sure, they would be changing the lives of everyone—persuading us persistently, throughout the day. He had previously worked on a course dedicated to "the psychology of mind control." In the fall of 2006, B.J. testified before the Federal Trade Commission (FTC), warning that there was a "potential dark side" looming, where it will be hard for you to tell "when you are being persuaded and when you are not." He assigned to Tristan and his other students a large amount of books that explained dozens of psychological insights and tricks that had been discovered about how to change human beings and to get them to do what you want. It was a treasure trove. One of the texts that most struck Tristan was based on the philosophy of B. F. Skinner, the man who, as I had learned earlier, had found a way to get pigeons and rats and pigs to do whatever he wanted by offering the right "reinforcements" for their behavior. After falling out of fashion for years, his ideas were back with full force.

"It really woke up the magic part of me," Tristan told me. "I was like—oh wow, there really are these invisible rules that govern what people do. And if there are rules that govern what people do, that's power. That's like Isaac Newton discovering the laws of physics. It felt like somebody's showing me the code—the code of how you can influence people. I remember the experience of sitting there in the graduate area of campus reading those books over the weekends, and underlining furiously these passages, and just being like—oh my God, I can't even believe that works." He was so intoxicated by the excitement of it that, he said, "I will admit, I don't think the ethical bells were firing in my brain yet."

As part of the class, he was paired with a young man named Mike Krieger, and they were tasked with designing an app. Tristan had been thinking for a while about something named "seasonal affective disorder"—a condition where, if you are stuck in gloomy weather for a long time, you are more likely to become depressed. How, they asked, could technology help with that? They came up with an app called Send the Sunshine. Two friends would choose to be connected through it, and it would track where they both were and the online weather reports for their locations. If the app realized that your friend was starved of sunshine, and you had some, it would prompt you to take a photo of the sun and send it to him. It showed that somebody cared; and it sent some sunshine your way. It was sweet, and simple, and it helped to spur Mike to think about the power of sharing photographs online. He was already thinking about another of the key lessons of the class, taken from B. F. Skinner: build in immediate reinforcements. If you want to shape the user's behavior, make sure he gets hearts and likes right away. Using these principles, he and another friend, Kevin Systrom, launched a new app of their own. They named it Instagram.

The class was filled with people who were going to use the techniques B.J. taught to change how we live our lives, and B.J. was dubbed "the millionaire maker." But something was starting to nag at Tristan. After a while, he noticed he had become obsessed with checking his email. He would do it repetitively, mindlessly, again and again, and he felt his attention span was beginning to atrophy. He realized, he told me, that the email app he was using "operates on a bunch of different levers, and it's very powerful, and it sucks, and it's super-stressful, and it ruins hours and hours of people's lives." He had learned at Stanford and elsewhere how to use technology to change people's behavior, but he came to ask a disconcerting question: Am I somehow being hacked by other tech designers myself? He wasn't yet sure how they might be doing it—but he began to have a strange feeling about it. B.J. taught his students that they should only use these powers for good, and he laced ethical debates throughout his course. Tristan told me: "B.J. is a good and ethical person who shouldn't bear the blame for what we're seeing take place." Yet Tristan was going to start to wonder: Were these radical new technologies actually being used ethically in the real world, by people who were leaving B.J.'s moral ambit, or had never heard his ethics lessons in the first place?

In the final class Tristan attended, all the students discussed ways in which these persuasive technologies could be used in the future. Professor Fogg led his students in a discussion, posing the question: "What if in the future you had a profile of every single person on earth?" As a designer, you would track all the information they offer up on social media and build a detailed profile of them. It's not just the simple stuff—their gender, or age, or interests. It would be something deeper. This would be a psychological profile—figuring out how their personality works, and the best ways to persuade them. It would know if the user was an optimist or pessimist, if they were open to new experiences or they were prone to nostalgia—it would figure out dozens of characteristics they have.

Think, the class wondered out loud, about how you could target people if you knew this much about them. Think about how you could change them. When a politician or a company wants to persuade you, they could pay a social-media company to perfectly target their message just for you. It was the birth of an idea—one that would be picked up in Silicon Valley later by different people far removed from B.J. and his warnings about ethics. Years later, when it was revealed that the campaign for Donald Trump had paid a company named Cambridge Analytica to do exactly that, Tristan would think of that final class discussion at Stanford. "This was the class that freaked me out," he told me. "I remember saying—this is horribly concerning."

But Tristan had a deep belief in the power of tech to do good. So he took what he had learned at Stanford and—under the mentorship of B.J., his former teacher at Stanford—designed an app with a straightforward positive purpose. He was trying to stop one of the ways the web screws with our attention. Let's say you are checking out the CNN site, and you start to read a news story about Northern Ireland, a topic you don't know much about. Normally, you will then open a new window and begin googling for info—and before you know it, you vanish down a rabbit hole and emerge half an hour later, lost in articles and videos about a totally different topic (usually cats playing the piano). Tristan's app was designed so that in this situation, you could do something different: you could highlight any phrase (say, "Northern Ireland"), and it would pull up a simple pop-up window giving you a straightforward summary of the topic. No clicking away from the site; no rabbit holes. Your attention is preserved. The app did well—it started to be used by thousands of websites, including the *New York Times,* and quite soon, Google made a substantial offer to buy the whole thing and for Tristan to come and work for them. They told him it was so he could integrate it into their web browser, Chrome, and make people less distracted. He jumped at the chance.

It is hard to convey, Tristan believes, quite what it was like to go to work for Google at that moment in history, in 2011. Every day, the company he worked for—from its base, the Googleplex in Palo Alto—was shaping and reshaping how one billion people navigated their way through the world: what they got to see, and what they didn't. He told one audience later: "I want you to imagine walking into a room. A control room, with a bunch of people, a hundred people, hunched over a desk with little dials—and that that control room will shape the thoughts and feelings of a billion people. This might sound like science fiction, but this actually exists right now, today. I know, because I used to work in one of those control rooms."

Tristan was assigned for a while to work on the development of

Gmail, Google's email system—precisely the app that was driving him wild, and that he suspected might be using some manipulative tricks he hadn't yet figured out. Even as he worked on it, he would obsessively check his email, making him less focused, and whenever he looked at a new message, he found it took him a long time to get his mind back to where it had been before. He started trying to think through how you might design a system of email that was less prone to nuking your attention—but whenever he tried to discuss this idea with his colleagues, the conversation didn't seem to go far. At Google, he quickly learned, success was measured, in the main, by what was called "engagement"—which was defined as minutes and hours of eyeballs on the product. More engagement was good; less engagement was bad. This was for a simple reason. The longer you make people look at their phones, the more advertising they see—and therefore the more money Google gets. Tristan's co-workers were decent people, struggling with their own tech distractions—but the incentives seemed to lead only one way: you should always design products that "engage" the maximum number of people, because engagement equals more dollars, and disengagement equals fewer dollars.

With each month that passed, Tristan became more startled by the casualness with which the attention of a billion people was being corroded at Google and the other Big Tech companies. One day he would hear an engineer excitedly saying: "Why don't we make it buzz your phone every time we get an email?" Everyone would be thrilled—and a few weeks later, all over the world, phones began to buzz in pockets, and more people found themselves looking at Gmail more times a day. The engineers were always looking for new ways to suck eyeballs onto their program and keep them there. Day after day, he would watch as engineers proposed more interruptions to people's lives—more vibrations, more alerts, more tricks—and they would be congratulated.

As the number of people using Google and Gmail continued to spike up, Tristan started to ask his colleagues: "How do you ethically persuade two billion people's minds? . . . How do you ethically structure two billion people's attention?" But instead, he found that most other people in the company were being pushed to ask simply, "How can we make this more engaging?" And that meant more attention-sucking, more interrupting—on and on it went, with better techniques being discovered every week. One day, when we were walking in San Francisco, Tristan said to me: "Things look pretty bad from the outside, but when you're on the inside, things can look even worse." Tristan was starting to realize: It's not your fault you can't focus. It's by design. Your distraction is their fuel.

After working intensively on the Gmail team, Tristan saw that when it came to questioning what they were doing to people's attention, "the conversation was not happening." He looked out across his friends now working in every part of Silicon Valley, and this grab-and-raid approach to our focus was being taken in almost all the companies they worked in. "What started to really concern me over the years," he told me, "was just watching my friends who had originally gotten into this business because they thought they could make the world better, [and now] were caught in this arms race to manipulate human nature."

To pluck one example out of dozens Tristan could offer, his friends Mike and Kevin had launched Instagram, and after a little while, "they added these filters, because it was a cool thing. So you could take a photo, and just have it look artistic instantly." It didn't cross their minds, he's sure, that it would start a race with Snapchat and others to see who could "provide better beautification filters"—and that this would, in turn, change how people thought of their own bodies so much that today there's a whole category of people who undergo surgery so they can look more like their filters. He could see that his friends were setting in motion changes that were transforming the world in ways they couldn't predict or control. "The reason we have to be so careful about the way that we design technology," he said, is that "they squeeze, they squish, the entire world down into that medium—and out the other end comes a different world."

But here was Tristan, at the center of the machine unleashing these transformations, and he could see that behind closed doors, the dials in the control room were being set to ten.

∽

After a few years at the heart of the Googleplex, Tristan couldn't take it anymore, and he decided to leave. As a final gesture, he put together a slide-deck for the people he worked with, to appeal to them to think about these questions. The first slide said simply: "I'm concerned about how we're making the world more distracted." He explained: "Distraction matters to me, because time is all we have in life. . . . Yet hours and hours can get mysteriously lost here." He showed a picture of a Gmail inbox. "And [on] feeds that suck huge chunks of time away here." He showed a Facebook feed. He said he was worried that the company—and others like it—was inadvertently "destroy[ing] our kids' ability to focus," pointing out that the average child between the ages of thirteen and seventeen in the U.S. was sending one text message every six minutes they were awake. People were, he warned, living "on a treadmill of continuous checking."

He asked: We know that interruptions cause a deterioration in people's ability to focus and think clearly—so why are we ramping up the interruptions? Why are we finding better and better ways to do it all the time? "Think about that," he told his colleagues. "We should feel an enormous responsibility to get this right." All humans have natural vulnerabilities, and instead of exploiting those vulnerabilities—like a malign magician—Google should be respecting them. He suggested some modest changes as a place to start. Instead of notifying someone every time they have a new email, he suggested, we could notify them once a day, in a batch—so it'd be like getting a newspaper in the morning, instead of constantly following the rolling news. Every time we prompt somebody to click over to a new photo their friend has posted, we could warn them—on the same screen—that the average person who clicks on a photo is pulled away for twenty minutes before they get back to their task. We could tell them: You think it'll only take a second, but it won't.

He suggested giving users a chance to pause every time they click to do something potentially seriously distracting, to check: Are you sure you want to do this? Do you know how much time it will take from you? "Humans make different decisions when we pause and consider," he said.

He was trying to give his colleagues a sense of the weight of the decisions they made every day: "We shape more than eleven billion interruptions to people's lives *every day*. This is nuts!" The people sitting around you in the Googleplex, he explained, control more than 50 percent of all the notifications on all the phones in the whole world. We are "creating an arms race that causes companies to find more reasons to steal people's time," and it "destroys our common silence and ability to think." He asked: "Do we really know what we're doing to people?"

This was an almost insanely bold thing to do. At the heart of the machine that was changing the world, here was a smart and talented but fairly junior engineer, still only twenty-nine years old, saying something that directly challenged the whole direction of the company. It would be like a junior exec in 1975 standing up in front of the whole of ExxonMobil and telling them that they were responsible for global warming by showing them images of the melting of the Arctic. Everyone in Silicon Valley was scrambling to get into and suck up to Google. But here was Tristan, with the ability to stay at its heart forever and make a lot of money, writing what seemed to be his own professional death certificate, because he believed somebody, somewhere, had to say something.

He shared his slide-deck with his colleagues, and went home, depressed. Then something unexpected happened.

⁓

With each hour that passed, more and more Google employees shared Tristan's slide-deck. The next day, he was inundated with messages from within the company enthusing about it. It turned out he had tapped into a latent mood. Just because you design these products, it doesn't mean you are more insulated than anyone else from becoming hooked on them. The workers at the Googleplex could feel this tsunami of distractions hitting them too. Many of them wanted to have a serious conversation about what they were doing to the world. People were drawn in particular to the question Tristan had put to them: "What if we designed [our products] to minimize stress and create calmer states of mind?"

There was some pushback too. A few of his colleagues said that every new technology brings with it a panic where people say it'll trash the world—after all, Socrates said writing things down would ruin people's memories. We were told that everything from the printed book to television would trash the minds of the young, but here we are, and the world survived. Some others responded from a libertarian perspective, saying that what he was suggesting would invite government regulation, which they believed was contrary to the whole spirit of cyberspace.

Tristan's presentation caused such a ruction within Google that he was asked to stay in a special new position, created just for him. They offered him the role of being Google's first "design ethicist." He was thrilled. Here was a chance to think through some of the most challenging questions of our time, in a place where—if he could get people to listen—he could make an enormous difference. For the first time in a long time, he felt optimistic. He thought his new appointment meant Google was serious about exploring these questions. He knew there was enthusism for it among his fellow workers, and he believed in the good faith of his bosses.

He was assigned a desk, and—in effect—left to think. So he started to research the effects of many things. For example, he looked at the way Snapchat hooks teenagers. The app had an option called "Snapchat streaks," where two friends—almost always teens—would check in with each other every day through the app. Every day they checked in, their streak got longer, so you would aim to build up a streak of two hundred, three hundred, four hundred days, all on a brightly colored display full of emojis. If you missed a single day, it would reset to zero. It was a perfect way to take the desire of teens for social connection and manipulate it to get them hooked. You came every day to extend your streak, and you stuck around to scroll, often for hours.

But whenever he came up with a specific proposal for how Google's own products could be less interrupting and presented it to people above him, he was told, in effect: "This is hard, it's confusing, and it's often at odds with our bottom line." Tristan realized he was bumping up against a core contradiction. The more people stared at their phones, the more money these companies made. Period. The people in Silicon Valley did not want to design gadgets and websites that would dissolve people's attention spans. They're not the Joker, trying to sow chaos and make us dumb. They spend a lot of their own time meditating and doing yoga. They often ban their own kids from using the sites and gadgets they design, and send them instead to tech-free Montessori schools. But their business model can only succeed if they take steps to dominate the attention spans of the wider society. It's not their goal, any more than ExxonMobil deliberately wants to melt the Arctic. But it's an inescapable effect of their current business model.

When Tristan warned about these negative effects, most people inside the company sympathized and agreed. When he suggested alternatives, people changed the subject. To give you a sense of the money involved: the personal wealth of Larry Page, one of the founders of Google, is $102 billion; his colleague Sergey Brin is worth $99 billion; and their colleague Eric Schmidt is worth $20.7 billion. That's separate from Google's wealth as a company, which as I write stands at $1 trillion. These three men alone are worth roughly the same as the total combined wealth of every single person, building, and bank account in the oil-rich country of Kuwait, and Google is worth roughly the entire wealth of the whole of Mexico or Indonesia. Telling them to distract people less was like telling an oil company not to drill for oil—they didn't want to hear it. "You don't even really get to make that ethical decision" to improve people's attention spans, Tristan realized, "because your business model and your incentives are making that decision for you." Years later, testifying before the U.S. Senate, he explained: "I failed because companies don't [currently] have the right incentive to change."

Tristan was in the ethicist job for two years, and toward the end, as he told an audience later, "I felt completely hopeless. There were literally days when I went to work and I would read Wikipedia all day and check my email and I would have no idea how, once you see something as massive as the attention economy and its perverse incentives, a system this big could ever change. I truly felt hopeless. I felt depressed." So, finally, he quit Google, and went out into a Silicon Valley where, as he put it to me, "everything is a race for attention." In that lonely time in Tristan's life, he was about to team up with another person who felt depressed and lost—and who felt guilty about what he personally had done to you, me, and everyone we know.

⁓

You probably haven't heard of Aza Raskin, but he has directly intervened in your life. He will, in fact, probably affect how you spend your time today. Aza grew up in the most elite sliver of Silicon Valley, at the height of its confidence that it was making the world better. His dad was Jef Raskin, the man who invented the Apple Macintosh for Steve Jobs, and he built it around one core principle: that the user's attention is sacred. The job of technology, Jef believed, was to lift people up and make it possible to achieve their higher goals. He taught his son: "What is technology for? Why do we even make technology? We make technology because it takes the parts of us that are most human and it extends them. That's what a paintbrush is. That's what a cello is. That's what language is. These are technologies that extend some part of us. Technology is not about making us superhuman. It's about making us extra-human."

Aza became a precocious young coder, and he gave his first talk about user interfaces when he was ten years old. By the time he was in his early twenties, he was at the forefront of designing some of the first internet browsers, and he was the creative lead on Firefox. As part of this work, he designed something that distinctly changed how the web works. It's called "infinite scroll." Older readers will remember that it used to be that the internet was divided into pages, and when you got to the bottom of one page, you had to decide to click a button to get to the next page. It was an active choice. It gave you a moment to pause and ask: Do I want to carry on looking at this? Aza designed the code that means you don't have to ask that question anymore. Imagine you open Facebook. It downloads a chunk of status updates for you to read through. You scroll down through it, flicking your finger—and when you get to the bottom, it will automatically load another chunk for you to flick through. When you get to the bottom of that, it will automatically load another chunk, and another, and another, forever. You can never exhaust it. It will scroll infinitely.

Aza was proud of the design. "At the outset, it looks like a really good invention," he told me. He believed he was making life easier for everyone. He had been taught that increased speed and efficiency of access were always advances. His invention quickly spread all over the internet. Today, all social media and lots of other sites use a version of infinite scroll. But then Aza watched as the people around him changed. They seemed to be unable to pull themselves away from their devices, flicking through and through and through, thanks in part to the code he had designed. He found himself infinitely scrolling through what he often realized afterward was crap, and he wondered if he was making good use of his life.

One day, when he was thirty-two, Aza sat down and did a calculation. At a conservative estimate, infinite scroll makes you spend 50 percent more of your time on sites like Twitter. (For many people, Aza believes, it's vastly more.) Sticking with this low-ball percentage, Aza wanted to know what it meant, in practice, if billions of people were spending 50 percent more on a string of social-media sites. When he was done, he stared at the sums. Every day, as a direct result of his invention, the combined total of 200,000 more human lifetimes—every moment from birth to death—is now spent scrolling through a screen. These hours would otherwise have been spent on some other activity.

When he described this to me, he still sounded a little stunned. That time is "just completely gone. It's like their entire life—poof. That time, which could have been used for solving climate change, for spending time with their family, for strengthening social bonds. For whatever it is that makes their life well-lived. It just . . ." He trailed off. I pictured my young godson Adam and all his teenage friends, scrolling, scrolling, infinitely scrolling.

Aza told me he felt "sort of dirty." He realized: "These things we do, they really can change the world. Then the question immediately follows: In what way did we change the world?" He realized he thought making tech easier to use meant the world would get better. But he began to think that "one of my biggest learnings as a designer or technologist is—making something easy to use doesn't mean it's good for humanity." He thought about his father—who had since died—and his commitment to make tech that set people free to be better, and he wondered if he was living up to his dad's vision. He began to ask if he and his generation in Silicon Valley were actually "mak[ing] technology that tears us, rips us, and breaks us."

He carried on designing more things in the vein of infinite scroll, and getting more and more uncomfortable. "It was about the time that we were getting to be really successful at this that my stomach started to drop," he told me. He felt that he was seeing people become more unempathetic, angry, and hostile as their social-media use went up. At the time, he was running an app he had designed named Post-Social, which was a social-media site designed to help people interact more in the real world, away from their devices. He was trying to raise money for the next phase of its development, and all any investor wanted to know was: How much of people's attention do you capture and run through your app? How often? How many times a day? That's not what Aza wanted to be—a person who thought solely about how to drain away people's time. But "you could see this gravity, pulling this product back to everything that we were trying to fight against."

The logic of the underlying system was being laid bare for Aza. Silicon Valley sells itself by articulating "a big, lofty goal—connecting everyone in the world, or whatever it is. But when you're actually doing the day-to-day work, it's about increasing user numbers." What you are selling is your ability to grab and hold attention. When he tried to discuss this, he thwacked into raw denial. "Say you were baking bread," he said to me, "and you had this incredible bread, and you used this secret substance—and all of a sudden, you're making free bread for the world, and everyone's eating it. Then one of your scientists comes and says: 'By the way, we think it causes cancer, this secret substance.' What do you do? You would almost certainly say: 'That can't be right. We need more research. Maybe it's something [else] that the people out there are doing. Maybe there's some other factor.'"

All throughout the industry, Aza kept meeting people who were going through similar crises. "There were a number of dark nights of the soul that I personally witnessed," he says. He watched as Silicon Valley's own inhabitants seemed to be hijacked by their own creations, and then tried to escape. When I met with several of these tech dissidents, it struck me how young they were—like they were almost children who had invented toys and watched their toys conquer the world. Everyone was scrambling to meditate in an attempt to resist the programs they had invented. He realized "one of the ironies is there are these incredibly popular workshops at Facebook and Google about mindfulness—about creating the mental space to make decisions nonreactively—and they are also the biggest perpetrators of non-mindfulness in the world."

When Tristan and Aza started to speak out, they were ridiculed as wildly over-the-top Cassandras. But then, one by one, all over Silicon Valley, people who had built the world we now live in were beginning to declare in public that they had similar feelings. For example, Sean Parker, one of the earliest investors in Facebook, told a public audience that the creators of the site had asked themselves from the start: "How do we consume as much of your time and conscious attention as possible?" The techniques they used were "exactly the kind of thing that a hacker like myself would come up with, because you're exploiting a vulnerability in human psychology. . . . The inventors, creators—it's me, it's Mark [Zuckerberg], it's Kevin Systrom on Instagram, it's all of these people—understood this consciously. And we did it anyway." He added: "God only knows what it's doing to our children's brains." Chamath Palihapitiya, who had been Facebook's vice president of growth, explained in a speech that the effects are so negative that his own kids "aren't allowed to use that shit." Tony Fadell, who co-invented the iPhone, said: "I wake up in cold sweats every so often thinking, what did we bring to the world?" He worried that he had helped create "a nuclear bomb" that can "blow up people's brains and reprogram them."

Many Silicon Valley insiders predicted that it would only get worse. One of its most famous investors, Paul Graham, wrote: "Unless the forms of technological progress that produced these things are subject to different laws than technological progress in general, the world will get more addictive in the next forty years than it did in the last forty."

~

One day, James Williams—the former Google strategist I met—addressed an audience of hundreds of leading tech designers and asked them a simple question: "How many of you want to live in the world you are designing?" There was a silence in the room. People looked around them. Nobody put up their hand.

CHAPTER SEVEN

Cause Six: The Rise of Technology That Can Track and Manipulate You (Part Two)

Tristan said to me that if you want to understand the deeper problems in the way our tech currently works—and why it is undermining our attention—a good place to start is with what seems like a simple question.

Imagine you are visiting New York and you want to know which of your friends are around in the city so you can hang out with them. You turn to Facebook. The site will alert you about lots of things— a friend's birthday, a photo you've been tagged in, a terrorist attack— but it won't alert you to the physical proximity of somebody you might want to see in the real world. There's no button that says "I want to meet up—who's nearby and free?" This isn't technologically tricky. It would be really easy for Facebook to be designed so that when you opened it, it told you which of your friends were close by and which of them would like to meet for a drink or dinner that week. The coding to do that is simple; Tristan and Aza and their friends could probably write it in a day. And it would be hugely popular. Ask any

Facebook user: Would you like Facebook to physically connect you to your friends more, instead of keeping you endlessly scrolling?

So—it's an easy tweak, and users would love it. Why doesn't it happen? Why won't the market provide it? To understand why, Tristan and his colleagues explained to me, you need to step back and understand more about the business model of Facebook and the other social-media companies. If you follow the trail from this simple question, you will see the root of many of the problems we are facing.

Facebook makes more money for every extra second you are staring through a screen at their site, and they lose money every time you put the screen down. They make this money in two ways. Until I started to spend time in Silicon Valley, I had only naively thought about the first and the most obvious. Clearly—as I wrote in the last chapter—the more time you look at their sites, the more advertisements you see. Advertisers pay Facebook to get to you and your eyeballs. But there's a second, more subtle reason why Facebook wants you to keep scrolling and desperately doesn't want you to log off. When I first heard about this reason, I scoffed a little—it sounded far-fetched. But then I kept talking with people in San Francisco and Palo Alto, and every time I expressed skepticism about it, they looked at me like I was a maiden aunt in the 1850s who had just heard the details of sex for the first time. How, they asked, did you *think* it worked?

Every time you send a message or status update on Facebook, or Snapchat, or Twitter, and every time you search for something on Google, everything you say is being scanned and sorted and stored. These companies are building up a profile of you, to sell to advertisers who want to target you. For example, starting in 2014, if you used Gmail, Google's automated systems would scan through all your private correspondence to generate an "advertising profile" exactly for you. If (say) you email your mother telling her you need to buy diapers, Gmail knows you have a baby, and it knows to target ads for baby products straight to you. If you use the word "arthritis," it'll try to sell you arthritis treatments. The process that had been predicted in Tristan's final class back in Stanford was beginning.

Aza explained it to me by saying that I should imagine that "inside of Facebook's servers, inside of Google's servers, there is a little voodoo doll, [and it is] a model of you. It starts by not looking much like you. It's sort of a generic model of a human. But then they're collecting your click trails [i.e., everything you click on], and your toenail clippings, and your hair droppings [i.e., everything you search for, every little detail of your life online]. They're reassembling all that metadata you don't really think is meaningful, so that doll looks more and more like you. [Then] when you show up on [for example] YouTube, they're waking up that doll, and they're testing out hundreds of thousands of videos against this doll, seeing what makes its arm twitch and move, so they know it's effective, and then they serve that to you." It seemed like such a ghoulish image that I paused. He went on: "By the way—they have a doll like that for one in four human beings on earth."

At the moment these voodoo dolls are sometimes crude and sometimes startlingly specific. We've all had one kind of experience of searching online for something. I recently tried to buy an exercise bike, and still, a month later, I am endlessly being served advertisements for exercise bikes by Google and Facebook, until I want to scream, "I bought one already!" But the systems are getting more sophisticated every year. Aza told me: "It's getting to be so good that whenever I give a presentation, I'll ask the audience how many think Facebook is listening to their conversations, because there's some ad that's been served that's just too accurate. It's about a specific thing they never mentioned before [but they happen to have talked about offline] to a friend the day before. Now, it's generally one-half to two-thirds of the audience that raises their hands. The truth is creepier. It's not that they are listening and then they can do targeted ad serving. It's that their model of you is so accurate that it's making predictions about you that you think are magic."

It was explained to me that whenever something is provided by a tech company for free, it's always to improve the voodoo doll. Why is Google Maps free? So the voodoo doll can include the details of where you go every day. Why are Amazon Echo and Google Nest Hubs sold for as cheap at $30, far less than they cost to make? So they can gather more info; so the voodoo doll can consist not just of what you search for on a screen but what you say in your home.

This is the business model that built and sustains the sites on which we spend so much of our lives. The technical term for this system—coined by the brilliant Harvard professor Shoshana Zuboff—is "surveillance capitalism." Her work has made it possible for us to understand a lot of what is happening now. Of course, there have been increasingly sophisticated forms of advertising and marketing for over a hundred years—but this is a quantum leap forward. A billboard didn't know what you googled at three in the morning last Thursday. A magazine ad didn't have a detailed profile of everything you've ever said to your friends on Facebook and email. Trying to give me a sense of this system, Aza said to me: "Imagine if I could predict all your actions in chess before you made them. It would be trivial for me to dominate you. That's what is happening on a human scale now."

Once you understand all this, you can see why there is no button that suggests you meet up with your friends and family away from the screen. Instead of getting us to maximize screen time, that would get us to maximize face-to-face time. Tristan said: "If people used Facebook just to quickly get on, so they could find the amazing thing to do with their friends that night, and get off, how would that [affect] Facebook's stock price? The average amount of time people spend on Facebook today is something like fifty minutes a day. . . . [But] if Facebook acted that way, people would spend barely a few minutes on there per day, in a much more fulfilling way." Facebook's share price would collapse; it would be, for them, a catastrophe. This is why these sites are designed to be maximally distracting. They need to distract us, to make more money.

Tristan has seen, on the inside, how these business incentives work in practice. Imagine this, he said to me: An engineer proposes a tweak that improves people's attention, or gets them to spend more time with their friends. "Then what happens is they will wake up two weeks to four weeks later, and there'll be some review on their dashboard looking at the metrics. [Their manager will] be saying, 'Hey, why did time spent [on the site] go down about three weeks ago? Oh, it'll be [because] we added these features. Let's just roll back some of those features, to figure out how we get that number back up.'" This isn't some conspiracy theory, any more than it's a conspiracy theory to explain that KFC wants you to eat fried chicken. It's simply an obvious result of the incentive structure that has been put in place and that we allow to continue. "Their business model," he says, "is screen time, not life time."

It was at this point in learning Tristan's story—from him, his friends, his colleagues, and his critics—that I realized something so simple that I am almost embarrassed to say it. For years, I had blamed my deteriorating powers of attention simply on my own failings or on the existence of the smartphone itself as a technology. Most of the people I know do the same. We tell ourselves: The phone arrived, and it ravaged me. I believed any smartphone would have done the same. But what Tristan was showing is that the truth is more complicated. The arrival of the smartphone would always have increased to some degree the number of distractions in life, to be sure, but a great deal of the damage to our attention spans is being caused by something more subtle. It is not the smartphone in and of itself; it is the way the apps on the smartphone and the sites on our laptops are designed.

Tristan taught me that the phones we have, and the programs that run on them, were deliberately designed by the smartest people in the world to maximally grab and maximally hold our attention. He wants us to understand that this design is not inevitable. I had to really think this over, because, of all the things I learned from him, this seemed the most important.

The way our tech works now to corrode our attention was and remains a choice—by Silicon Valley, and by the wider society that lets them do it. Humans could have made a different choice then, and they can make a different choice now. You could have all this technology, Tristan told me, but not design it to be maximally distracting. In fact, you could design it with the opposite goal: to maximally respect people's need for sustained attention, and to interrupt them as little as possible. You could design the technology not so that it pulls people away from their deeper and more meaningful goals, but so that it helps them to achieve them.

This was shocking to me. It's not just the phone; it's the way the phone is currently designed. It's not just the internet; it's the way the internet is currently designed—and the incentives for the people designing it. You could keep your phone and your laptop, and you could keep your social-media accounts—and have much better attention, if they were designed around a different set of incentives.

Once you see it in this different way, Tristan came to believe, it opens up a very different path forward, and the beginnings of a way out of our crisis. If the existence of the phone and the internet is the sole driver of this problem, we're trapped and in deep trouble—because as a society, we're not going to discard our tech. But if it's the current *design* of the phones and the internet and the sites we run on them that is driving a lot of the problem, there's a very different way they could work that would put us all in a very different position.

After you've adjusted your perspective in this way, seeing this as a debate between whether you are pro-tech or anti-tech is bogus and lets the people who stole your attention off the hook. The real debate is: *What* tech, designed for *what* purposes, in *whose* interests?

∿

But when Tristan and Aza said that these sites are designed to be as distracting as possible, I still didn't really understand how. It seemed like a big claim. To grasp it, I had to first learn something else embarrassingly basic. When you open your Facebook feed, you see a whir of things for you to look at—your friends, their photos, some news stories. When I first joined Facebook back in 2008, I naively thought that these things appeared simply in the order in which my friends had posted them. I'm seeing my friend Rob's photo because he just put it up; then my auntie's status update comes next because she posted it before him. Or maybe, I thought, they were selected randomly. In fact, I learned over the years—as we all became more informed about these questions—that what you see is selected for you according to an algorithm.

When Facebook (and all the others) decide what you see in your news feed, there are many thousands of things they could show you. So they have written a piece of code to automatically decide what you will see. There are all sorts of algorithms they could use—ways they could decide what you should see, and the order in which you should see them. They could have an algorithm designed to show you things that make you feel happy. They could have an algorithm designed to show you things that make you feel sad. They could have an algorithm to show you things that your friends are talking about most. The list of potential algorithms is long.

The algorithm they actually use varies all the time, but it has one key driving principle that is consistent. It shows you things that will keep you looking at your screen. That's it. Remember: the more time you look, the more money they make. So the algorithm is always weighted toward figuring out what will keep you looking, and pumping more and more of that onto your screen to keep you from putting down your phone. It is designed to distract. But, Tristan was learning, that leads—quite unexpectedly, and without anyone intending it—to some other changes, which have turned out to be incredibly consequential.

Imagine two Facebook feeds. One is full of updates, news, and videos that make you feel calm and happy. The other is full of updates, news, and videos that make you feel angry and outraged. Which one does the algorithm select? The algorithm is neutral about the question of whether it wants you to be calm or angry. That's not its concern. It only cares about one thing: Will you keep scrolling? Unfortunately, there's a quirk of human behavior. On average, we will stare at something negative and outrageous for a lot longer than we will stare at something positive and calm. You will stare at a car crash longer than you will stare at a person handing out flowers by the side of the road, even though the flowers will give you a lot more pleasure than the mangled bodies in a crash. Scientists have been proving this effect in different contexts for a long time—if they showed you a photo of a crowd, and some of the people in it were happy, and some angry, you would instinctively pick out the angry faces first. Even ten-week-old babies respond differently to angry faces. This has been known about in psychology for years and is based on a broad body of evidence. It's called "negativity bias."

There is growing evidence that this natural human quirk has a huge effect online. On YouTube, what are the words that you should put into the title of your video, if you want to get picked up by the algorithm? They are—according to the best site monitoring YouTube trends—words such as "hates," "obliterates," "slams," "destroys." A major study at New York University found that for every word of moral outrage you add to a tweet, your retweet rate will go up by 20 percent on average, and the words that will increase your retweet rate most are "attack," "bad," and "blame." A study by the Pew Research Center found that if you fill your Facebook posts with "indignant disagreement," you'll double your likes and shares. So an algorithm that prioritizes keeping you glued to the screen will—unintentionally but inevitably—prioritize outraging and angering you. If it's more enraging, it's more engaging.

~

If enough people are spending enough of their time being angered, that starts to change the culture. As Tristan told me, it "turns hate into a habit." You can see this seeping into the bones of our society. When I was a teenager, there was a horrific crime in Britain, where two ten-year-old children murdered a toddler named Jamie Bulger. The Conservative prime minister at the time, John Major, responded by publicly saying that he believed we need "to condemn a little more, and understand a little less." I remembered thinking then, at the age of fourteen, that this was surely wrong—that it's always better to understand why people do things, even (perhaps especially) the most heinous acts. But today, this attitude—condemn more, understand less—has become the default response of almost everyone, from the right to the left, as we spend our lives dancing to the tune of algorithms that reward fury and penalize mercy.

In 2015 a researcher named Motahhare Eslami, as part of a team at the University of Illinois, took a group of ordinary Facebook users and explained to them how the Facebook algorithm works. She talked them through how it selects what they see. She discovered that 62 percent of them didn't know their feeds were filtered at all, and they were astonished to learn about the algorithm's existence. One person in the study compared it to the moment in the film *The Matrix* when the central character, Neo, discovers he is living in a computer simulation.

I called several of my relatives and asked them if they knew what an algorithm was. None of them—including the teenagers—did. I asked my neighbors. They looked at me blankly. It's easy to assume most people know about this, but I don't think it's true.

When I pieced together what I'd learned, I could see that—when I broke it down—the people I interviewed had presented evidence for six distinct ways in which this machinery, as it currently operates, is harming our attention. (I will come to the scientists who dispute these arguments in chapter eight; as you read this, remember that some of it is controversial.)

First, these sites and apps are designed to train our minds to crave frequent rewards. They make us hunger for hearts and likes. When I was deprived of them in Provincetown, I felt bereft, and had to go through a painful withdrawal. Once you have been conditioned to need these reinforcements, Tristan told one interviewer, "it's very hard to be with reality, the physical world, the built world—because it doesn't offer as frequent and as immediate rewards as this thing does." This craving will drive you to pick up your phone more than you would if you had never been plugged into this system. You'll break away from your work and your relationships to seek a sweet, sweet hit of retweets.

Second, these sites push you to switch tasks more frequently than you normally would—to pick up your phone, or click over to Facebook on your laptop. When you do this, all the costs to your attention caused by switching—as I discussed in chapter one—kick in. The evidence there shows this is as bad for the quality of your thinking as getting drunk or stoned.

Third, these sites learn—as Tristan put it—how to "frack" you. These sites get to know what makes you tick, in very specific ways— they learn what you like to look at, what excites you, what angers you, what enrages you. They learn your personal triggers—what, specifically, will distract *you*. This means that they can drill into your attention. Whenever you are tempted to put your phone down, the site keeps drip-feeding you the kind of material that it has learned, from your past behavior, keeps you scrolling. Older technologies— like the printed page, or the television—can't target you in this way. Social media knows exactly where to drill. It learns your most distractible spots and targets them.

Fourth, because of the way the algorithms work, these sites make you angry a lot of the time. Scientists have been proving in experiments for years that anger itself screws with your ability to pay attention. They have discovered that if I make you angry, you will pay less attention to the quality of arguments around you, and you will show "decreased depth of processing"—that is, you will think in a shallower, less attentive way. We've all had that feeling—you start prickling with rage, and your ability to properly listen goes out the window. The business models of these sites are jacking up our anger every day. Remember the words their algorithms promote—attack, bad, blame.

Fifth, in addition to making you angry, these sites make you feel that you are surrounded by other people's anger. This can trigger a different psychological response in you. As Dr. Nadine Harris, the surgeon general of California, who you'll meet later in this book, explained to me: Imagine that one day you are attacked by a bear. You will stop paying attention to your normal concerns—what you're going to eat tonight, or how you will pay the rent. You become vigilant. Your attention flips to scanning for unexpected dangers all around you. For days and weeks afterward, you will find it harder to focus on more everyday concerns. This isn't limited to bears. These sites make you feel that you are in an environment full of anger and hostility, so you become more vigilant—a situation where more of your attention shifts to searching for dangers, and less and less is available for slower forms of focus like reading a book or playing with your kids.

Sixth, these sites set society on fire. This is the most complex form of harm to our attention, with several stages, and I think probably the most harmful. Let's go through it slowly.

~

We don't just pay attention as individuals; we pay attention together, as a society. Here's an example. In the 1970s, scientists discovered that all over the world, people were using hairsprays that contained a group of chemicals named CFCs. These chemicals were then entering the atmosphere and having an unintended but disastrous effect—they were damaging the ozone layer, a crucial part of the atmosphere that protects us from the sun's rays. Those scientists warned that, over time, this could pose a serious threat to life on earth. Ordinary people absorbed this information and saw that it was true. Then activist groups—made up of ordinary citizens—formed, and demanded a ban. These activists persuaded their fellow citizens that this was urgent and made it into a big political issue. This put pressure on politicians, and that pressure was sustained until those politicians banned CFCs entirely. At every stage, averting this risk to our species required us to be able to pay attention as a society—to absorb the science; to distinguish it from falsehood; to band together to demand action; and to pressure our politicians until they acted.

But there is evidence that these sites are now severely harming our ability to come together as a society to identify our problems and to find solutions in ways like this. They are damaging not just our attention as individuals, but our collective attention. At the moment false claims spread on social media far faster than the truth, because of the algorithms that spread outraging material faster and farther. A study by the Massachusetts Institute of Technology found that fake news travels six times faster on Twitter than real news, and during the 2016 U.S. presidential election, flat-out falsehoods on Facebook outperformed all the top stories at nineteen mainstream news sites put together. As a result, we are being pushed all the time to pay attention to nonsense—things that just aren't so. If the ozone layer was threatened today, the scientists warning about it would find themselves being shouted down by bigoted viral stories claiming the threat was all invented by the billionaire George Soros, or that there's no such thing as the ozone layer anyway, or that the holes were really being made by Jewish space lasers.

If we are lost in lies, and constantly riled up to be angry with our fellow citizens, this sets off a chain reaction. It means we can't understand what is really going on. In those circumstances, we can't solve our collective challenges. This means our wider problems will get worse. As a result, the society won't just *feel* more dangerous—it will actually *be* more dangerous. Things will start to break down. And as real danger rises, we will become more and more vigilant.

One day, Tristan was shown how this dynamic works when he was approached by a man named Guillaume Chaslot, who had been an engineer designing and administering the algorithm that picks out the videos that are recommended to you on YouTube when you watch a video there. Guillaume wanted to tell him what was happening behind closed doors. Just like Facebook, YouTube makes more money the longer you watch. That's why they designed it so that when you stop watching one video, it automatically recommends and plays another one for you. How are those videos selected? YouTube also has an algorithm—and it too has figured out that you'll keep watching longer if you see things that are outrageous, shocking, and extreme. Guillaume had seen how it works, with all the data YouTube keeps secret—and he saw what it means in practice.

If you watched a factual video about the Holocaust, it would recommend several more videos, each one getting more extreme, and within a chain of five or so videos, it would usually end up automatically playing a video denying the Holocaust happened. If you watched a normal video about 9/11, it would often recommend a "9/11 truther" video in a similar way. This isn't because the algorithm (or anyone at YouTube) is a Holocaust denier or 9/11 truther. It was simply selecting whatever would most shock and compel people to watch longer. Tristan started to look into this, and concluded: "No matter where you start, you end up more crazy."

It turned out, as Guillaume leaked to Tristan, that YouTube had recommended videos by Alex Jones and his website Infowars 15 *billion* times. Jones is a vicious conspiracy theorist who has claimed that the 2012 Sandy Hook massacre was faked, and that the grieving parents are liars whose children never even existed. As a result, some of those parents have been inundated with death threats and have had to flee their homes. This is just one of many insane claims he has made. Tristan has said: "Let's compare that—what is the aggregate traffic of the *New York Times,* the *Washington Post,* the *Guardian*? All that together is not close to fifteen billion views."

The average young person is soaking up filth like this day after day. Do those feelings of anger go away when they put down their phone? The evidence suggests that for lots of people, they don't. A major study asked white nationalists how they became radicalized, and a majority named the internet—with YouTube as the site that most influenced them. A separate study of far-right people on Twitter found that YouTube was by far the website they turned to the most. "Just watching YouTube radicalizes people," Tristan explained. Companies like YouTube want us to think "we have a few bad apples," he explained to the journalist Decca Aitkenhead, but they don't want us to ask: "Do we have a system that is systematically, as you turn the crank every day, pumping out more radicalization? We're growing bad apples. We're a bad-apple factory. We're a bad-apple farm."

I saw a vision of where this could take us all when in 2018, I went to Brazil in the run-up to their presidential election, in part to see my friend Raull Santiago, a remarkable young man I got to know when I was writing the Brazilian edition of my book about the war on drugs, *Chasing the Scream*.

Raull grew up in a place named Complexo do Alemão, which is one of the biggest and poorest favelas in Rio. It's a huge, jagged ziggurat of concrete and tin and wire that stretches far up on the hills, way above the city, until it seems to be almost in the clouds. At least 200,000 people live there, in narrow concrete alleyways that are crisscrossed with makeshift wires providing electricity. The people here built this whole world brick by brick, with little support from the state. The alleyways of Alemão are surreally beautiful: they look like Naples after some undefined apocalypse. As a child, Raull would fly kites high above the favela with his best friend, Fabio, where they could see out all across Rio, toward the ocean and the statue of Christ the Redeemer.

Often the authorities would send tanks rolling into the favela. The attitude of the Brazilian state toward the poor was to keep them suppressed with periodic threats of extreme violence. Raull and Fabio would regularly see bodies in the alleyways. Everyone in Alemão knew that the cops could shoot poor kids and claim they were drug dealers, and plant drugs or guns on them. In practice, the police had a license to murder the poor.

Fabio always seemed like the kid most likely to get away from all of this. He was great at math, and determined to earn money for his mother and disabled sister. He was always figuring out deals—he persuaded the local bars to let him buy their bottles so he could sell them in bulk, for example. But then, one day, Raull was told something terrible: Fabio had—like so many kids before him—been shot dead by the police. He was fifteen years old.

Raull decided he couldn't just watch his friends being killed one by one—so, as the years passed, he decided to do something bold. He set up a Facebook page named Coletivo Papo Reto, which gathered cellphone footage from across Brazil of the police killing innocent people and planting drugs or guns on them. It became huge, their videos regularly going viral. Even some people who had defended the police began to see their real behavior and oppose it. It was an inspiring story about how the internet made it possible for people who have been treated like third-class citizens to find a voice, and to mobilize and fight back.

But at the same time as the web was having this positive effect, the social-media algorithms were having the opposite effect—they were supercharging anti-democratic forces in Brazil. A former military officer named Jair Bolsonaro had been a marginal figure for years. He was way outside the mainstream because he kept saying vile things and attacking large parts of the population in extreme ways. He praised people who had carried out torture against innocent people when Brazil was a dictatorship. He told his female colleagues in the senate that they were so ugly he wouldn't bother raping them, and that they weren't "worthy" of it. He said he would rather learn his son was dead than learn his son was gay. Then YouTube and Facebook became one of the main ways people in Brazil got their news. Their algorithms prioritized angry, outrageous content—and Bolsonaro's reach dramatically surged. He became a social-media star. He ran for president openly attacking people like the residents of Alemão, saying the country's poorer, blacker citizens "are not even good for breeding," and should "go back to the zoo." He promised to give the police even more power to launch intensified military attacks on the favelas—a license for wholesale slaughter.

Here was a society with huge problems that urgently needed to be solved—but social-media algorithms were promoting far-right-wingers and wild disinformation. In the run-up to the election, in favelas like Alemão, many people were deeply worried about a story that had been circulating online. Supporters of Bolsonaro had created a video warning that his main rival, Fernando Haddad, wanted to turn all the children of Brazil into homosexuals, and that he had developed a cunning technique to do it. The video showed a baby sucking a bottle, only there was something peculiar about it—the teat of the bottle had been painted to look like a penis. This, the story that circulated said, is what Haddad will distribute to every kindergarten in Brazil. This became one of the most-shared news stories in the entire election. People in the favelas explained indignantly that they couldn't possibly vote for somebody who wanted to get babies to suck these penis-teats, and so they would have to vote for Bolsonaro instead. On these algorithm-pumped absurdities, the fate of the whole country turned.

When Bolsonaro unexpectedly won the presidency, his supporters chanted "Facebook! Facebook! Facebook!" They knew what the algorithms had done for them. There were, of course, many other factors at work in Brazilian society—this is only one—but it is the one Bolsonaro's gleeful followers picked out first.

Not long afterward, Raull was in his home in Alemão when he heard a noise that sounded like an explosion. He ran outside and saw that a helicopter was hovering above the favela and firing down at the people below—precisely the kind of violence Bolsonaro had pledged to carry out. Raull screamed for his kids to hide, terrified. When I spoke to Raull on Skype later, he was more shaken than I had seen him before. As I write, this violence is being ramped up more and more.

When I thought about Raull, I could see the deeper way the

rage-driven algorithms of social media and YouTube damages attention and focus. It's a cascading effect. These sites harm people's ability to pay attention as individuals. Then they pump the population's
heads full of grotesque falsehoods, to the point where they can't
distinguish real threats to their existence (an authoritarian leader
pledging to shoot them) from nonexistent threats (their children
being made gay by penises painted on baby bottles). Over time, if
you expose any country to all this for long enough, it will become a
country so lost in rage and unreality that it can't make sense of its
problems and it can't build solutions. This means that the streets and
the skies actually become more dangerous—so you become hypervigilant, and this wrecks your attention even more.

This could be the future for all of us if we continue with these
trends. Indeed, what happens in Brazil alone directly affects your life
and mine. Bolsonaro has dramatically stepped up the destruction of
the Amazon rain forest, the lungs of the planet. If this continues for
much longer, it will tip us into an even worse climate disaster.

When I was discussing all this with Tristan one day back in San
Francisco, he ran his fingers through his hair and said to me that
these algorithms are "debasing the soil of society. . . . You need . . . a
social fabric, and if you debase it, you don't know what you are going
to wake up to."

This machinery is systematically diverting us—at an individual and a
social level—from where we want to go. James Williams, the former
Google strategist, said to me we should imagine "if we had a GPS
and it worked fine the first time. But the next time, it took you a few
streets away from where you wanted to go. And then later, it took you
to a different town." All because the advertisers who funded GPS
had paid for this to happen. "You would never keep using that." But
social media works exactly this way. There's a "destination we want to
get to, and most of the time, it doesn't actually get us there—it takes

us off track. If it was actually navigating us not through informational space but through physical space, we would never keep using it. It would be, by definition, defective."

~

Tristan and Aza started to believe that all these effects, when you add them together, are producing a kind of "human downgrading." Aza said: "I think we're in the process of reverse-engineering ourselves. [We discovered a way to] open up the human skull, find the strings that control us, and start pulling on our own marionette strings. Once you do that, an accidental jerk in one direction causes your arm to jerk further, which pulls your marionette string farther. . . . That's the era that we're headed into now." Tristan believes that what we are seeing is "the collective downgrading of humans and the upgrading of machines." We are becoming less rational, less intelligent, less focused.

Aza told me: "Imagine if you have worked your entire career toward a technology that you feel is good. It's making democracy stronger. It's changing the way you live. Your friends value you because of these things you've made. All of a sudden you're like— that thing I've been working on my entire life is not just meaningless. It's tearing apart the things you love the most."

He told me that literature is full of stories where humans create something in a burst of optimism and then lose control of their creation. Dr. Frankenstein creates a monster only for it to escape from him and commit murder. Aza began to think about these stories when he talked with his friends who were engineers working for some of the most famous websites in the world. He would ask them basic questions, like why their recommendation engines recommend one thing over another, and, he said to me, "they're like: 'We're not sure why it's recommending those things.'" They're not lying—they have set up a technology that is doing things they don't fully comprehend. He always says to them: "Isn't that exactly the moment, in the allegories, where you turn the thing off—[when] it's starting to do things you can't predict?"

When Tristan testified about this before the U.S. Senate, he asked: "How can we solve the world's most urgent problems if we've downgraded our attention spans, downgraded our capacity for complexity and nuance, downgraded our shared truth, downgraded our beliefs into conspiracy-theory thinking, where we can't construct shared agendas to solve our problems? This is destroying our sense-making, at a time when we need it the most. And the reason why I'm here is because every day it's incentivized to get worse." He said he was especially worried about this, he told me later, because we are now, as a species, facing our biggest challenge ever—the fact that we are destroying the ecosystem we depend on for life by triggering the climate crisis. If we can't focus, what possible hope do we have to solve global warming?

So Tristan and Aza started to ask with increasing urgency: How, in practice, do we change the machinery that is stealing our attention?

CHAPTER EIGHT

Cause Seven: The Rise of Cruel Optimism

(or: Why Individual Changes Are an Important Start, but Not Enough)

I was with my daughter that afternoon," the Israeli American tech designer Nir Eyal said to me, as he looked back on the day that it hit him that something had gone really wrong. "We had this beautiful afternoon planned"—they were going through a daddy-and-daughter book, and she got to a page that asked: If you could have any superpower, which one would you choose? As she was contemplating this, Nir received a text, and "I started looking at my phone, as opposed to being fully present with her." When he looked up, she was gone.

A childhood is made up of small moments of connection between a child and their parent. If you miss them, you don't ever get them back. Nir realized with a lurch: "She got the message that whatever was on my phone was more important than she was."

This wasn't the first time. "I realized—wow, I really need to reconsider my relationship with distraction." Except Nir's relationship to the technology causing this was different from yours or mine in a crucial way. Like Tristan, he had learned from B. J. Fogg, attending a retreat at his home and sitting in on some of his lectures, and then he went on to work with some of the most influential companies in Silicon Valley, helping them figure out how to get their users "hooked." Now he was seeing it happen even to his own young daughter. She would scream at him: "iPad time! iPad time!" and demand to go online. Nir realized he needed to figure out a strategy for how to overcome this—for her, for himself, and for all of us.

He offers one particular way of dealing with this crisis that I want to engage with in detail. It is very different from the approach that Tristan and Aza have developed. Nir's approach is important because it's pretty clear this is going to be the approach that the wider tech industry offers us for the attention problems they are, in part, causing.

Somewhere at the back of his mind, Nir already had a template for what he believed he had to do. When he was young, Nir had been seriously overweight—something that shocked me when he said it, because he is now lean, bordering on buff. He was sent to "fat camp," and tried all sorts of diets and detoxes, stripping out sugar or fast food. Nothing worked. Then, finally, he realized: "As much as I would have loved to blame McDonald's for the problem, that wasn't the problem. I was eating my feelings. I was using food as a coping mechanism." Once he knew this, he said, he could "actually tackle the problem." He got in touch with his own anxieties and unhappiness, and he took up wrestling, and slowly began to change his body. "Clearly, food had a role," he said, "but it wasn't the root cause of my problem." He said he had learned a key lesson: "In my life, I had something that felt like it controlled me, and I controlled it."

Nir came to believe that if we are going to overcome this process of becoming hooked on our apps and devices, we have to develop individual skills to resist the part inside all of us that succumbs to these distractions. He argues that to do that, we primarily have to look inward—to the reasons why we want to use them compulsively in the first place. People like Tristan and Aza, he said, "tell me about how bad these companies are. I say, well, what have you tried? Right? What have you done? Often, it's nothing." He believes individual changes should be "the first line of defense," and "it has to begin with a bit of introspection, with a bit of understanding ourselves." Yes, he says, the environment changed: "You [the average tech user] didn't make the iPhone. It's not your fault. I never said it's your fault. I'm saying it's your responsibility. This stuff isn't going away. In some form or other, it's here to stay. What choice do we have? We have to adapt. That's our only option."

So how can we adapt? What can we do? He began to read through the social-science literature, to find evidence for individual changes you can make. He laid out what he sees as the best answers in his book *Indistractible*. There is one tool in particular that he believes can get us out of this problem. All of us have "internal triggers"— moments in our lives that push us to give in to bad habits. Nir realized that for him, it's "when I'm writing—it's never come easy. It's always difficult." When he sat at his laptop and tried to write, he would often start to feel bored or stressed. "All of these bad things come bubbling up when I'm writing." When that happened, it would trigger something inside him. To get away from these uncomfortable feelings, he would tell himself there was something else he had to do, for just a moment. "The easiest thing to do would be—let me just check email real quick. Let me just open my phone real quick." He said: "I would think of every single conceivable excuse." He would compulsively check the news, telling himself that's what a good citizen does. He would google a fact supposedly relevant to his writing, and two hours later he would find himself at the bottom of a rabbit hole, looking at something totally irrelevant.

"An internal trigger is an uncomfortable emotional state," he told me. "It's all about avoidance. It's all about—how do I get out of this uncomfortable state?" He believes we all need to explore our triggers nonjudgmentally, think about them, and find ways to disrupt them.

So whenever he felt that prickling feeling or boredom or stress come to him, he identified what was happening, and picked up a pack of Post-it notes, and he wrote on it what he wanted to know. Later, when he had finished a good stretch of writing, he would let himself google it—but only then.

It worked for him. This taught Nir that "we're not beholden to habits. They can be interrupted. They get interrupted all the time. We can change habits. The way we change a habit is by understanding what the internal trigger is, and making sure that there's some kind of break between the impulse to do a behavior and the behavior itself." He developed a range of techniques like this. He believes we should all try adopting a "ten-minute rule"—if you feel the urge to check your phone, wait ten minutes. He says you should "time-box"—which means you should draw up a detailed schedule of what you are going to do each day, and stick to it. He recommends changing the notification settings on your phone, so that your apps can't interrupt you and kill your focus throughout the day. He says you should delete all the apps you can from your phone, and if you have to keep some, then you should schedule the time you are willing to spend on them in advance. He advises that you unsubscribe from email lists, and—if you can—have "office hours" on your email, when you check it a few times a day, and ignore it the rest of the time.

By laying out these tools, he told me, "I wanted to empower people to realize—Look, this isn't that hard. It's not that tough. If you know what to do, it's pretty simple how to handle distraction." He seemed puzzled that more people don't do it: "Two-thirds of people with a smartphone never change their notification settings. What? Right? This is not hard stuff. We just need to do this kind of stuff." Instead of railing against the tech companies, he says, we need to ask what we have done as individuals. He asked me: "Why isn't the beginning of the discussion—'Okay, have we exhausted everything you can do right now? Can we do that stuff first?' . . . Change your notification settings! Come on, this is basic stuff, right? Turn off the fucking Facebook notifications every five minutes! How about planning your day, you know? How many of us plan our day? We just let our time be usurped by the news or whatever's on Twitter or whatever's happening in the world outside us, as opposed to saying— 'Actually what do I want to do with my time?'"

~

I felt conflicted as Nir explained this to me. I realized he was articulating precisely the logic that had taken me to Provincetown. Something deep inside me thought like this. Like him, I believed: this is a problem in you, and you need to change yourself. There was clearly some truth in it. Every specific intervention Nir recommends is, I believe, helpful. I tried each one of them after going through his work, and several of them made a small but real difference to me.

But there was something about what he said that made me feel uncomfortable, and for a while, I couldn't articulate it. Nir's approach is absolutely in line with how the tech companies want us to think about our attention problems. They can no longer deny the crisis, so they are doing something else: subtly urging us to see it as an individual problem that has to be solved with greater self-restraint on my part and yours, not theirs. That's why they began to offer tools they argued would help you to strengthen your willpower. All new iPhones have an option where you can be told how much Screen Time you have spent that day and that week, and a Do Not Disturb function where you can block out incoming messages. Facebook and Instagram introduced their own modest equivalents. Mark Zuckerberg even started using Tristan's slogan, promising that time on Facebook would be "time well spent"—except for him, it was all about Nir-style tools where you reflect on what's gone wrong with your own motives. I am writing this chapter about Nir not because he is unusual, but because he is the most candid of the people putting forward the dominant view in Silicon Valley about what you and I should do now.

Nir kept insisting that the tech companies have done a lot to make it easy for us to unplug. To explain this, he gave the example of a company boardroom he had been to where the boss took out his phone in a meeting, so everyone else felt free to do it. "I don't know why that's the tech company's responsibility. In fact, if anything, the tech company gives you this beautiful little function here that [says] 'do not disturb.' The tech company gave us a button. All you have to do is that. What more responsibility do we want from Apple? For God's sake, push the fucking button that says 'do not disturb' for an hour if you're going to have a meeting with your colleagues. Is that so difficult?"

My unease about this approach only became clear to me when I turned to the book Nir wrote a few years before he produced his work about how to beat distraction. It was written for an audience of tech designers and engineers, and it was named *Hooked: How to Build Habit-Forming Products*. He described it as a "cookbook" containing "a recipe for human behavior." Reading *Hooked* as an ordinary user of the internet is strange—it's like the moment in an old Batman movie when the villain is caught and reveals everything he did all along, step by step. Nir writes: "Let's admit it: we are all in the persuasion business. Innovators build products meant to persuade people to do what we want them to do. We call these people users and even if we don't say it aloud, we secretly wish every one of them would become fiendishly hooked to whatever we're making."

He lays out the methods to achieve this, which he describes as "mind manipulation." The goal, Nir says, is to "create a craving" in human beings—and he cites B. F. Skinner as a model for how to do it. His approach can be summarized by the headline on one of his blog posts: "Want to Hook Your Users? Drive Them Crazy."

The goal of the designer is to create an "internal trigger" (remember them?) that will keep the user coming back again and again. To help the designer picture the kind of person they are targeting, he says they should imagine a user he names Julie, who "fears being out of the loop." He comments: "Now we've got something! Fear is a powerful internal trigger, and we can design our solution to help calm Julie's fear." Once you have succeeded in playing on feelings like this, "a habit is formed, [and so] the user is automatically triggered to use the product during routine events such as wanting to kill time while waiting in line," he writes approvingly.

Designers should get you and me "to repeat behaviors for long periods, ideally for the rest of their lives," he writes. He says he believes this makes people's lives better, but he also notes: "Habits can be very good for the bottom line." Nir says there should be some ethical limits to this: it is wrong to target children, and he believes designers need to "get high on their own supply" and use their own apps themselves. He is not opposed to all regulations—he believes it should be legally required that if you spend more than thirty-five hours on Facebook a week, you should see a pop-up saying you might have a problem and directing you toward a place to get help.

But as I read all this, I was troubled. Nir's "cookbook" for how to design apps became hugely successful—a senior executive at Microsoft, for example, held it aloft and told her staff to read it, and Nir is a hugely popular speaker at tech conferences. Many apps inspired by his techniques were built. Nir was one of the people who led Silicon Valley in the charge to "drive them crazy"—and yet when people like my godson Adam were, in fact, driven crazy, he told me that the solution was primarily to change our individual behavior, not the actions of the tech companies.

When we talked, I explained to him that, for me, it seemed like there was a worrying mismatch between his two books. In *Hooked* he talks about using ferociously powerful machinery to get us "fiendishly hooked" and in "pain" until we get our next techno-fix. Yet in *Indistractible* he tells us that when we feel distracted by this machinery, we should try gentle personal changes. In the first book, he describes big and powerful forces used to hook us; in the second, he describes fragile little personal interventions that he says will get us out.

"I see exactly the opposite, in fact," he said in response. "Everything I talked about in *Hooked,* you can turn off with the tap of one thumb. Fuck them."

⁓

I understood my growing discomfort with Nir's approach more fully when I talked it over with several other people. One was Ronald Purser, who is professor of management at San Francisco State University. He introduced me to an idea I hadn't heard before—a concept named "cruel optimism." This is when you take a really big problem with deep causes in our culture—like obesity, or depression, or addiction—and you offer people, in upbeat language, a simplistic individual solution. It sounds optimistic, because you are telling them that the problem can be solved, and soon—but it is, in fact, cruel, because the solution you are offering is so limited, and so blind to the deeper causes, that for most people, it will fail.

Ronald gave lots of examples of this idea, which was first coined by the historian Lauren Berlant. I started to really grasp this idea when he applied this concept to one that's related to attention but separate from it—stress. I think it's worth taking a little time to go through it, because I believe it can help us see a mistake that Nir— like many of us—is making when it comes to focus.

Ronald talked to me about a bestselling book by a *New York Times* reporter that tells its readers: "Stress isn't something imposed on us. It's something we impose on ourselves." Stress is a feeling. Stress is a series of thoughts. If you just learn how to think differently—to quiet down your rattling thoughts—your stress will melt away. So you just need to learn to meditate. Your stress comes from a failure to be mindful.

This message sings off the page with optimistic promise—but Ronald points out that in the real world, the top causes of stress in the U.S. have been identified by scientists at Stanford Graduate School of Business in a major study. They are "a lack of health insurance, the constant threat of lay-offs, lack of discretion and autonomy in decision-making, long working hours, low levels of organizational justice, and unrealistic demands." If you don't have health insurance and you have diabetes and you can't afford insulin, or if you are forced to work sixty hours a week by a bullying boss, or if you are watching your colleagues get laid off one by one and you suspect with a sickening feeling that you will be next, your stress is not "something we impose on ourselves." It is something imposed on you.

Ronald thinks that meditation can help some people, and I agree, but that this typical bestselling book, which tells you to meditate your way through stress and humiliation, is "bullshit. . . . Tell it to Hispanic women working three jobs with four kids." The people who say stress is just a matter of changing your thoughts are, he says, talking "from a privileged position. It's easy for them to say that." He gave me the example of a company that was cutting back on providing healthcare to some people—and was, at the same time, congratulated by the same *New York Times* writer for providing meditation classes to its employees. You can see clearly how this is cruel. You tell somebody there's a solution to their problem—just think differently about your stress and you'll be fine!—and then leave them in a waking nightmare. We won't give workers insulin, but we'll give them classes on how to change their thinking. It's the twenty-first-century version of Marie Antoinette saying, "Let them eat cake." Let them be present.

While at first glance, cruel optimism seems kind and optimistic, it often has an ugly aftereffect. It ensures that when the small, cramped solution fails, as it will most of the time, the individual won't blame the system—she will blame herself. She will think she screwed up and she just wasn't good enough. Ronald told me, "it deflects attention away from the social causes of stress," like overwork, and it can quite quickly turn into a form of "victim-blaming." It whispers: the problem isn't in the system; the problem is in you.

As he said this, I thought about Nir again, and the wider Silicon Valley approach he exemplifies. He makes his living from marketing and promoting a digital model that "hooks" us and plays on our fears and that even he says is designed to make us "crazy." That model, in turn, hooked him. But because he is in a position of incredible privilege—in terms of wealth, and knowledge of these systems—he was able to use his own techniques to regain some sense of control. Now he thinks the solution is simply for all of us to do the same.

Set aside the fact that it's very convenient for him if we all blame ourselves rather than tackling the deeper problems—after all, his income depends on the tech industry. Look at something more basic. The truth is that it's not so easy for everyone else to do what he has done. This is one of the problems with cruel optimism—it takes exceptional cases, usually achieved in exceptional circumstances, and acts as if they can be commonplace. It's easier to find serenity through meditation when you haven't just lost your job and you aren't wondering how you're going to avoid being evicted next Tuesday. It's easier to say no to the next hamburger, or the next Facebook notification, or the next tab of OxyContin if you aren't exhausted and stressed, and in desperate need of some kind of salve to get you through the next few stress-filled hours. To tell people—as Nir does, and as the wider tech industry increasingly does—that it's "pretty simple" and that they should just "push the fucking button" is to deny the reality of most people's lives.

And, most importantly, people shouldn't have to do it. Cruel optimism takes it for granted that we can't significantly change the systems that are wrecking our attention, so we have to mainly focus on changing our isolated selves. But why should we accept these systems as a given? Why should we accept an environment full of programs designed to "hook" us and drive us "crazy"?

I could see this most clearly when I thought about Nir's own analogy with the obesity he experienced when he was a kid. I think it's worth taking a moment to think through this comparison, because I think it tells us a lot about where we are going wrong now. It seems incredible to us today, but fifty years ago, there was very little obesity in the Western world. Look at a photograph of a beach taken back then: everyone is, by our standards, slim. Then a whole series of changes took place. We replaced a food-supply system based around fresh, nutritious food with one consisting mainly of processed junk. We massively stressed out our populations, making comfort eating a whole lot more appealing. We built cities that are often impossible to walk or bike around. In other words, the environment changed, and that—not any individual failing on the part of you or me—changed our bodies. We gained mass, en masse. The average weight gain for an adult between 1960 and 2002 was twenty-four pounds.

Then what happened? Rather than acknowledge the wider forces that have done this to us, take them on, and build a healthy environment in which it's easier to avoid obesity, we were taught by the diet industry to blame ourselves as individuals. We learned to think: I got fat because of a personal failing. I chose the wrong food. I got greedy, I got lazy, I didn't get a handle on my feelings properly, I'm not good enough. We resolved to count the calories better next time. (I've been there.) Individual diet books and diet plans became the primary answer offered by the culture to a crisis with primarily social causes.

How is that working out for us? The scientists who have studied this have discovered that 95 percent of people in our culture who lose weight on a diet regain it within one to five years. That's nineteen out of every twenty people. Why? It's because this way of approaching the problem misses most of why you (and I) gained weight in the first place. It has no systemic analysis. It doesn't talk about the crisis in our food supply, which surrounds us with addictive, highly processed foods that bear no relationship to what previous generations of humans ate. It doesn't explain the crisis of stress and anxiety that drives us to overeat. It doesn't address the fact that we live in cities where you have to squeeze yourself into a steel box to get anywhere. Diet books ignore the fact that you live in a society and culture that are shaping and pushing you, every day, to act in certain ways. A diet doesn't change your wider environment—and it's the wider environment that is the cause of the crisis. Your diet ends, and you're still in an unhealthy environment that's pushing you to gain weight. Trying to lose weight in the environment we've built is like trying to run up an escalator that is constantly carrying you down. A few people might heroically sprint to the top—but most of us will find ourselves back at the bottom, feeling like it's our fault.

If we listen to Nir and the people like him, I fear we will respond to the rise of attention problems in the same way that we responded to the rise in weight problems—and we will end up with the same disastrous outcomes. It's not just Silicon Valley that pushes this approach. Almost all the existing books about attention problems (and I read a lot as research for this book) present them simply as individual flaws requiring individual tweaks. They are digital diet books. But diet books didn't solve the obesity crisis and digital diet books won't solve the attention crisis. We have to understand the deeper forces at work here.

There was a different way we could have reacted to the obesity crisis when it began forty or so years ago. We could have listened to the evidence that purely practicing individual restraint—in an unchanged environment—rarely works for long, except in one in twenty cases like Nir's. We could have looked instead at what does work: changing the environment in specific ways. We could have used government policy to make fresh, nutritious food cheap and accessible, and sugar-filled junk expensive and inaccessible. We could have reduced the factors that cause people to be so stressed that they comfort eat. We could have built cities people can easily walk or bike through. We could have banned the targeting of junk food ads at children, shaping their tastes for life. That's why countries that have done some of this—like Norway, or Denmark, or the Netherlands—have much lower levels of obesity, and countries that have focused on telling individual overweight people to pull themselves together, like the U.S. and U.K., have very high levels of obesity. If all the energy people like me have put into shaming and starving ourselves had been put instead into demanding these political changes, there would be far less obesity now, and a lot less misery.

Tristan believes we need a similar shift in consciousness around tech. When he testified before the Senate, he told them: "You can try having self-control, but there are a thousand engineers on the other side of the screen working against you." This is precisely what Nir refuses to fully acknowledge—even though he has been one of those designers himself. I stress again: I am in favor of each individual piece of advice he offers. You really should take out your phone now and turn off your notifications. You really should figure out your internal triggers. And on, and on. (Tristan believes this too.) But it's not "pretty simple" to get from that to being able to pay attention in an environment designed—in part by Nir himself—to invade and raid your focus.

My discussion with Nir got a little heated as we spoke more. Because this is one of the only contentious interviews in this book, to be fair to him, I have posted the full audio on the book's website, so you can hear his responses—including the ones I don't have space to quote here—in full. Our conversation clarified my thinking in a really helpful way. He made me realize that to get our attention back, we are going to have to adopt some individual solutions, to be sure—but we have to be honest enough to tell people that they alone probably won't be enough to get most of us out of this hole. We are also going to have to collectively take on the forces that are stealing our focus and compel them to change.

There is an alternative to cruel optimism, which offers inadequately small solutions. It is authentic optimism. This is where, together, we build a solution that actually deals with the underlying causes of the problem. I felt this was a breakthrough in my understanding, and I felt a little glow that I saw it clearly—but I only felt smug for a few minutes.

~

Then I realized I was now left with a really difficult question: How, precisely, do we start to do that?

CHAPTER NINE

The First Glimpses of the Deeper Solution

After learning so much about how our technology works, I was left with two clear and urgent questions. Firstly: what are the specific changes to this invasive tech that could be made, in practice, to prevent it from harming our attention and focus? And secondly: how do we compel these huge corporations to introduce these changes in the real world?

Tristan and Aza—drawing on their own experiences, and the essential work of Professor Shoshana Zuboff—believe that if we are going to find a lasting solution, we need to go right to the root cause of the problem. That's why, one morning, Aza said to me starkly: "We could just ban surveillance capitalism." I paused to try to process what he was saying. This would mean, he explained, that the government would ban any business model that tracks you online in order to figure out your weaknesses and then sells that private data to the highest bidder so they can change your behavior. This model is, Aza says, "just fundamentally anti-democratic and anti-human," and it has to go.

This sounded dramatic and frankly impossible when I first heard it, but Tristan and Aza explained that there are plenty of historical precedents for something becoming so widespread, only for society to discover it actually causes a lot of harm and ban the market in it. Think about lead paint. It was in a majority of American homes—then it was discovered to damage the brains of kids and adults, making it harder for them to focus. As one of Tristan's mentors, Jaron Lanier, pointed out to me, when we found that out, we didn't say nobody could paint their homes ever again. We just banned the lead in the paint. Your home is still painted today—just with much better products. Or think about CFCs. As I mentioned before, when I was a child in the hairspray-obsessed 1980s, it was discovered that a substance in hairsprays was destroying the ozone layer that protects us from the sun's rays. It terrified us all. We banned CFCs. We still have hairsprays, they just work differently, and today, the ozone layer is healing. There are all sorts of things that we have decided, as a civilized society, can't be bought and sold, like (for example) human organs.

So, I asked them, let's say we banned surveillance capitalism. What would happen to my Facebook and Twitter accounts the following day, the following week, the following year? "I think they would have a crisis moment, in the same way that Microsoft had a crisis moment," Aza told me. In 2001, Microsoft was ruled by the U.S. government to have become a monopoly. That company reinvented itself, and now "they're sort of like the benevolent adult in the room. I think the same transformation would happen to Facebook."

In practice, the day after a ban, these companies would have to find different ways to fund themselves. One model that is obvious—and an alternative form of capitalism that everyone reading this will have some experience of—is subscription. Let's imagine each of us had to pay fifty cents or a dollar every month to use Facebook.

Suddenly, Facebook would no longer be working for advertisers and offering up your secret wishes and preferences as their real product. No. It would be working for you. Its job, for the first time, would be to actually figure out what makes you happy, and to give it to you—instead of figuring out what makes advertisers happy, and how they can manipulate you to give it to them. So if, like most people, you want to be able to focus, the site would have to be redesigned to facilitate that. If you want to be socially connected, instead of isolated in front of your screen, it would have to figure out how to make that possible.

There's another obvious way that these companies could survive, which is for them to be bought by the government and taken into public ownership. This would take social media out of the capitalist part of the economy. This can sound drastic, but every single person reading this book benefits today, directly, from exactly the same model. We all agree we need to have sewers—they are an unavoidable necessity, unless we want to go back to the world of cholera outbreaks and feces in the streets. So in virtually every country, the government owns, maintains, and regulates the sewers, and even hardcore anti-government activists agree that this is a good use of state power.

Using the same model, our governments could acknowledge that social media is now an essential public utility, and explain that when it is run according to the wrong incentives, it causes the psychological equivalents of cholera outbreaks. It would be a bad idea for the government to run it—it's easy to imagine how authoritarian leaders could abuse that. Fortunately, there's a better option: you can have public ownership, independent of the government. In Britain, the BBC is owned and funded by the British public, and it is run in the interests of the British public—but its day-to-day running is independent of the government. It's not perfect, but this model works so well that it is the most respected media organization in the world.

Once the financial incentives are changed—either through subscription, or public ownership, or another model—then the nature of these sites can change, in ways we can actually begin to envision already. Aza told me that "it's actually technically not hard" to redesign the major social-media sites so that, instead of trashing your attention span and our societies, they would be designed to heal them, once the financial incentives to do that are in place. This was difficult for me to grasp at first, so I asked what social media would look like after the changes they would like to see. Tristan, Aza, and others began by explaining minor changes, then built up to big changes, then told me what has to occur to make any of these changes happen.

They started by talking about how these companies could, overnight, remove a lot of the aspects of these apps and sites that deliberately scramble our heads and keep us online longer than we really want. Aza said: "For instance, Facebook tomorrow could start batching your notifications, so you only get one push notification a day. . . . They could do that tomorrow." (This was something Tristan had proposed in his explosive slide-deck back when he was still at Google.) So instead of getting "this constant drip of behavioral cocaine," telling you every few minutes that somebody liked your picture, commented on your post, has a birthday tomorrow, and on and on and on—you would get one daily update, like a newspaper, summarizing it all. You'd be pushed to look once a day, instead of being interrupted several times an hour.

"Here's another one," he said. "Infinite scroll." That's his invention, where when you get to the bottom of the screen, it automatically loads more and more, forever. "What's going on there is it's catching your impulses before your brain has a chance to really get involved and make a decision." Facebook and Instagram and the others could simply turn off infinite scroll—so that when you get to the bottom of the screen, you have to make a conscious decision to carry on scrolling.

Similarly, these sites could simply switch off the things that have been shown to most polarize people politically, stealing our ability to pay collective attention. Since there's evidence YouTube's recommendation engine is radicalizing people, Tristan told one interviewer: "Just turn it off. They can turn it off in a heartbeat." It's not as if, he points out, the day before recommendations were introduced, people were lost and clamoring for somebody to tell them what to watch next.

Once the most obvious forms of mental pollution have been stopped, they said, we can begin to look deeper, at how these sites could be redesigned to make it easier for you to restrain yourself and think about your longer-term goals. "It doesn't take much work to start imagining what would be different interfaces," Aza said. The most obvious example takes us back to where I started with Tristan, in our very first conversation: there could be a button that says, "Here are all your friends who are nearby and are indicating they'd like to meet up today." You click it, you connect, you put down your phone and hang out with them. Instead of being a vacuum sucking up your attention and keeping it away from the outside world, social media would become a trampoline, sending you back into that world as efficiently as possible, matched with the people you want to see.

Similarly, when you set up (say) a Facebook account, it could ask you how much time you want to spend per day or per week on the site. You might name ten minutes, or two hours—it's up to you—and then the website could help you to achieve your goal. One way could be that when you hit that limit, the website could radically slow down. In tests, Amazon found that even one hundred milliseconds of delay in the pace at which a page loads results in a substantial drop-off in people sticking around to buy the product. Aza said: "It just gives your brain a chance to catch up to your impulse and [ask]—do I really want to be here? No."

In addition, Facebook could ask you at regular intervals: What changes do you want to make to your life? Maybe you want to exercise more, or take up gardening, or become vegetarian, or start a heavy-metal band. It could then match you up with other people nearby—friends, or friends of friends, or interested strangers in your neighborhood—who say they also want to make that change and have indicated they are looking for the equivalent of gym buddies. Facebook would become, Aza says, "a way of socially surrounding yourself with the behavior that you want." A battery of scientific evidence shows that if you want to succeed in changing something, you should meet up with groups of people doing the same.

At the moment, they said, social media is designed to grab your *attention* and sell it to the highest bidder, but it could be designed to understand your *intentions* and to better help you achieve them. Tristan and Aza told me that it's just as easy to design and program this life-affirming Facebook as the life-draining Facebook we currently have. I think that most people, if you stopped them in the street and painted them a vision of these two Facebooks, would say they wanted the one that serves their intentions. So why isn't it happening? It comes back, Tristan and Aza said, to the business model. If right now these social-media companies made the changes that you just read about, they would lose an enormous amount of money. Within the existing economic structure of the companies, they can't do the right thing by your attention span or the wider society. This—above everything else—is the rock-solid reason why you have to change the business model, if you want to change the way social media affects us.

The business model can only be changed by regulation imposed on these companies by governments, they said. Then the changes I just described would cease to be impossible threats to the bottom line and start to become very exciting ways to tempt subscribers. At the moment there is a fundamental clash between your interests—to be able to focus, to have friends you see offline, to be able to discuss things calmly—and the interests of the social-media companies. With the introduction of a ban on surveillance capitalism and a move to a different business model, that clash ends. As Tristan put it, you'd be paying for the interests to be aligned between you and the product you use. Suddenly that team of Silicon Valley engineers behind the screen wouldn't be working against you and your deeper intentions; they'd be working *for* you and trying to *serve* your deeper intentions.

One day, Aza said to me: "The fundamental thing is that no one likes the way that they are spending time or making decisions with the way technology currently is. It's hard to get from that hill to this hill, because we have to go through a valley. That's the role of regulation—to help making crossing that valley easier. But the hill on the other side is much, much nicer."

⁓

I found so much of what Aza and Tristan had taught me persuasive— but I was wary about their argument that we need to use the law to stop these companies from continuing as they are. I wondered if they were overstating the problem. When I spoke with Nir Eyal, he said: "Every generation has these moral panics, where we only want to look at the negative sides" of an issue. He told me, "Tristan is reading, literally verbatim, from the 1950s about the comic-book debate," when many people believed that children were being made violent by a new wave of gory comics. In the 1950s, "people like Tristan went to the Senate and told the senators that comic books are turning children into addicted, hijacked [zombies]— literally, it's the same stuff. . . . Today, we think of comic books as so innocuous."

On this basis, he argues—and here he's not alone—that the science that Tristan and Aza and other critics of the current tech business model draw on is incorrect. He believes that some of the social science I have drawn on in the past two chapters is garbled or wrong.

I'll give you one detailed example, so you get a sense of this controversy. Tristan argues YouTube is radicalizing people, based on an array of evidence I mentioned before. Nir responds by pointing to a recent study by the coder Mark Ledwich suggesting that, in fact, watching YouTube had a slightly *deradicalizing* effect on its users. Tristan, in response, directs people toward the Princeton academic

Professor Arvind Narayanan, and many other critics of this study, who say that the research Nir is citing here is worthless. Let's go through this, step by step. The people who say YouTube radicalizes you argue that this effect happens over time. You create a profile, you log in, and gradually YouTube builds up knowledge of your preferences, and to keep you watching, the content it feeds you gets more extreme. But the research Nir cites didn't study *any* logged-in users. All they did was go to a video on YouTube—say, Boris Johnson giving a speech—and without logging in, they looked at the recommendations that appeared along the side. If you use YouTube in this highly unusual way, the videos don't become more extreme over time, and it might be fair to say YouTube is deradicalizing. But huge numbers of YouTube users *do* log in. (We don't know exactly how many, because YouTube keeps that information secret.)

For every conceivable way the tech companies could be screwing with us, there is a back-and-forth like this, with Tristan and Nir each citing rigorous social scientists who have reached opposing conclusions. Tristan draws on academics from Yale and New York University and Harvard; Nir draws on academics like Professor Andrew Przybylski at Oxford University, who agrees with Nir that Tristan's warnings are overheated. So what's happening? It's not that either of them is being disingenuous—it's that measuring the changes these sites are triggering is really complicated, and hard to figure out. We have to be honest that we are making decisions based on a lot of uncertainty here. In the long sweep of history, there will likely be some areas where it turns out Nir is right, and some where Tristan is right. That still leaves us with a basic dilemma. Right now, we need to make choices about whether to let social-media companies continue behaving as they have been. We have to figure out the balance of risk.

There are two things that helped me make up my mind about what I think we should do next. One was a thought experiment, and the other was hard evidence from inside Facebook itself.

Let's imagine Nir is wrong, and we all follow his advice anyway—

we allow surveillance capitalism to continue getting us "fiendishly hooked," with only light regulation. Then let's imagine Tristan is wrong, and we all follow his advice anyway—we regulate the Big Tech companies to stop their invasive practices.

If Tristan is wrong and we still follow his advice, you would have been tricked into creating a world where you get targeted with a lot less advertising, you spend less, you get spied on less, and in return, you have to pay a small sum each month to subscribe to a few social-media companies, or those companies have in some way been taken over as public utilities run in our collective interests, like the sewers or the highways. Now imagine if we did what Nir wants. What happens if he's wrong? What are we left with? Attention shrinks even more, political extremism expands, and the disturbing trends we see around us continue to rise.

The second thing that persuaded me was even more decisive. One day, in the spring of 2020, it was revealed what Facebook actually thinks about these questions, in private, when they think we will never be able to hear them. A large number of internal Facebook documents and communications were leaked to the *Wall Street Journal*. It turns out that behind closed doors, the company had responded to the claims that their algorithms had damaged our collective attention and helped the rise of Trump and Brexit by convening a team of some of their best scientists and tasking them with figuring out if this was really true, and if it was, to figure out what they could do about it. The unit was called Common Ground.

After studying all the hidden data—the stuff that Facebook doesn't release to the public—the company's scientists reached a definite conclusion. They wrote: "Our algorithms exploit the human brain's attraction to divisiveness," and "if left unchecked," the site would continue to pump its users with "more and more divisive content in an effort to gain user attention and increase time on the platform." A separate internal Facebook team, whose work also leaked to the *Journal,* had independently reached the same conclusions. They found that 64 percent of all the people joining extremist groups were finding their way to them because Facebook's algorithms were directly recommending them. This meant that across the world, people were seeing in their Facebook feeds racist, fascist, and even Nazi groups next to the words: "Groups You Should Join." They warned that in Germany, one-third of all the political groups on the site were extremist. Facebook's own team was blunt, concluding: "Our recommendation systems grow the problem."

After carefully analyzing all the options, Facebook's scientists concluded there was one solution: they said Facebook would have to abandon its current business model. Because their growth was so tied up with toxic outcomes, the company should abandon attempts at growth. The only way out was for the company to adopt a strategy that was "anti-growth"—deliberately shrink, and choose to be a less wealthy company that wasn't wrecking the world.

Once Facebook was shown—in plain language, by their own people—what they were doing, how did the company's executives respond? According to the *Journal*'s in-depth reporting, they mocked the research, calling it an "Eat Your Veggies" approach. They introduced some minor tweaks, but dismissed most of the recommendations. The Common Ground team was disbanded and has ceased to exist. The *Journal* reported dryly: "Zuckerberg also signaled he was losing interest in the effort to recalibrate the platform in the name of the social good . . . asking that they not bring him something like that again." I read this and I thought of my friend Raull Santiago, in his favela in Rio, being terrorized by helicopters sent by the far-right government that was elected with the help of these algorithms—algorithms so powerful that Bolsonaro's supporters responded to his victory by chanting, "Facebook! Facebook!"

I realized that if Facebook won't stop promoting fascism—promoting Nazism *in Germany*—they will never care about protecting your focus and attention. These companies will never restrain themselves. The risks of letting them continue behaving the way they have are greater than the risks of overreacting. They have to be stopped. They have to be stopped by us.

⁓

I was daunted. For a while, I felt I had no idea how we could achieve such a goal. Many people go this far in the argument, and then sputter to a pessimistic halt. They say that, yes, this system is messing with us in terrible ways, but we'll just have to adjust, because nothing and nobody can stop it. We live in a culture where there is a sense of deep political fatalism at every turn. I saw this when I wrote my book about the war on drugs, *Chasing the Scream,* and I traveled all over the world talking about it. Especially in the U.S., I kept hearing: Yes, you're right that the drug war is a disaster and failure. (Over 80 percent of Americans agree.) Yes, you're right that decriminalization or legalization would be better. But no, it will never happen—so do you know a good lawyer or rehab facility for an addicted relative? Political pessimism keeps people trapped in a search for purely personal and individual solutions.

But here's the truth: this despair isn't just self-defeating; I think it's actually empirically wrong. I reminded myself—forces as powerful as the tech companies have been defeated many times in human history, and it always happens in the same way. It is when ordinary people form movements and demand something better, and they don't give up until they have achieved it. I know that could sound vague or idealistic, so I want to give a very practical example of a change that happened in my family, and very likely in your family, in the past three generations.

I am forty-one years old. My grandmothers were the age I am now in the year 1962. In that year, my Scottish grandmother, Amy McRae, was living in a working-class tenement in Scotland, and my Swiss grandmother, Lydia Hari, was living on a mountain in the Swiss Alps. Amy had been forced to leave school when she was thirteen, because nobody thought it was worth educating girls. While her brother stayed in education, she was sent to work cleaning toilets, which she did all her working life. She had wanted to work with homeless people, but in practice women were locked out of jobs like that, and she was told to know her place as a woman and shut up. Lydia grew up in a Swiss village, and as a teenager she was constantly drawing and painting. She wanted to be an artist. She was told that girls couldn't be artists. She got married young, and was told to obey her husband. I would sit in their kitchen years later, when her husband would hold out an empty mug and yell *"Kaffee!"* (coffee), and she was expected to scramble to fetch it. She would sometimes sketch, but she said it made her depressed, because it reminded her of what her life might have been.

My grandmothers lived in societies in which women were excluded from almost all systems of power and almost all choices about their lives. In 1962 there were no women in the British cabinet, the U.S. cabinet, or the Swiss government. Women made up less than 4 percent of the members of the British Parliament and the U.S. Senate, and less than 1 percent of Switzerland's Federal Assembly, where women weren't even allowed to vote in seventeen out of the country's twenty cantons (including the one where my grandmother lived). This meant that the rules were written by men for men. American and British women were banned from getting mortgages or opening bank accounts unless they were married and had written permission from their husbands. Swiss women were banned from getting jobs at all without the written permission of their spouses. There were no domestic-violence shelters anywhere on earth, and it was legal everywhere for a man to rape his wife. (When, in the 1980s, there were moves to ban rape within marriage, one California Assembly member objected, saying, "But if you can't rape your wife, who can you rape?") In practice, men could beat their wives, because the police did not regard this as a crime, and they could molest their daughters, since it was so taboo to speak out about this that nobody ever went to the police to report it.

As I type out those facts, I keep thinking about my fifteen-year-old niece. Like her great-grandmother, she loves to draw and paint, and every time I see her doing it, I think of Lydia, doing the same thing in her Swiss village eighty-five years before. Lydia was told to stop wasting her time and start serving men. My niece is told: You're going to be a great artist—let's start looking at art schools. My niece never met my grandmother, but I believe that Lydia would have been happy to know the ways in which feminism changed the world.

I know it's exceptionally irritating for a male to mansplain this topic in this way, especially when so much sexism and misogyny remains, and when women still face huge barriers. I know the advance of women's rights is far from won, and many of the advances that have been made are under threat. I know only one thing here that is definitely true: the difference between the lives of my grandmothers and the life of my niece is a stunning achievement, and it happened for one reason, and one reason only. There was an organized movement of ordinary women who banded together and fought for it, and continued fighting even when it was really hard.

There are, of course, many differences between the fight for feminism and the fight for our focus. But nonetheless, I kept returning to this example in my mind for a very basic reason. The feminist movement teaches us that huge and seemingly immovable forces can be challenged by ordinary people—and that when they are, it can lead to real change. The concentrated power of men in 1962 was vastly greater than the power of Big Tech as I write this in 2021. Men controlled almost everything—every parliament, every corporation, every police force—and they had for as long as those institutions had existed. It would have been very easy, in that situation, to say: Nothing can change; give up; women will just have to learn to live a life of subordination. Many people are tempted to think that now, when they contemplate the huge forces stealing our focus. But that's the thing about the pessimistic belief that we are powerless and can't change anything. It's false.

Think about another historical example. I'm gay. In 1962, I would have been put in jail for it. Now I can get married. Homophobia ruled for 2,000 years, and then it didn't. The difference—the only difference—was a movement of ordinary people demanding an end to the forces thwarting their lives. I am free because the people who came before us didn't give up; they got up. Again, of course, there are big differences between the struggle for equality for gay people, and this fight. But there is a key parallel: no source of power, no set of ideas, is so large it can't be challenged. Facebook would love us to believe that their power is impregnable and there's no point fighting for change because that never works. But these companies are as fragile as every other powerful force that was torn down in the end.

If we don't form a movement and fight, what is the alternative? Tristan and Aza warned me that right now, we are only at the start of what unregulated surveillance capitalism will do to us. It is only going to become more sophisticated and more invasive. They gave me lots of examples. Here's one. There's a technology that exists called "style transfer." If you use it, you can show a computer lots of paintings by Van Gogh and then you point it at a new scene, and it can re-create it in the style of Van Gogh. Aza told me how "style transfer" could quite soon be used against you or me: "Google today could read all of your Gmail, come up with a model that can mimic your style, and then sell that to an advertiser. [You, as the user] don't even know what's going on," but you will start to receive emails that are unusually welcoming and persuasive, because they sound just like you. Aza explained: "Even worse, they could look at all of your Gmail, look at all the emails you responded to quickly and positively, and learn that style. So [they] learn the style that is uniquely persuasive to you. There is nothing illegal about that. There are no laws to protect you against that. Is it breaking your privacy? They're not selling your data. They're just selling an asymmetric knowledge about how you work—even more than you know about yourself—to the highest bidder."

It's an asymmetry so extreme that it will hack vulnerabilities you don't even know are vulnerabilities. There are technological innovations coming that will make the current forms of surveillance capitalism look as crude as Space Invaders looks to a kid raised on Fortnite. Facebook, in 2015, filed a patent for technology that will be able to detect your emotions from the cameras on your laptop and phone.

If we don't regulate, Aza warns, "our supercomputers are going to test their way to finding all our vulnerabilities, without anyone ever stopping to ask—is that right? It'll feel to us a little bit like we're still making our own decisions," but it will be "a direct attack against agency and free will."

Tristan's mentor, Jaron Lanier—a veteran Silicon Valley engineer—told me he used to be a consultant for loads of dystopian Hollywood movies, like *Minority Report,* but he had to stop because he kept designing ever-more-frightening technologies to warn people of what was coming—and designers kept responding by saying: That's so cool; how do we make that?

"Sometimes I hear people say it's too late to make certain changes to the web or platforms or digital technology," James Williams told me. But the ax, he said, existed for 1.4 million years before anybody thought to put a handle on it. The web, by contrast, is "less than ten thousand days old."

We are, I realized, in a race. To one side there is the rapidly escalating power of invasive technologies, which are figuring out how we work and fracking our attention. On the other side there needs to be a movement demanding technologies that work for us, not against us; technologies that feed our ability to focus, instead of fracturing it. At the moment, the movement for humane technology consists of a few brave people like Professor Shoshana Zuboff, Tristan, and Aza. They are the equivalent of the scattered bands of brave feminists of the early 1960s. We all need to decide—are we going to join them and put up a fight? Or are we going to let the invasive technologies win by default?

CHAPTER TEN

Cause Eight: The Surge in Stress and How It Is Triggering Vigilance

When I first admitted to myself I had an attention problem and fled to Provincetown, I had a simple story about what had happened to my focus—the internet and cellphones had broken it. I now knew that this was too simplistic—that the business model behind the tech was more important than the tech itself—but I was about to learn something even more important. These technologies arrived in our lives at a moment when we were unusually vulnerable to them—when our collective immune system was down, for reasons that are totally separate from the technology and its design.

At some level, many of us can sense some of the reasons for this. In early 2020 I decided to team up with the Council for Evidence-Based Psychiatry, and together we commissioned YouGov—one of the world's leading polling companies—to carry out (so far as I can tell) the first scientific opinion poll ever conducted on attention, in both the U.S. and Britain. The poll identified people who felt their attention was getting worse, and then it asked them why they believed this was happening. It gave them ten options to choose from, and asked them to select any and all that they felt applied to them. The number-one reason people gave for their problems focusing was not their phones. It was stress, which was chosen by 48 percent. The number-two reason was a change in life circumstances, like having a baby or getting older, also chosen by 48 percent. The number-three reason was difficult or disturbed sleep, which was named by 43 percent. Phones came fourth, chosen by 37 percent.

When I started to study the science of this in more detail, I learned that the hunches of ordinary people are not wrong. There are deeper forces than our phones and the web at work—and those forces led us, in turn, to develop a dysfunctional relationship with the web.

I began to understand the first dimension of this when I spent time with the woman who later became the surgeon general of California, who has made a key breakthrough on these questions. Of all the people I met for this book, she is perhaps the one I most admire. At first, when you read her story, it might seem like the situation she is describing is so extreme that it doesn't have much to do with your own life—but stick with me, because what she discovered can help us understand a force that is fracturing the attention of many of us.

$\sim$

In the 1980s, in the suburbs of Palo Alto in California, a young Black girl named Nadine felt anxious as she made her way home from school. She loved her mother—her mom had taught her some ferocious moves on the tennis court, and she was always telling Nadine to get herself an education, because once you have it, nobody can take it away from you. But there were times when—through no fault of her own—her mother behaved very differently. "The problem was," Nadine wrote later, "that we never knew which mother we were going to get. Every day after school it was a guessing game—are we coming home to happy Mom or scary Mom?"

Two decades later, Dr. Nadine Burke Harris looked at the two children sitting in front of her in her examination room and felt something in her body—an old, familiar ache. The kids were seven and eight years old, and a few hours before, their father had pulled them into his car, deliberately failed to put on their seatbelts, and driven off, until he found a wall. Then he aimed his car at it and drove forward as fast as he could. Nadine watched the kids and thought about how afraid they must have been. "I knew intuitively what that type of fear felt like," she told me when we sat together. "I could empathize on a physiological level, if that makes any sense. I know what happens in those moments." These children, it turned out, also had a parent with paranoid schizophrenia.

Nadine had coped with her mother's mental illness by always being an A student, just as her mom, in her healthier moments, had taught her to. She got into Harvard, and then she studied public health and pediatrics. When it came to making a decision about what to do with everything she had learned, she realized she wanted to help children. While many of her classmates went on to provide medicine for rich people, Nadine went to Bayview, one of the last non-gentrified parts of San Francisco, which is a really poor, struggling neighborhood with a lot of violence. Not long after she started there, Nadine was with some friends when she heard a cracking sound. She ran toward it, and found a seventeen-year-old boy who had been shot and was bleeding out. She learned that grandmothers in her new neighborhood sometimes slept in their bathtubs because they were afraid of stray bullets hitting them in their sleep. She reflected later on what it's like to live in the middle of random violence like this all the time. To live in Bayview, she realized, was to constantly soak up fear and stress.

One day, a fourteen-year-old boy who had been diagnosed with ADHD, who I'll call Robert, was brought to see Nadine. (I have also changed some other details throughout this chapter, at Nadine's request, to protect the medical confidentiality of her patients.) For a while, Robert had been prescribed the stimulant drug Ritalin, but it didn't seem to be making any difference for him. He said he didn't like how it made him feel, and he wanted to stop, but his previous doctors had insisted that he carry on taking it at higher and higher doses.

Nadine asked Robert and his mother when his attention problems had first begun. It was when he was ten. She asked: What happened then? Well, they explained, that was when he was sent to live at his dad's house. They talked about the divorce, and the boy's life in general—and then Nadine asked gently: Why was Robert sent to live with his dad? It took a while for them to tell the story, but in fits and starts, it tumbled out. Robert's mother had a boyfriend, and one day when she came home, she found him in the shower, sexually abusing her son. She had been sexually abused all throughout her own childhood, and she had been groomed to be terrified of abusive men and to submit to their demands. In that moment, she felt powerless—so she did something she was deeply ashamed of. Instead of calling the police, she sent her son away to live with his dad. Whenever Robert came back to visit, his abuser was still there, waiting.

Nadine thought a lot about this case, and she began to wonder if it might connect to a wider problem she was seeing. When she arrived at the medical center in Bayview, she had noticed that the kids there were being diagnosed as having attention problems at a staggering rate—dramatically higher than in wealthier neighborhoods—and that the first and usually only response was to drug them with very powerful stimulants like Ritalin or Adderall. Nadine is a believer in the power of medication to solve all sorts of problems—it's why she went into medicine—but she started to wonder: What if we are misdiagnosing the problem a lot of these kids are facing?

Nadine knew that decades before, scientists had discovered something significant. When human beings are in a terrifying environment—like a war zone—we often flip into a different state. She gave me an example, one I briefly referred to a little earlier. Imagine that you are walking in the woods and you are confronted by a grizzly bear that looks like it's angry and about to attack you. In that moment, your brain stops worrying about what you're going to eat that night, or how you're going to pay the rent. It becomes narrowly and entirely focused on one thing: danger. You track every movement of the bear, and your mind starts scanning for ways to get away from it. You become highly vigilant.

Now imagine that these bear attacks happen a lot. Imagine if three times a week, an angry bear suddenly appeared on your street and swiped one of your neighbors. If this happened, you would likely develop a state known as "hypervigilance." You would start to look out for danger all the time—whether there's a bear right in front of you or not. Nadine explained to me: "Hypervigilance is essentially when you're looking out for the bear around every corner. Your attention is focused on cues for potential danger, as opposed to being focused on being present with what's going on, or the lesson you're supposed to be learning, or doing the work you were supposed to be doing. It's not that [people in this state are] not paying attention. It's that they're paying attention to any cues or signs of threat or danger in their environment. That is where their focus is."

She pictured Robert sitting in a classroom trying to learn math, but knowing that in a few days he will be seeing the man who sexually abused him and might do it again. How, Nadine wondered, could he bring the power of his mind to bear on sums in these circumstances? It was primed instead to do one thing—to detect danger. This wasn't a failing in his brain—it was a natural and necessary response to intolerable circumstances. She wanted to know how many of the kids who she was treating, who were being told they had some inherent defect, might in fact be in a position like this. With the team at her clinic, she decided to scientifically investigate this question. She began to read the relevant scientific studies, and she learned that there was a standard way to identify if a child has been traumatized, and by how much. It's named the Adverse Childhood Experiences Study. It's quite straightforward. It asks: Have you experienced any of these ten bad things in your childhood—factors like physical abuse, cruelty, and neglect? Then it asks about any problems you might be having now—like obesity, addiction, and depression.

Nadine decided her team was going to study all of the more than 1,000 children in their care in this way, to figure out how much childhood trauma they had experienced, and to see if that correlated with any of the other problems they might be having—including headaches, abdominal pains, and (crucially) attention problems. With every child, they went through this detailed assessment.

Children who had experienced four or more types of trauma were 32.6 *times* more likely to have been diagnosed with attention or behavior problems than children who had not experienced any trauma. Other scientists across the U.S. have backed up the broad finding that kids are far more likely to have problems focusing if they experience trauma. For example, Dr. Nicole Brown, in a separate body of research, found that childhood trauma tripled the development of ADHD symptoms. A large study by the British Office of National Statistics found that if there's a financial crisis in the family, a child's chances of being diagnosed with attention problems go up 50 percent. If there's a serious illness in the family, it goes up 75 percent. If a parent has to make a court appearance, it goes up nearly 200 percent. This evidence base is small, but it is growing, and it seems to broadly back up what Nadine found in Bayview.

She believed she had uncovered a key truth about focus: To pay attention in normal ways, you need to feel safe. You need to be able to switch off the parts of your mind that are scanning the horizon for bears or lions or their modern equivalents, and let yourself sink down into one secure topic. In Adelaide, in Australia, I met with a child psychiatrist named Dr. Jon Jureidini, who has specialized in this question, and he told me that narrowing your focus is "a really good strategy in a safe environment, because it means you can learn things and flourish and develop. But if you are in a dangerous environment, selective attention [where you focus on just one thing] is a really dumb strategy. What you need instead is to evenly spread vigilance around your environment, looking for cues for danger."

After she learned this, Nadine realized that with Robert, the response by his previous doctors had been a serious error. She told me: "Guess what? Ritalin does not treat sexual assault." For these kids, "the medications are treating the surface symptoms and not the root cause. . . . If a child is having horrific behavior, most of the time, it's the child's really great way of alerting the system that something is not right." She came to believe that when children can't pay attention, that's often a signal that they are under terrible stress. Jon, the doctor in Adelaide who specialized in this subject, told me: "If you're medicating a child in that situation, you're colluding with them remaining in a violent or unacceptable situation." One study compared children who had been sexually abused with a group of children the same age who hadn't been abused, and found that the sexual-abuse survivors had double the usual rate of diagnosable ADHD. (This is not the only cause of ADHD—I'll come to the others later.)

The approach that was taken with Robert can lead to horrendous outcomes. In Norway, I went to interview the politician Inga Marte Thorkildsen, who started to investigate these questions—and wrote a book about it—after she was shaken by the case of one of her constituents. He was an eight-year-old boy whose teachers identified him as showing all the signs of hypervigilance. He wouldn't sit still; he was running around all the time; he refused to do what he was told. So he was diagnosed with ADHD, and given stimulants. Not long afterward he was found dead, with a seventeen-centimeter gap in his skull. He had been murdered by his father, who, it emerged, had been violently abusing him all along. When I sat with her in Oslo, Inge told me: "Nobody did anything because they just said, 'Wow, he has problems with attention,' blah blah. They didn't even talk to him during [the period when he was being given] medication."

Nadine began to ask: If that is the wrong approach, what's the right way to respond? How could she help Robert, and all the other kids in her care like him? She told me that she starts by explaining to parents: "I believe this [inability to focus] is being caused by your [child's] body making too many stress hormones. So here's how we fix them. We have to create an environment. We have to limit the amount of scary or stressful things that [your child] is experiencing and witnessing. And we have to layer on lots of buffering, lots of caregiving, lots of nurturing. In order for you to be able to do that, you, Mom, have to recognize and address your own history of what's gone on in your life."

There's no point saying this if you can't then offer them practical ways to do it. So she worked really hard to get funding from Bay Area philanthropists so that she could turn this proposal into a reality. In a case like Robert's, Nadine explained, there are lots of steps that have to be taken. They had to help the mother get therapy, so she could understand why she felt powerless to challenge his abuser. They had to connect the family with legal help so they could get a restraining order on the abuser, so he was out of Robert's life forever. They had to prescribe yoga for both the abused child and mother, so they could reconnect with their bodies. They had to help them to improve their sleep and their nutrition.

Nadine told me that you have to "scale the tools that you offer to be the same scale as the problems folks are having." These deeper solutions are, she stressed, really hard work—but she has seen them transform children. "I think it's easy for people to hear that when you've experienced childhood trauma, you're broken or damaged," she said, but in reality, "we have an ability to change." She sees it all the time in her practice: "The number of kids who have gone from failing to honor roll when they have the right diagnosis and the right support is nuts." That's why, for her, this is "joyful work," because "it shows us the profound potential for change. That's what I see in my clinical practice. This is eminently treatable. It's nuts how treatable it is. And there's so much low-hanging fruit." She believes that if we work hard enough to inform people, "we're going to get there; we're going to get to the place where we've transformed the landscape of how society and medicine—all of us—respond to this issue."

∽

Nadine believes she can only do this work because of the scared child she was in the suburbs of Palo Alto all those years before. She told me: "There's a Buddhist saying—be grateful for your suffering, because it allows you to empathize with the suffering of others."

Not long before I saw her last, Nadine had just been appointed surgeon general of California, the most senior medical position in the state. But as prestigious and powerful as that is, she told me she is more proud of something else. She had recently met with Robert and his mother. She saw how—as a result of the extensive help they have been given—they were slowly changing. He was no longer drugged for attention problems, nor was he showing difficulty focusing. They were developing empathy for each other. They were healing at a deep level, in a way that drugging the child could never have achieved. Robert's mother was able to see how her own sexual abuse had left her unable to protect her own child, and she was able, for the first time in her life, to see herself differently—and to have compassion for herself. This in turn meant she could start to have compassion for her son. They are both, Nadine said, "recognizing how the story can unfold differently" from now on.

∽

Nadine could see that the severe trauma that Robert experienced had been devastating, but she also came to believe that ordinary life in Bayview—with all the stress that entails—corrodes attention. Her patients who weren't abused as kids were still worried a lot of the time about being evicted, or going hungry, or being shot. They were under constant low-level pressure.

When she explained this to me, I wanted to understand—do other forms of stress affect attention? How about ones that are vastly less harrowing than sexual abuse? I found that the scientific evidence on this is a little bit complicated. The evidence in labs shows if you are put under mild to moderate stress, you will perform *better* on some tasks that require attention in the short term. We've all had that experience. Before I go onstage to give a speech, I feel a surge of pressure, but it makes me wake up, pull myself together, and perform at my best.

But what if that stress is protracted? In those circumstances, even mild levels of stress "can significantly alter attentional processes," as one scientific team found in a typical study. The science is so clear on this that a recent summary explained: "It is now obvious that stress can cause structural changes in the brain with long-term effects."

I started to ask: Why would this be? One reason is that stress often triggers other problems that we know undermine attention. For example, Professor Charles Nunn—a leading evolutionary anthropologist—investigated the rise of insomnia, and found that we struggle to sleep when we experience "stress and hyper-vigilance." If you don't feel safe, then you'll be unable to wind down, because your body is saying to you: You're in danger; stay alert. So the inability to sleep, he explained, isn't a malfunction—it's "an adaptive trait, under circumstances of perceived threat." To really deal with insomnia, Charles concluded, we "need to alleviate the sources of the anxiety and stress to effectively treat insomnia." They have to come to grips with the causes.

What might those deeper causes be? Here's one. Six out of every ten U.S. citizens have less than $500 in savings for if a crisis comes along, and many other countries in the Western world are moving in the same direction. As a result of big structural changes in the economy, the middle class is collapsing. I wanted to understand: What happens to your ability to think clearly when you become more financially stressed? I learned that this has been studied carefully by Sendhil Mullainathan, professor of computational science at the University of Chicago. He was part of a team that studied sugar-cane harvesters in India. They tested their thinking skills before the harvest (when they were broke), and after the harvest (when they had a fair bit of money). It turned out that when they had the financial security that came at the end of the harvest, they were on average thirteen IQ points smarter—an extraordinary gap. Why would that be? Anyone reading this who's ever been financially stressed knows part of the answer instinctively. When you are worried about how to survive financially, everything—from a broken washing machine to a child's lost shoe—becomes a threat to your ability to get through the week. You become more vigilant, just like Nadine's patients.

As I studied this big cause of stress, I kept thinking about something Nadine said to me: You have to "scale the tools that you offer to be the same scale as the problems folks are having." I wondered: What would this mean if we applied it to our financial stress? It turns out there is a place that answered that very question. In Finland in 2017, a coalition government, consisting of both centrist and right-wing parties, decided to try an experiment. Every now and then, politicians and citizens across the world have suggested that we should give everyone a small guaranteed basic income every month. The government would say to you: We're giving you a small amount of money to cover the basics (food, housing, heat), but no more. You don't have to do anything for it—we just want you to be secure and have the basic minimum necessary to survive. This idea has been touted by everyone from Republican president Richard Nixon to the Democratic presidential candidate Andrew Yang.

Finland decided to stop talking and actually try it. They selected 2,000 of their citizens at random, aged between twenty-five and fifty-eight, and told them: For the next two years, every month, we're going to give you €560 (which is about $650 U.S.), no strings attached. The government set up alongside it a rigorous scientific program to see what happened next, and once the project was over, the results were published. I interviewed two of the lead scientists who worked on it, Olavi Kangas, who is a professor in the Department of Social Research at the University of Turku, and Dr. Signe Jauhiainen, and they talked me through their findings.

Olavi told me that when it came to attention and focus, "the differences were very significant"—once people received a basic income, their ability to focus improved dramatically. Signe said they couldn't figure out the exact reason why, but they found that "problems with money are really not good for concentration. . . . If you have to worry about your financial situation . . . it takes a lot of the capacity of your brain. If you don't have to worry, then it improves your capacity to think about other things."

What the guaranteed basic income seems to have done—even though it was quite small—is give the recipients a sense they were standing on stable ground at last. How many people in the world feel that at the moment? Anything that reduces stress improves our ability to pay deep attention. Finland showed that a universal basic income—enough to give a baseline of security, but not so much that it disincentivizes work—improves people's focus by dealing with one of the causes of our hypervigilance.

This made me think again about our problems with our phones and with the web. The internet arrived for most of us in the late 1990s, into a society where the middle class was starting to crumble, and where financial insecurity was rising, and we were sleeping an hour less than people did in 1945. A more stressed society will be less able to resist distractions. It would always have been hard to resist the sophisticated human-hacking of surveillance capitalism, but it appeared we were already getting weaker, and we were easier to hack than we would have been otherwise. I was about to investigate other causes that also made us increasingly vulnerable.

꒰

I want to be honest here about something that complicates the argument I am putting forward in this book. There's one way in which what Nadine had to teach me—and the wider science of stress that I learned later—is a challenge to the broader thrust of what I'm writing here.

As you saw in the introduction, I believe it is reasonable to argue that our attention problems are getting worse, even though we don't have any long-term studies tracking changes in people's ability to focus over time. I came to this conclusion because we can prove that there are several factors that damage focus and attention, and those factors are rising.

But there's one counterargument to that. You might ask: What if there are counterveiling trends, happening at the same time, which make our attention better? Nadine has shown that experiencing violence damages your ability to focus. But over the past century, there has been a big fall in violence in the Western world. I know this runs contrary to what we read in the news, but it's true—Professor Steven Pinker, in his book *The Better Angels of Our Nature,* lays out the evidence for this very clearly. This seems counterintuitive, in part because we are constantly fed images of violence and threat on television and the web, but it is a fact that you are far less likely to be violently attacked or murdered than your ancestors. Not very long ago, the whole world—in terms of violence and fear—looked more like Bayview, or worse.

The threat of being beaten up or killed is surely the largest source of stress any person can face. Since that has fallen, we would expect this trend to have *improved* attention and focus. I want to be candid about this fact.

Do I think this sole—but highly significant—trend improving our focus outweighs all the other factors dragging it down? Does it outweigh the effects of a huge increase in switching, a decline in sleep, the effects of the vast machinery of surveillance capitalism, the rise in financial insecurity? I think—on balance—it doesn't. But this isn't something we can put into a computer and crunch the numbers on—it's too hard to quantify and compare each of these effects. So reasonable people could disagree with me. It is possible that Nadine's evidence suggests our attention, as a society, should be improving.

But I then learned about another attention-wrecking force in our culture—one that has been rising throughout my lifetime.

ᔐ

As a culture, in the Western world, we work longer with each decade that passes. Ed Deci, a professor of psychology who I interviewed at the University of Rochester in upstate New York, has shown that an extra month per year has been tacked on to what, in 1969, was considered a full-time job. As the twenty-first century began, the Canadian health service decided to study how people in their country spent their time at work. They studied over 30,000 people in over one hundred workplaces—public and private, large and small—and they ended up producing some of the most detailed research anywhere on how we work. They explained that as work hours swell and swell, people get more distracted and less productive, and concluded: "These workloads are not sustainable."

I only understood the full implications of this for our attention when I went to two places that had experimented with ways to radically reduce the amount of stress people experience at work. They are 10,000 miles apart, and their experiments are quite different—but I believe they have big implications for how we could reverse the damage that is being done to our attention today.

CHAPTER ELEVEN

The Places That Figured Out How to Reverse the Surge in Speed and Exhaustion

ndrew Barnes never stopped. He was working in the City of London—Britain's Wall Street—in the aftermath of the financial sector being deregulated in 1987. So companies could really let rip, and there was an explosion of financial swagger, with men in suits yelling at each other across the floor of the stock exchange as they traded billions. In this world, you were a wimp if you arrived later than 7:30 a.m., and you were a fool if you left before 7:30 p.m. So for half of the year, Andrew woke up in the dark and arrived home in the dark. He missed feeling the sun on his face.

In the City, everyone believed working better meant working more, until work consumed your whole life. He moved between various ball-breaking corporations. At one of them, all the new employees were called in on their first day to find that on the table in front of them there was a pre-typed resignation letter. They were ordered to sign it, and they were told: If you ever displease the boss, we'll pull out this letter, and you will be out. Andrew slowly realized that he hated this exhausting existence. "If I look back, I sacrificed my twenties on the altar of ambition, and later in life, I probably sacrificed my family," he told me. His wild overwork "cost me some relationships along the way," and it was only many years later that "I'm now having to build relationships with my kids."

Andrew left England for Australia and New Zealand, where over time he became really successful, rising to own a series of large businesses. When I went to see him, we met in his penthouse apartment looking out over the city of Auckland—but the memory of those sunless years in the City of London never left him.

One day, in 2018, he was on a plane when he happened to see a report in a business magazine about research into productivity at work. It contained some figures that intrigued him. The average British worker, the research had found, was only actually engaged with their job for less than three hours a day. This meant that most of the time people were at work, they were mentally checked out. They were in the office for a lot of hours, with their lives passing them by, but they weren't getting much done.

Andrew kept thinking about this. The company he ran in New Zealand, named Perpetual Guardian, had over a dozen offices employing over 240 people, in a business that drew up wills and ran and managed trusts. He wondered if these poor productivity figures applied to his own staff. In this situation, everyone is losing out. The workers are bored and distracted and worried about other things, particularly the families they don't get to see as much as they should. At the same time, the employer isn't getting a workforce that's focused on the task at hand. At the back of Andrew's mind, there was a memory of the years he himself had worked in a dysfunctional way, and he felt his own focus and judgment had been thrown off.

So one day he asked himself: What if I changed my entire company so that from now on, every employee worked only four days a week, for the same wages? It would free up time for them to rest, have a proper social life, and be with their families—the things they are often trying to squeeze into the cracks of their work time. What if giving them all this meant that, in return, the workers were able to focus on their tasks for just forty-five minutes more a day? His back-of-the-envelope calculations suggested to him that, in this scenario, the company's productivity would actually go up. Giving people more time to rest and enjoy life might mean they worked more productively when they were in the office.

To see if this could be right, he started to look back over the history of experiments in changing people's work hours. For example, in Britain during the First World War, there had been a munitions factory that made people work seven days a week. When they cut back to six days, they found, the factory produced more overall. How far, Andrew wondered, could that principle be extended?

So he decided to try something bold. He arranged a conference call and told all his employees that starting soon, they were going to be paid the same wage they currently got for a five-day week, but they would only be asked to work four days. However, he told them, in return, you have to find ways to genuinely get the job done. My hunch is you'll be more productive—but you have to show me I'm right. We'll try this change for two months. If, in that period, we don't see a fall in productivity, I will make the four-day week permanent.

"I was like—what? Am I hearing this right?" I was told by Amber Taare when I went to interview everyone at the offices Perpetual has in a town named Rotorua, which is well away from the corporate headquarters. The workers were excited but wary. How could a plan like this really succeed? Was there some catch they couldn't see? Gemma Mills, who also works in the Rotorua offices, told me: "I didn't have a lot of faith that it was going to work." Andrew's management team was also highly skeptical. "My head of HR literally fell over," Andrew said. The managers felt sure that productivity would be dented, and the blame would come back to them.

He gave the company a month to prepare, in which everyone had to think about how they could work better, and he called in a team of academic researchers to measure the real outcomes. Niggling drains on productivity that had been dragging on for years were identified and finally dealt with. One person, for example, had a job where she had to enter data, and it was wasting an hour of her day to have to enter it twice because two different systems weren't talking to each other. Now she went to IT and insisted they sort it out. There were hundreds of changes like this happening across the company. In another office, the staff bought a little pot of flags, and everyone agreed that if you didn't want to be interrupted, you would put a flag on your desk, to show you were focusing.

"It took a while to get your head around the concept, because it's so challenging," I was told by Russell Bridge, another Perpetual Guardian employee. "If you've worked on an eight-to-five model for so long, it's so ingrained and entrenched." But the change happened. With a whole extra day to themselves, people spent this time in different ways. Amber took her three-year-old daughter out of daycare for one day a week, and played with her more. Gemma said, "It just gives you that extra day to recuperate," and as a result, "I just felt genuinely better overall." Russell started to do DIY repairs around his home, and spent "quality time with the family." He told me it helped him to realize that "the way humans are designed is to have downtime and [then] you will be more productive." He found that when he came back to work, he was "fresher."

Almost everyone I spoke to who went through this experiment stressed that they noticed one change above all the others. As Gemma put it to me: "I was less likely to be distracted." Why? She said that, for her, it was about decompression. "I think your brain doesn't necessarily switch off as easily if you're going, going, going. You don't take that time to switch off and relax. . . . Your brain becomes accustomed to thinking constantly." But she found that with "that extra day to relax," she could start to wind down—and so when she came back to work, her mind was clearer.

Of course, the workers had a vested reason to believe this—they wanted to keep the extra time off. What mattered more was more objective measurements. What did the academics who studied the changes find? All signs of distraction, they found, were radically down.

For example, the time people spent on social media at work—which was measured by monitoring their computers—fell by 35 percent. At the same time, levels of engagement, teamwork, and stimulation at work—some of which were measured by observing the workers, and some by how the workers described themselves—went up by between 30 and 40 percent. Stress levels were down by 15 percent. People told me they slept more, rested more, read more, relaxed more. Andrew's management team—who had initially been highly skeptical—reached a surprising conclusion: they conceded that the company was achieving as much in four days as they had before in five. The changes have now been made permanent.

Dr. Helen Delaney, who studied these changes as part of her work in the Faculty of Business and Economics at the University of Auckland, told me with a laugh: "It wasn't a monstrous failure— I think we can say that. The work got done, clients were happy, staff were happy." When she interviewed them in depth, she found that "overwhelmingly, employees really liked their four-day workweek. . . . They loved it. Who wouldn't?" Helen found this extra time gave them two things. Firstly, it "allowed them to nurture relationships with other people that are lost in the frenzy of modern living." One senior manager told her he had struggled to connect with his son, but now that he had started spending a lot of his freed-up time with him, he "realized actually I like being with my son, and he quite likes me, and this is a nice time to be together." Secondly, "they also talked a lot about having what they called 'me time.'" They told her, "With no one around me, no kids, no partner, no one—I got to be myself."

Something similar has been tried in many other places, and even though the experiments are quite different, they keep finding similar outcomes. In 1920s Britain, W. G. Kellogg—the manufacturer of cereals—cut his staff from an eight-hour day to a six-hour day, and workplace accidents (a good measure of attention) fell by 41 percent. In 2019 in Japan, Microsoft moved to a four-day week, and they reported a 40 percent improvement in productivity. In Gothenberg in Sweden around the same time, a care home for elderly people went from an eight-hour day to a six-hour day with no loss of pay, and as a result, their workers slept more, experienced less stress, and took less time off sick. In the same city, Toyota cut two hours per day off the workweek, and it turned out their mechanics produced 114 percent of what they had before, and profits went up by 25 percent.

All this suggests that when people work less, their focus significantly improves. Andrew told me we have to take on the logic that more work is always better work. "There's a time for work, and there's a time for not having work," he said, but today, for most people, "the problem is that we don't have time. Time, and reflection, and a bit of rest to help us make better decisions. So, just by creating that opportunity, the quality of what I do, of what the staff does, improves." Andrew followed his own advice. Now he takes every weekend off— something he had never done before in his life—and goes away to his home on a nearby island without any devices connected to the internet. Gemma, one of the workers who told me that she had been wary at the start, said to me gently: "You know, there's so much more than working until twelve o'clock at night. . . . You've got to have a life outside of it."

Later, at Stanford University, I discussed these questions with Jeffrey Pfeffer, who is a professor of organizational behavior there. He said the reason it works is blindingly obvious. Ask any sports fan, he said. "If I want to win a football game, [or] if I want to win a baseball game, do I really want my team to be exhausted?" He let this question hang in the air. Why, he asked, would the rest of us be any different?

One day I went for a walk along the shore in Auckland, thinking about what I had seen—and it struck me that this was the first place I had been to that had directly challenged the logic of our ever-accelerating society. We live in a culture that gets us to walk faster, talk faster, work longer, and we are taught to think that is where productivity and success come from. But here was a group of people saying: No. We are going to slow down and create more space for rest and attention.

At the moment, this sane decision looks like an impossible luxury to the majority of us. Most people can't slow down, because they fear that if they do, they'll lose their jobs or their status. Today, only 56 percent of Americans take even one week of vacation a year. This is why telling people what they need to do to improve their attention—do one thing at a time, sleep more, read more books, let your mind wander—can so easily curdle into cruel optimism. The way our society works at the moment means they can't do those things. But it doesn't have to be this way. Our society can change. As I reflected on this, I felt a little uneasy, because there are a few reasons why telling you the story of what happened in New Zealand in this way could leave you with a misleading impression. I like Andrew Barnes a lot—he's an unusually enlightened and decent employer—but I don't want you to imagine you too can wait for your boss to have an epiphany and hand you a four-day week. If we want this change to happen, you will very likely have to take a different route.

Think about the weekend, which for more than a hundred years gave most workers a guaranteed slice of rest and reflection. How did that come to pass? In the eighteenth century, as the Industrial Revolution surged, many workers found themselves forced by their employers to work for ten hours a day, six days a week. It was breaking them, physically and mentally. So they began to band together and demanded time to live. The first strike demanding shorter working hours took place in Philadelphia in 1791. The police beat the workers to a pulp, and afterward, many of them were fired. But the workers didn't give up. They fought harder. By 1835 they were organizing a general strike for an eight-hour day. Only decades of campaigns like this finally yielded an eight-hour day and a weekend for almost everyone.

With a few honorable exceptions like Andrew, the owners of corporations will not voluntarily take less of your time, any more than Facebook will. They have to be compelled to do it. The introduction of the weekend was the biggest challenge to the speeding-up of society that has ever happened. Only a comparable fight will deliver a four-day week.

This insight is connected to another big obstacle to achieving this goal. A four-day week can be applied to salaried workers—but increasingly, many people are being forced into the "gig economy," where they scramble to do several jobs without any contracts or fixed work hours at all. This is happening as a result of a very specific change: in countries like the U.S. and Britain, governments broke up and largely destroyed labor unions. They made it harder and harder for workers to band together and demand things like contracts and fixed work hours. The only long-term solution to this is to steadily rebuild unions—so people have the power to demand these basic rights. This has already begun. For example, all over the U.S., workers in fast-food restaurants are unionizing and demanding a $15 minimum wage per hour, with incredible success. They have secured wage raises for over 22 million workers and have pulled off the difficult job of winning majority support both in states that voted for Donald Trump and in states that voted for Joe Biden.

But I think we won't only have to take on employers—we'll also have to fight something inside ourselves. When I spent time with the workers at Perpetual Guardian, I found what they said persuasive—but in my gut, I kept pushing back, looking for flaws in what they were telling me. At first I couldn't figure out why. Then I realized that I often only feel I have worked enough if, at the end of the day, I am bone-tired and wrung out. The team who designed the original Macintosh computer wore T-shirts boasting WORKING 90 HOURS A WEEK AND LOVING IT! This could be the insane slogan for our professional class. Many of us have built our identities around working to the point of exhaustion. We call this success. In a culture built on ever-increasing speed, slowing down is hard, and most of us will feel guilty about doing it. That's one reason why it's important we all do it together—as a societal, structural change.

⌇

When Covid-19 spread across the world, lots of people thought—amid all the tragedy and horror—that there might at least be one good outcome. Many people (not all) were freed from the daily commute and from the pressure to be seen at their desks all the time. So it was assumed that there might be a little space created for more rest. But work hours actually went *up* during Covid—in the first month and a half of lockdown alone, the average U.S. worker clocked in three extra hours a day. In France, Spain, and Britain, people worked two hours more a day on average. It's not totally clear why. Some people think it's because Zoom meetings take so damn long; others reckon it's because, given all the economic insecurity, people were even more keen to show they were working so they didn't get laid off.

What this shows is that no big outside force is going to come along and free us from the ratchet to work more and more hours—not even a global pandemic. We will only get it through a collective struggle to change the rules.

But Covid also showed us something else that is relevant to a four-day week. It demonstrated that businesses can change their working practices radically, in a very short period of time, and continue to function well. When I caught up with him on Zoom in early 2021, Andrew Barnes said to me: "If a chief executive of a British bank had said, 'We could run a 60,000-person bank from home' a year and a half ago, you'd have said: 'No chance.' Right?" And yet it happened, pretty seamlessly. "So . . . surely you can run a business in four days, not five?" Andrew told me other managers used to say to him that a four-day week couldn't possibly work because they wouldn't be able to trust their staff if they couldn't see them. Andrew called them back and said they should think again now: "They all work from home. Amazingly, the work got done."

The way we work seems fixed and unchangeable—until it changes, and then we realize it didn't have to be like that in the first place.

Ten thousand miles away, in Paris, workers had come up with a parallel proposal to help slow their lives down. Before the rise of smartphones, it was unusual for a boss to contact her worker once she had left the office and gone home. As a kid, plenty of my friends had parents with demanding jobs—but I almost never saw them get phoned by their employer once they got home. This was rare in the 1980s: when work was over, it was over. The only people who lived on permanent call were doctors, presidents, and prime ministers.

But since our work lives came to be dominated by email, there's a growing expectation that workers will respond at any time, day or night. One study found that a third of French professionals felt they could never unplug, for fear of missing out on an email they were expected to reply to. Another study found that just the expectation that you should be on call causes workers anxiety, even if they don't actually get contacted on any given night. In effect, the idea of work hours has disappeared, and we are all on call all the time. By 2015, French doctors explained they were seeing an explosion in patients suffering from *"le burnout,"* and voters started to demand action—so the French government commissioned Bruno Mettling, the head of the telecom company Orange, to study the evidence and figure out a solution. He concluded that this constantly-on-call way of working was disastrous for people's health and their ability to do their jobs. He proposed a significant reform: everyone should have a "right to disconnect."

This right is simple. It says that you are entitled to clearly defined work hours—and you are entitled, when those work hours are over, to unplug and not to have to look at email, or to have any other work contact. So in 2016, the French government passed this into law. Now any company with more than fifty people has to formally negotiate with its workers to agree on the hours in which they can be contacted—and all other hours are out of bounds. (Smaller companies can draw up their own charters but don't have to formally consult their workers.) Since then, several companies have faced penalties for trying to force people to respond to email out of hours. For example, the pest-control company Rentokil had to pay a local branch manager €60,000 (around $70,000 in the U.S.) in compensation after it had complained he didn't respond to off-hour emails.

In practice, when I went to Paris and spoke to my friends who work for companies there, they said change is happening too slowly on this—the law is not being enforced by a tough regulator, so most French people haven't yet experienced a big shift. But it's a first step in the direction we all need to travel.

Sitting in a café in Paris, I thought about what I had seen. There's no point giving people sweet self-help lectures about the benefits of unplugging unless you give them a legal right to do it. In fact, lecturing about the benefits of unwinding to people whose bosses don't allow them to unwind becomes a kind of maddening taunt—it's like lecturing famine victims on how they'd feel better if they had dinner at the Ritz. If you have an independent fortune and you don't need to work, then you can probably make these changes now. But for the rest of us, we need to be part of a collective struggle in order to reclaim the time and space that has been taken from us—so we can finally rest, and sleep, and restore our attention.

CHAPTER TWELVE

Causes Nine and Ten: Our Deteriorating Diets and Rising Pollution

For every summer of my childhood and my teenage years, I was banished from my home in suburban London to a place that seemed as alien to me as the rings of Saturn. My dad had been born in a wooden farmhouse on a mountain in the Swiss Alps. "You must go to the farm," my father yelled, "it will teach you how to be a man!" And so, for six weeks of the year, I would be woken up every morning by the crowing of a cockerel, in a fog of deep confusion, in the tiny room my father had shared as a kid with his four brothers.

The first summer I spent alone with my Swiss grandparents was when I was nine years old. I learned that all through their lives, they had mostly eaten food that they had grown, raised, or killed themselves. They had a huge garden, where they planted their own fruit and vegetables, and they raised their own animals for meat. But when they put their food on the table in front of me, I stared at it and struggled to recognize that it was even edible. Back home, my mother and my other grandmother were working-class Scottish women, and they had raised me on a diet of chips, fried food, supermarket-bought processed meals, and vast amounts of Kinder Egg chocolate. We got a microwave when I was about seven, and from that point on I lived primarily on radiated pizza and zapped French fries. So for the first few weeks I was in Switzerland, I pleaded for chips, pizza, anything that I saw as food, and I refused to eat what my grandmother prepared. *"Ce n'est pas nourriture!"* I said sincerely: "It's not food."

My grandparents were baffled. One day my grandmother caved in and took me into the city several hours away for McDonald's. She didn't order anything for herself, and she watched me eat my Big Mac and fries with a look of compassionate disgust. Years later, in Las Vegas, I stumbled one day upon a very mentally unwell homeless person who was eating rotting maggot-filled food from the garbage behind the Rio casino. I realized my facial expression was exactly the same as my grandmother's had been that day in the McDonald's in Zurich.

In the two generations that had passed from my grandparents to me, there had been a dramatic transformation in one of the most basic elements of being a human—what we put into our bodies for fuel. All over the world I interviewed experts who said that we all know this change has been bad for our waistlines and our hearts, but we have been neglecting another key effect: it is stealing large parts of our ability to pay attention.

Dale Pinnock is one of the best-known nutritionists in Britain, and when we sat down together for a meal in London, I tried not to look at the juicy hamburgers on the menu, and ordered tofu and vegetables instead, just to impress him. He told me that if you want to understand why so many of us are struggling to focus, you might want to think about it this way: "If you put shampoo into a car engine, you're not going to scratch your head when the thing conks out," he said. Yet every day, all over the Western world, we are putting into our bodies substances "which are so far removed from what was intended for human fuel." Achieving sustained attention, he said, is a physical process that requires your body to be able to do certain things. So if you disrupt your body—by depriving it of the nutrients it needs, or by pumping it full of pollutants—your ability to pay attention will also be disrupted.

Dale, and other experts on this question I spent time with across the world, went on to outline three broad ways in which how we eat now is harming our focus. The first is that we currently eat a diet that causes regular energy spikes and energy crashes. If you eat (say) a Twinkie, he said, your "blood sugar is going through the roof, and then crashing back down again. That's going to affect how you can actually physically focus, because if your energy is through the floor, you're not going to be able to give things your full attention." But most of us now start the day with the equivalent of a Twinkie, though we don't realize it. "Think about that typical pattern. People will eat maybe a bowl of cereal and a slice of toast in the morning. It's usually Frosties and white bread." Because there's very little fiber in there, glucose—which gives you energy—"will be released very, very rapidly. So your blood sugar goes really high, really quickly, which is great—for about twenty minutes." Then "it crashes down, and when it crashes down, that's when you're knackered," and at this point "you get brain fog."

When that happens, you sit at your desk and you struggle to think. Your child experiences that crash sitting at school, and she isn't able to listen to the teacher. This is where "you have very, very low energy, and you constantly feel like you need a pick-me-up. . . . That is the blood sugar crashing." When this happens, you and your kid want more sugary-carby treats in order to get another short burst of focus. "If every mealtime you're consuming those cheap, shitty carbohydrates, then you're going to be going on that roller coaster over and over again." He added that if you're consuming those kinds of foods with caffeine, the effect on blood sugar is exaggerated even further: "If you had a croissant on its own, your blood sugar will obviously spike, but if you had it with a coffee, it would spike even higher, and you would get a much more aggressive crash." These spikes and crashes take place throughout the day, leaving us so depleted that we can't focus well for long stretches. He said that all this—shifting metaphor slightly—is "like putting rocket fuel into a mini. It would just burn out and bust very quickly—because it can't handle that. But put in the petrol it's designed to take, and it'll go along nicely."

There is such a strong scientific consensus that our current diets cause these energy crashes that the British National Health Service's carefully fact-checked official website warns about it. So, Dale said, if we want to improve our kids' focus and attention, our first step should be to "stop feeding them fucking Coke for breakfast and a bowl of sugar and milk. Try giving them proper food first." If we do, he said, we'll see rapid results, because "the developing brain is so responsive to change." (He later explained that, at the moment, parents have to fight against an army of advertisers trying to get their kids to eat badly, and a food-supply system that is designed to hack our weaknesses—I'll come to that soon.)

The second way in which our diets affect our focus is that most of us now eat in a way that deprives us of the nutrients we need for our brains to develop and function fully. For almost all of our history, human beings ate, roughly, like my grandparents—they consumed fresh food that they knew the origin of. As the great food writer Michael Pollan, who's a big influence on Dale, has explained, in the two generations between them and me, food went through a profound degeneration. In the mid-twentieth century there was a rapid move from fresh food toward precooked, processed food that was sold in supermarkets and created in order to be reheated. This food had to be prepared for sale in a completely different way. It was pumped full of stabilizers and preservatives to make sure it didn't go bad as it sat on supermarket shelves, and this industrial process has, it turns out, stripped food of a lot of its nutritional value.

Then, as we became more accustomed to food that was radically different from what had gone before, the food industry began to find more and more sophisticated ways to directly target our primitive pleasure centers. They pumped our foods full of sugars in quantities that never occur in nature, and trans fats, and various unprecedented new inventions. In the U.S. and Britain, most of what we eat now falls into the category of "ultra-processed food"—which is, as Michael Pollan has pointed out, so removed from anything in nature that it's very hard to figure out what the original ingredients even were.

There's some uncertainty about precisely how this has affected our focus, but we have some pretty strong clues. Since the 1970s there have been several scientific studies designed to figure out what happens to your attention when you change your diet. To give one example, in 2009 a team of Dutch scientists took a group of twenty-seven children who had been identified as having trouble focusing, and they split them into two groups. Fifteen of them were assigned to an "eliminationist" diet, which meant they couldn't consume the junk most of us eat every day—preservatives, additives, synthetic dyes—and so instead they had to eat the kind of food my grand-parents would have recognized. The other twelve carried on eating the usual Western diet. The team then monitored them for several weeks to see what happened. It turned out that more than 70 percent of the kids who cut out the preservatives and dyes improved their ability to pay attention, and the average improvement was a remarkable 50 percent.

But this was a small study—so the same team decided to follow up. This time, they took a hundred children, and they did the experiment again, following kids over five weeks. Once again, it turned out that most of the kids who stuck to the eliminationist diet saw a big improvement in their attention and focus, and more than half got dramatically better.

The scientists doing these studies have mostly been investigating the notion that these kids can't focus because they are allergic to something in our everyday diets. That's possible. But their experiments seem to me more likely to fit with this wider way of thinking that I was learning about: that when you consume the kind of foods we evolved to eat, your brain will function better. In New York, I went for breakfast with Dr. Drew Ramsay, who's one of the pioneers of "nutritional psychiatry"—a new field that is teasing out

the connection between the way we eat and our psychological challenges. He said if anyone doubts these insights, he would ask them
where "they think attention comes from. . . . The brain gets built
from foods. So there's that very fundamental connection." Your brain,
he told me, can only grow and thrive if it gets a broad range of key
nutrients. To give one well-studied example, if you eat a diet that's
deprived of omega-3s—which are largely found in fish—your brain
will suffer. And it's not good enough to replace these foods with
supplements—your body absorbs nutrients much more effectively
from real food than from capsules.

The third reason our food harms our focus is different. Our current diets aren't just lacking in what we need—they also actively contain chemicals that seem to act on our brains almost like drugs. For
example, in 2007 a group of scientists in Southampton in Britain got
297 normal kids, who were either three years old or between eight
and nine, and they split them into two groups. One group was given
a drink containing common food additives that appear regularly in
our diets, and the other group was given a drink that didn't contain
them. They were then monitored to see how they behaved. The kids
who drank the food dyes were significantly more likely to become
hyperactive. The evidence for this was strong and decisive enough
that in the aftermath of this discovery, many European countries
banned these dyes—but the U.S. regulators refused to, and they are
still being consumed every day in some of the country's most popular
cereals and snacks. I wondered if this could help to explain some of
the gap in ADHD rates between Europe and the U.S.

Dale told me that if you want to understand what's really going
on here, you should look out across the world at the places where
people are physically and mentally fitter than we are, with lower levels of diagnosed ADHD and dementia. If you do that, he said, at
first it'll seem puzzling, because the diets they eat are actually very
different—some of them are heavy on fish, some have very little fish;
some have a lot of plants, some don't have many plants; some have
lots of carbohydrates and some have none at all. If you're looking for

a magic ingredient, you won't find it. But "there's one thing that uni-
fies every single one of them. They're all leaving out the crap that's
making us sick in the first place. They're all leaving out the refined
carbohydrates, the processed food, the junk oils. They're all building
their foundations on whole foods. . . . That's the key. That's the magic
bullet—just go back to whole foods. Foods as they were originally
intended." He quoted Michael Pollan, who says we should eat only
food that our grandparents would have recognized as food, and we
should shop primarily around the outer edges of the supermarket—
the fruit and veg at the front, and the meat and fish at the back. The
stuff in the middle, he warned, isn't really food at all.

Yet instead of promoting healthy food to children, we often push
the worst food on them. In Boston another nutritional psychiatrist,
Dr. Umadevi Naidoo, told me that a few years before, the funding for
school lunches in the U.S. had been cut, and "the food companies
moved in and provided vending machines." Now, "the obvious connection is that if they're getting candy bars and cookies, which were
processed," there will "definitely" be a link to the rise in attention
problems in children. These reasons—and many more—are why
Professor Joel Nigg, the ADHD expert I interviewed in Portland, has
written: "A sea change is under way. . . . If you think your child's
ADHD may have something to do with food, science now agrees
with you."

⁀

I liked all the people I was meeting—but part of me felt really uncomfortable as I had these conversations. So many of my emotions are
tied up with the foods that they were explaining to me are focus-
killers. I was raised to find comfort in unhealthy food. I pine for it
when I feel down. As I reflected on how this diet might be affecting
me, I started to think again about my time in Provincetown. There
are no fast-food chains there—no McDonald's! No KFC! Not even
Burger King! There's only a single pizza place, Spiritus Pizza. So for
three months, I ate almost nothing but healthy, fresh food—which

is two months and thirty days longer than at any other point in my life, other than those long Swiss summers. I wondered if that too had played a role in why I focused so easily and so well there.

As I investigated all this, I kept thinking about the last time I ever saw my Swiss grandmother. She was in her mid-eighties, and we walked up her mountain together, with her walking faster than me. She led me into her huge garden, and she tended to it—ripping out weeds, observing the progress of her carrots and leeks—while her chickens scratched freely all around us. Then, with brisk hand movements, she picked out the food we were going to eat together that night, and I watched her cook it. To her, this was as natural as breathing. To me, I realize now, it should have been a revelation.

Yet I can imagine presenting this evidence to people in a way that reeks of cruel optimism. You can picture Instagram influencers taking these points and posting: Look! Just change what you eat and your focus will return! I did it! Now you can too! But the truth is that this—like so much of what I was learning about for this book—is primarily a structural problem. Nobody I know has a mountain and a farm like my grandparents did—they have to get their food at supermarkets. Those supermarkets are full of cheap processed food, which is promoted to us from the moment we are born by enormous advertising budgets. If we are going to overcome this problem, there is some role for each of us making individual changes, but there's a bigger need to deal with the larger forces behind it. Today, just like—as Tristan had taught me—every time you try to put down your phone, there are a thousand engineers behind the screen trying to get you to pick it up again, every time you try to give up processed food, there's a team of expert marketers trying to get you to crack and come back to it. From long before you were even consciously aware of it, they have been working at getting you to associate positive feelings with unhealthy food. They programmed me perfectly to feed their profit margins rather than my brain health, and I'm not alone. That machinery needs to be turned off, so it can't distort the tastes and steal the focus of another generation.

∿

The next cause of our attention crisis is, out of all the factors I have written about in this book, potentially the biggest. We all know that being exposed to pollution and to industrial chemicals—in the air, or in the products we buy—is bad for us. If you'd asked me when I started researching this book, I could have explained to you, in pretty basic terms, that air pollution causes asthma and other breathing problems, for example. But I was startled to learn that there is growing evidence suggesting that this pollution is seriously damaging our ability to focus.

To understand this, I read widely about the science surrounding this question, and I interviewed scientists who have been at the cutting edge of discovering these effects. Professor Barbara Demeneix—a prestigious scientist in France who has won several major awards, including the Légion d'honneur, the country's highest civilian prize—explained to me: "At every stage of your life, different forms of pollution will affect your attention span," and she has concluded this is a factor in why "we've got neurodevelopmental disease increasing exponentially . . . [including] ADHD across the board." She said that we are now surrounded by so many pollutants that "there is no way we can have a normal brain today."

The form of pollution we, as ordinary citizens, know most about is in the air all around us, so I interviewed Barbara Maher, who is a professor of environmental science at the University of Lancaster in England, and has been carrying out potentially game-changing research on how it is affecting our brains. She explained to me that if you live in a major city today, every day you are breathing in a chemical soup—a mixture of many different contaminants, including those spewed from car engines. Your brain did not evolve to absorb these chemicals, like iron, through the respiratory system, and it doesn't know how to handle them. So just by living in a polluted city, she said, you are experiencing a "repeated chronic insult to your brain," and it will react by becoming inflamed. I asked her: What happens if that goes on for months and years? She said it "is going to lead to damage to the nerve cells, to the neurons. Depending on the dose [i.e., how bad the pollution is], depending on your genetic susceptibility, eventually, over time, your brain cells will be damaged."

She has found that the worse the pollution, the worse the damage to your brain. After soaking up this damage for years, you are more likely to develop one of the worst forms of brain degeneration, dementia. In Canada, a study found that people who lived within fifty meters of a major road were 15 percent more likely to develop dementia than people who didn't. But I asked Barbara: What does that inflammation do to your mental functioning earlier in life? "It's probable that if there's a chronic impact, that can cause aggression, loss of control, attention deficit."

The evidence is especially worrying when it comes to children's brains, which are still developing, she said. "We've now seen evidence for the onset of these degenerative diseases in really, really young children in highly polluted environments. That's your next generation. . . . My colleague in Mexico [has] been doing MRI scans, and they can already see shrinking volumes of brain tissue in badly affected young people." The more polluted an area is, the worse the harm—to the point where some have "lesions. You can actually see plaques and tangles [in the brain, like in dementia patients], even in very young cases." A scientist in Barcelona, Professor Jordi Sunyer, tested schoolchildren's ability to pay attention across the city—and found that the worse the pollution, the worse the kids performed.

This seemed really daunting. It told me there's a focus-killer literally all around us, and I felt overwhelmed. How can we fight it? I began to get some clues once I had learned some history. I started by looking at the effect of one specific pollutant on our attention: lead. As far back as ancient Rome, it was known that lead was poisonous to human beings. The architect Vitruvius, for example, begged the Roman authorities to not use it to build the city's pipes. Yet for centuries lead was used to paint homes and in water pipes, and then in the early twentieth century it was added to petrol, which meant it was pumped into the air of every city in the world and breathed in by its inhabitants. Scientists warned almost at once that leaded gasoline was likely to produce disaster. When in 1925 General Motors announced that putting lead in gasoline was a "gift of God," its CEO was warned by Dr. Alice Hamilton, the leading expert on lead in the U.S., that he was playing with fire. "Where there is lead," she said, "some case of lead poisoning sooner or later develops." It was clear this could have a terrible effect on people's brains: in high doses, lead poisoning makes people hallucinate, lose their minds, or die. The factories where leaded petrol was developed had outbreaks of staff members going violently insane and dying because of their exposure to it.

There was always a non-leaded form of gasoline available that didn't carry these risks, but the big corporations resisted it fiercely, seemingly for a commercial reason: they could patent the leaded version, and so make more money from it. For forty years, the lead industry funded all the scientific research into whether it was safe— and assured the world that their scientists had discovered it was.

It turns out this decision to allow leaded petrol to dominate the market stole a large amount of focus from people all over the world. I went to interview Bruce Lanphear, who is professor of health sciences at Simon Fraser University in Canada. He explained that as a young academic in the 1980s, he was offered a position in Rochester in upstate New York to study the effects of lead on children's cognitive abilities. He knew that kids were still being exposed to a lot of lead, even though lead paint had been banned in 1978, because millions of people still lived in homes full of it, and leaded petrol continued to be used everywhere. He wanted to know what this was doing to them.

As part of the project he worked with, all the kids in Rochester were given blood tests to see just how much lead they were carrying in their bodies. When Bruce saw the results, he was taken aback. One in three of the children in the city had lead poisoning. For Black children, it was one in two. Rochester wasn't unusual—separate research a few years before found that modern Americans by the 1970s were carrying more than six hundred times more lead in their bodies than preindustrial humans, and the Environmental Protection Agency estimates that 68 million children were exposed to toxic levels of lead in the U.S. from leaded petrol alone between 1927 and 1987.

Bruce and other scientists showed that lead severely stunts your ability to focus and pay attention. If you are exposed to lead as a child, he explained to me, you are "two and a half times more likely to meet criteria for ADHD." The effect becomes even bigger if it is combined with other forms of pollution. For example, if your mother was exposed to lead during pregnancy and she smoked cigarettes, you are *eight times* more likely to be diagnosed with ADHD.

Before Bruce arrived, the mothers of Rochester—like mothers across the United States—had been warned about the dangers of lead poisoning, and then told that it was their fault. The authorities said to them: Your kids are being exposed in this way because, as mothers, you have failed to dust your homes enough. Do more housework and get your kids to wash their hands more. This was part of a wider push. The lead industry itself claimed the problem lay mainly with "uneducable Negro and Puerto Rican" parents who "failed" to protect their kids from the lead in their homes.

But when Bruce studied it, he found that all this dusting and handwashing made no difference at all. He could see that a whole city, and a whole generation of children, had been poisoned, and the families had been told it was on them because they weren't clean enough. Some scientists went even further in blaming the victims. They said the problem wasn't that the families were living with high levels of a brain-damaging metal, but that the children had a mental illness. They said the kids had a psychological disorder named "pica," which was making toddlers irrationally stick chunks of lead paint in their mouths. These children were labeled as having a "perverted appetite," and it was (again) claimed that this problem seemed to be suffered mainly by Black and Brown children.

At every stage, right from the 1920s onward, the lead industry created and encouraged these diversionary tactics. They also bought the loyalty of some scientists, who systematically cast doubt on the evidence that lead harmed people's brains. Right at the start, in the 1920s, one scientist, named Thomas Midgley, announced at a press conference that it was perfectly safe to use leaded products. He didn't tell the gathered journalists he had just recovered from a terrible dose of lead poisoning himself, caused by the very products he was now promoting. At every stage, the lead industry insisted, in effect: If there is any doubt about the danger, we should be allowed to carry on pumping lead into people's bodies.

All through the research for this book, I had an ongoing struggle to hold clearly in my mind the structural nature of our attention crisis. We live in an extremely individualistic culture, where we are constantly pushed to see our problems as individual failings, and to seek out individual solutions. You're unable to focus? Overweight? Poor? Depressed? We are taught in this culture to think: That's my fault. I should have found a personal way to lift myself up and out of these environmental problems. Now, whenever I feel that way, I think about the mothers in Rochester whose kids were being poisoned by lead, and they were simply told they should dust their homes more, or that their kids had a "perverted" desire to suck on chunks of lead paint. We can see clearly now there was a huge problem with a deep cause in the environment—and yet the primary response was to tell people to throw all their energy into a frantic individual displacement activity that made no difference at all, or (even worse) to blame their own poisoned children.

When the problem was blamed on isolated individuals, and they were told to solve it by simply tweaking their own behavior, the problem only got worse. So I investigated—what did end it? I learned it was one thing, and one thing only. It stopped when ordinary citizens learned the scientific evidence and banded together to demand their governments change the law to stop these companies from poisoning them. In Britain, for example, the campaign against leaded petrol was led by a housewife named Jill Runnette, who succeeded in getting the government to cut the amount of lead in petrol by two-thirds in 1981. (It was later banned altogether.) She did it to protect herself and the children of her society.

In a way, this felt to me like a metaphor for our whole attention crisis. Our attention and focus have been raided, pillaged, and poisoned by huge external forces—and we have been told to do the equivalent of dusting our homes and washing our hands more, when we should have been doing the equivalent of banning lead paint and petrol all along. In many ways, the story of resistance to lead poisoning is a model for us to follow now. The dangers were clear for decades—Dr. Alice Hamilton accurately documented them in the mid-1920s—but things only changed when there was a dedicated democratic movement of ordinary citizens taking on the forces that stole their focus. In 1975 the average American had a blood lead level of 15 micrograms per deciliter. Today it's 0.85 micrograms per deciliter. The IQ of the average preschooler is estimated by scientists at the U.S. Centers for Disease Control and Prevention to have risen by five points as a result of the ban. It's proof that it's possible to make dramatic progress on fighting an attention-killer.

$\backsim$

But Barbara Demeneix warned me that since then, "there are so many other [attention-damaging] chemicals that . . . are increasing on the market" that she fears this is now dwarfing the benefit of ditching lead. So I asked her: What chemicals are we being exposed to today that have potential effects on attention? "Let's start with the main culprits: Pesticides. Plasticizers. Flame-retardants. Cosmetics." She said, "Of over two hundred pesticides on the market in Europe, about two-thirds affect either brain development or thyroid hormone signaling." When monkeys are exposed to the same level of the common pollutant polychlorinated biphenyls (PCBs) as humans currently are, they develop serious problems with their working memory and mental development. A team of scientists studied the amount of a pollutant named bisphenol A, or BPA—which is used to coat 80 percent of metal cans—that mothers are exposed to. They found that exposure to the chemical predicts which of them will have kids with behavior problems.

Barbara has been engaged for nearly twenty years in developmental neurotoxicity testing—the science that figures out how the chemicals we are exposed to, both in the products that we buy and in the food that we eat, affect the development of fetuses and babies. She was commissioned by the European Parliament to do major research on this question, and she has coordinated many other research projects—in the course of her research, there was one area in particular that worried her most. She explained to me that from the moment you are conceived, your development is shaped by hormones, which "regulate early development." So she began to research whether these chemicals have any effect on these endocrine signals. What she discovered is that many of them create an effect that's like "radio interference," screwing with the system that guides how a human should develop, especially the brain, and making parts of it go astray. This affects attention, she explained, because this whole system guides how a person's brain will develop. If your brain doesn't develop normally, your attention can seriously suffer.

Between 2005 and 2012, she tested many common substances that are all around us—and the more substances her team tested, the more evidence she gathered that the endocrine system is being messed with by our current environment. She warns that all children today are being born "precontaminated" by a "toxic cocktail."

This is disputed. Some scientists believe that these dangers are being hugely overstated. For example, the American Council on Science and Health has ridiculed Barbara's claims, arguing that you would have to be exposed to a massive dose of some of these chemicals for them to have the effects she describes. This group has been funded by chemical companies and large agricultural corporations with a vested interest in this debate, which means we should handle their skepticism with some skepticism of our own—but it doesn't necessarily mean they are wrong. There needs to be more funding to study these questions in detail.

It sometimes seems like the same story that played out with lead is now happening with other attention-damaging chemicals. The industries that profit from using them fund the vast majority of the research into them; they systematically promote doubt about the possible harms; and they argue that if there's any doubt at all about the danger of their products, they should be allowed to carry on using them.

I felt tempted, when I heard all this, to keep asking the scientists I interviewed: Okay, what products contain these pollutants, and how do I cut them out of my life? You say BPA coats metal cans—should I avoid metal cans? But Barbara Demeneix told me that trying to personally avoid pollutants today, at an individual level, is largely a fool's errand in a landscape so filled with them. "We can eat bio [i.e., organic]. We can air our homes as often as possible. [We can] live in the countryside." But when it comes to these endocrine disruptors, "there's no escape. There's no escape." Not at the level of the isolated individual.

To understand what we can actually do to solve the damage pollution is doing to our attention, I went to meet up with Bruce Lanphear by the rocks in Horseshoe Bay, on the West Coast of Canada, on a foggy day. He had just been out kayaking, and in the water in front of us, there were seals flapping around and vanishing under the waves. "Look at that," he said. "The clouds. The water. The greenery."

From our conversation, I learned that there were two ways we need to respond now. Firstly, when it comes to new chemicals, we need a new approach. He told me that at the moment, "chemicals are assumed to be innocent until study after study shows they're toxic." So if you want to put a product on the market containing a new chemical, you can use whatever you want, and, in the years that follow, poorly funded scientists have to scramble to figure out if it's safe. "That's because who's calling the shots? Industry." We need to do it differently, he said. "Basically, we should treat new chemicals, new pollutants, as though they are like drugs." The chemical should have to be tested for safety *before* it starts being used by ordinary people—and only if it passes stringent tests should it end up in your home and in your bloodstream.

Second, for the chemicals that are already widely used, we need to do these tests, and this research needs to be carried out by scientists who are not funded by industry. Then, if we discover that any of them are harmful, we need to band together as citizens and demand that they be prohibited, like lead is—finally—today. Barbara Demeneix later told me bluntly: "We've got to get this under control very soon."

Barbara Maher told me that when it comes to her area of expertise, air pollution, we need to pressure our governments to bring forward the transition to electric cars by law, because they massively reduce this problem. She stressed, in addition, that there are interim steps we can push our leaders to take: if we plant trees in pollution hotspots, they will soak up a lot of the contamination, and clean the air of many toxins.

～

As I absorbed all this, I kept thinking about what Barbara Demeneix said to me: "There is no way we can have a normal brain today." It's possible that a hundred years from now, when they look back at us and ask why we struggled to pay attention, they will say, "They were surrounded by pollutants and chemicals that inflamed their brains and harmed focus. They walked around exposed to BPA and PCBs, and breathing in metals. Their scientists knew what it did to their brains and their ability to focus. Why were they surprised they struggled to pay attention?" Those people in the future will know whether, after learning this, we banded together to protect our brains—or whether we allowed them to continue to degrade.

CHAPTER THIRTEEN

Cause Eleven: The Rise of ADHD and How We Are Responding to It

Something strange started to happen around fifteen years ago, when my nephews were small. Their teachers believed that large numbers of kids in their classes were becoming more restless and unable to focus. They didn't want to sit still or attend to their lessons. Around this time, an idea that didn't exist in Britain when I was a child—or, at least, was exceptionally rare—started to spread through the country. It was argued by some researchers and doctors that these children had a biological disorder, and that is why they weren't paying attention. This idea proliferated with incredible speed across the English-speaking world. Between 2003 and 2011 alone, diagnoses of attention deficit hyperactivity disorder (ADHD) soared in the United States by 43 percent overall, and by 55 percent among girls. It has now reached the point that 13 percent of adolescents in the U.S. have been given this diagnosis, and of them, a majority are given powerful stimulant drugs as a result.

In Britain, the increase has also been extraordinary: for every child who was diagnosed with ADHD when I was seven years old, in 1986, there are now one hundred kids in this position. Between 1998 and 2004 alone, the number of children being given stimulants doubled.

When it comes to our own attention problems as adults, we often readily acknowledge a whole range of influences on us—the rise of invasive technologies, stress, lack of sleep, and so on. But when our children face the same challenges, over the past twenty years we have been drawn to a starkly simple story: that this problem is largely the result of a biological disorder. I wanted to investigate this in depth. Of all the chapters in this book, this is the one I've found hardest to write, because it's the topic about which serious scientists disagree the most. By interviewing them, I learned that they don't agree on even the most basic questions—including whether ADHD actually exists in the way most people have been told it does, as a biological illness. So I want to go through this chapter slowly and carefully. This is the topic where I interviewed the most experts—over thirty of them—and I kept going back with more questions for a long time.

But I want to make clear a few things at the start that every expert I spoke with agreed on: Everyone being diagnosed with ADHD has a real problem. They aren't making it up or faking it. Whatever the cause, if you or your child is struggling to focus, it's not your fault; you're not incompetent or undisciplined or any of the other stigmatizing labels that might have been applied to you. You deserve compassion and practical help to find solutions. Most experts believed that for some children, there can be a biological contribution to their poor focus—though they disagreed on how large a contribution that is. We should be able to have a calm and honest conversation about the other aspects of the ADHD controversy while holding these truths in our minds.

∽

The question of whether kids who can't focus have a biological problem is, in fact, a fairly new debate, and it has changed a lot in the past few years. In 1952 the American Psychiatric Association first wrote a guide to all the things that can go wrong with a person's mental health, and the idea that kids who struggle to focus are suffering from a biological disorder was not included. By 1968, the idea had gained enough popularity among psychiatrists that they added it, but they believed it applied to a tiny number of children. With each passing year, the number of kids identified as having this problem has soared, to the point that in many parts of the South in the United States, 30 percent of boys are now diagnosed with ADHD by the time they turn eighteen. As I write, it is swelling even further—huge numbers of adults are now being told they have this disability, with over three million of them already being prescribed stimulants. The market for prescribed stimulants is now worth at least $10 billion.

As all this has exploded, a polarized argument has broken out over it. On one side, there are people saying ADHD is a disorder caused overwhelmingly by something going wrong within the individual's genes and brain, and that very large numbers of children and adults should be taking these stimulants to treat it. This side has largely prevailed in the U.S. On the other side, there are people saying that attention problems are real and painful, but it is incorrect and harmful to see them as a biological disorder that requires the mass prescription of drugs, and we should be offering different forms of help. This side has largely prevailed in places like Finland.

～

Let's start with the purely biological story, and why so many people find truth and relief in it. One day, on an Amtrak train, I got talking to a woman who asked me what I did for a job. When I told her I was writing a book about why people struggle to pay attention, she started to tell me about her son. I didn't write it down at the time, so I only remember the broad details of what she said—but he had a typical experience. Years before, he had been really struggling at school—he wasn't able to pay attention in class, and he was in trouble a lot. She felt concerned for him, and judged by the other parents. Finally, the school's teachers urged her to take him to the doctor. Their doctor spoke to her son and then told her that he had diagnosed him with ADHD. He told her that it meant her son had different genetics from other kids, and that as a result he had developed a different kind of brain, one that wasn't like most people's. This meant he found it much harder to sit still and focus. Stephen Hinshaw, a professor of psychology at Stanford University, similarly told me that genetics account for "75 to 80 percent" of ADHD, a ballpark figure that is based on a large series of scientific studies.

It's distressing to be told your child has a disability. She felt shocked—but at the same time as they are offered this message, parents are also told lots of positive things: Your son's behavior isn't your fault. In fact, you deserve sympathy; you've been coping with something really hard. And best of all, there is a solution. Her son was prescribed the stimulant drug Ritalin. When he started to take it, he stopped being so restless and bouncing off the walls. He said he didn't like how it made him feel, though—one child I know told me that he felt like his brain was turned off when he took the drug—so his mother felt genuinely conflicted. Ultimately, she decided to continue to give him the stimulant until he turned eighteen, because she felt that at least this would stop him from being thrown out of school. There's no dramatic aspect to this story: he didn't have a heart attack or start using meth. On balance, she thought she was doing the right thing.

I feel a lot of sympathy for her. But there are also several reasons why I also feel worried about the fact that there are more and more people like her, who now believe this is an overwhelmingly genetic problem that needs to be dealt with primarily with stimulants. I think the best way to start to explain why might be to step sideways for a moment, and to look at what happened when the concept of ADHD spread beyond kids, and even beyond adults, to a whole new category of living creatures.

One day in the 1990s, a nine-year-old beagle named Emma was led into a vet's surgery. Her stressed-out owner explained that she had a problem. The dog was anxious all the time—she ate constantly, and there were times when she would suddenly go ballistic, ricocheting off the walls and barking incessantly. If she was left alone in the house, the dog would freak out even more. The owner kept using one word to describe Emma: hyperactive. She implored the vet to help her figure out what to do.

The vet she had come to see was a man named Nicholas Dodman, an English immigrant who—over a thirty-year career—had become one of the leading veterinary specialists in the United States, and a professor at Tufts University. At first, Nicholas prescribed for Emma and her owner to go to dog training, where both of them could learn new skills to help them interact. It worked—but not completely. The owner said Emma's problems dipped by around 30 percent. When he heard this, Nicholas decided that Emma in fact had ADHD— a concept that, until he made his own breakthroughs in interpreting animal behavior, had only really been applied to humans. He prescribed the stimulant drug Ritalin for the dog, and told Emma's owner to smush it into her food twice daily. When she came back not long afterward, the owner was thrilled. The problem, she said, was solved. The dog had stopped bouncing around the house and trying to eat all the time. It was true that Emma still howled terribly when she was left alone, but otherwise, she was the dog her owner had always hoped for.

By the time I met Nicholas at his home in Massachusetts, this had become a normal day at his clinic. He regularly prescribes Ritalin and other stimulants to animals he diagnoses as having ADHD. Nicholas is a pioneer, and he's been called the "Pied Piper" of drugging animals for psychiatric problems.

I was curious about how he came to take this position. He told me it all began quite by accident, like many scientific breakthroughs. In the mid-1980s he was called as a vet to visit a horse named Poker, who had a problem. Poker was obsessively "cribbing"—a terrible compulsive behavior that around 8 percent of horses develop when they are shut away in stalls for most of the day. It's an awkward repetitive action, where the horse will grasp with his teeth onto something solid—like the fence in front of him—then arch his neck, swallow, and grunt hard. He'll do this again and again, compulsively. The so-called treatments for cribbing at that time were shockingly cruel. Sometimes vets would drill holes into the horse's face so he couldn't suck in air, or they would put brass rings in the horse's lips so he couldn't grasp the fence. Nicholas was appalled by these practices, and in his search for alternatives, he suddenly had an idea: What if we gave this horse a drug? He decided to inject the horse with naloxone, which is an opioid-blocker. "Within a few minutes, the horse just completely stopped," he told me. "The owner was like, 'Oh my God. Oh my God.'" After about twenty minutes the horse started cribbing again, but "we repeated that [injection] many times with many different horses subsequently, and had exactly the same result." He said: "It fascinated me that you could change behavior so dramatically by changing brain chemistry. . . . You know, that changed my career."

From that point on, Nicholas began to believe you could solve the problems of many animals by responding to them in ways that, until then, had only been applied to humans. For example, he was consulted by the Calgary Zoo about a polar bear that was endlessly pacing, and he recommended giving it a massive dose of Prozac. It stopped pacing and began to sit docilely in its cage. Today, thanks in part to Nicholas's shift in perspective, there are parrots on Xanax and Valium, there are many species from chickens to walruses being given antipsychotics, and there are cats on Prozac. One of the staff at the Toledo Zoo told a reporter that psychiatric drugs are "definitely a wonderful management tool, and that's how we look at them. To be able to just take the edge off puts us a little more at ease." Nearly half of all zoos in the U.S. now admit to giving psychiatric drugs to their animals, and 50 to 60 percent of the owners who come to Nicholas's clinic are seeking psychiatric meds for their pets. At times, it sounds like *One Flew over the Cuckoo's Nest* for actual cuckoos.

Before I went to meet Nicholas, I expected him to justify this in one particular way. I thought he would tell me the story that lots of doctors tell parents who have kids with attention problems—that this is a disorder with biological causes, which is why you need biological solutions in the form of drugs. But he didn't say that. In fact, his explanation started where his own journey into this science had begun—with cribbing horses. "No one's ever seen a horse in the wild do this. This is a condition of 'domestication,' keeping horses in unnatural situations," he told me. "If they'd never been put in a stall, and they'd never been subjected to that psychological pressure early on, they wouldn't develop it."

As he described what happened to these horses, he used a phrase that struck me. He said these horses are suffering from "frustrated biological objectives." Horses want to roam and run and graze. When they can't express their innate nature, their behavior and focus go awry, and they start to act out. He told me that "the pressure of having your biological objectives thwarted is such that it opens a Pandora's box," where you'll try to find any behavior that will "alleviate this crushing psychological pressure or inability to do anything. . . . Horses spend about 60 percent of their time in the wild grazing, so it's not surprising that one of the things that gives them release is a sort of fake grazing, which is what cribbing is."

He admitted freely that his approach of drugging animals for what's dubbed "zoochosis"—the madness animals often develop when they are caged—is an extremely limited solution. I asked him if, for example, drugging the polar bear had solved his problem. "No," he replied. "It's a Band-Aid. The problem is you've taken a polar bear out of the polar environment, and you've stuck it in a zoo. . . . Polar bears in nature will walk for miles across the Arctic tundra. They look for seal places, and they swim, and they eat seals. The exhibit [the cage where this polar bear was trapped] is nothing like real life.

So, just like the guy in jail, they pace to appease the inner pain of being denied a real life. . . . They've got all these instincts that are all intact, that they're unable to utilize."

The long-term solution is to shut down zoos, he said, and to let all animals live in an environment that is compatible with their natures. He told me about a dog that was unable to focus on anything and spent all its time obsessively chasing its own tail. It lived in a tiny apartment in Manhattan. Then, one day, its owners split up, and it was sent to live on a farm upstate—and its tail-chasing and apparent focus problems went away. All dogs should run for at least an hour off-leash every day, but "not many" pet dogs in the U.S. get that, he told me. They're frustrated, and it causes problems.

He can't magic that world into existence by himself. In the absence of those long-term solutions, he wanted to know, what would I have him do? We discussed this for a long time. I tried to explain to him that while I saw where he was coming from, I felt instinctively uncomfortable with it. These animals are showing these behaviors as a way of expressing distress—Poker the horse hated being shut away, and Emma the beagle hated being left alone, because horses need to run and dogs need a pack. I was worried that by muffling their signals with drugs, he might be encouraging their owners into a kind of fantasy—that they could take a creature, ignore its nature, and make it live a life that fits the owner's needs, not the animal's, without any cost. We need to hear the animal's distress, not suppress it.

He listened thoughtfully, and responded by describing to me pigs who live and die in brutal factory farms, ripped from their mothers as babies, spending their whole lives in carts where they can't turn around. He asked: "I could make this pig a lot better and tolerate this intolerable situation with less psychological pain if I was to put Prozac in the drinking line. Would you be against that?" But the choices he was confronting me with, I said, shouldn't exist. His hypothetical concedes too much—it takes a dysfunctional environment for granted, and assumes that all we can do is try to adapt to it and take the edge off. We need better choices than that. "I mean—reality shouldn't be the choice," he replied. "It's what we have, you know? So you have to work with what you've got."

$\backsim$

I began to ask myself: Is there any way in which children who struggle to focus are like Emma the beagle, and are being medicated for what is in fact an environmental problem? I learned that scientists fiercely disagree about this. We do know that the huge rise in children being diagnosed with attention problems has coincided with several other big changes in the way children live. Kids are now allowed to run around far less—instead of playing in the streets and in their neighborhoods, they now spend almost all their time inside their homes or school classrooms. Children are now fed a very different diet—one that lacks many nutrients needed for brain development, and is full of sugars and dyes that negatively affect attention. Children's schooling has changed, so it now focuses almost entirely on preparing them for high-stress testing, with very little space for nurturing their curiosity. Is it a coincidence that ADHD diagnoses are rising at the same time as these big changes are occurring, or is there a connection? I've already discussed the evidence that our dramatic changes in diet and rise in pollution are causing an increase in children's attention problems, and I'll come to the evidence about how the other changes might be affecting children's attention in the next chapter.

I want to start, though, with somebody who has pioneered a different way of responding to ADHD in children. Across three years, I repeatedly interviewed Dr. Sami Timimi, who is a leading child psychiatrist in Britain, and one of the most prominent and vocal critics in the world of the way we talk about ADHD today. I went to see him in Lincoln, a town that was built over a thousand years ago around a cathedral and seems to have been sighing back into the earth ever since. The old parts of the town have been taken over by chain stores paying minimum wage, and when Sami moved there, he discovered his practice was full of people who were really struggling, through no fault of their own, with low wages and little hope. He could see that people in Lincoln needed a lot of practical help—but he was surprised to find that they seemed to expect one thing from him. They thought, as he put it, "that a psychiatrist was basically somebody who does medication," and he was treated as a pill-dispenser. He inherited from his predecessor twenty-seven kids who were being prescribed stimulant drugs for ADHD, and local schools were pressing for more kids to be put on them. It would have been easy for Sami to just carry on with this approach.

But he was pensive. He believed that if he was going to take his responsibility as a doctor to these kids seriously, he had to take time to look in depth at their lives and their environments. One of the children who had been diagnosed with ADHD and given stimulants by Sami's predecessor was an eleven-year-old boy, who he called Michael to protect his confidentiality. After he was dragged into Sami's office by his mother, Michael refused to even talk to him. He just sat there, angrily sulking, as his mother explained that she didn't know what to do. She said that Michael kept acting up at school, refusing to focus, and becoming aggressive. As she explained all this, Michael kept interrupting her, sullenly demanding to leave.

Sami refused to decide anything based on just one session. He felt he needed to learn more—so he kept interviewing this mother and son over a period of several months. He wanted to understand when these problems began. As he probed into this, it slowly emerged that two years before, Michael's dad had moved to another town, and he hardly ever talked to his son anymore. It was in the aftermath of this that Michael started acting up at school. Sami wondered if he felt rejected. Sami told me: "When you're a child, you're not developed intellectually to take a step back and look at things from a more rational, objective point of view. . . . When a father says they're going to come and see you, but they never turn up, you imagine it's because there's something wrong with you. It's because they don't want to see you. It's because you're not very nice. It's because you cause problems."

So one day, Sami decided to phone Michael's dad. He agreed that he would come into the doctor's offices to see Sami, and they talked over the situation. The father was chastened, and decided to come back into his son's life in a structured and consistent way. Sami called Michael in and told him that there was nothing wrong with him. It wasn't his fault his dad had disengaged. He didn't have a disorder. He had been let down, and that wasn't his fault. Now it was going to change. As Michael reconnected with his dad, over several months they weaned him off his stimulant drugs. Sami did this gradually because the withdrawal effects can be severe and terrible. As time passed, several things changed for Michael. He had a male role model. He knew he wasn't a bad person who drove his dad away. He stopped acting out at school and started learning again. Sami felt he had identified the underlying problem and solved it—and so the attention problems gradually went away.

Another of the kids brought to Sami was a nine-year-old boy he called Aden, who behaved well at home, but seemed to be behaving badly at school. His teacher said he was hyperactive and kept distracting the other kids, and was urging that he be given stimulants. Sami decided to visit the school, and he was appalled by what he saw. Aden's teacher spent all her time yelling at the class to be quiet, and irrationally punishing Aden and a few other kids she seemed to have taken a dislike to. The classroom was in chaos, and Aden was being blamed. At first, Sami tried to help the teacher to change her story about Aden, but she wouldn't listen, so he helped Aden's parents move him to a new, less chaotic school. Once he got settled in, he started to thrive, and his attention problems also faded.

Sami does still occasionally continue the prescription of stimulants to children, but it's rare, it's short-term, and it's after trying all other options. He said that with the vast majority of cases of kids with attention problems that come into his office, if he listens carefully and offers practical support to change the child's environment, it almost always reduces or ends the problem they have.

He told me that when people hear a child has been diagnosed with ADHD, they often imagine this is like a diagnosis of, say, pneumonia—that a doctor has identified an underlying pathogen or illness, and is now going to prescribe something that can deal with that physical problem. But with ADHD, there are no physical tests a doctor can carry out. All she can do is talk to the child, and to people who know the child, and see if the kid's behavior matches a checklist drawn up by psychiatrists. That's it. Sami says: "ADHD is not a diagnosis. It's not a diagnosis. It's just a description of certain behaviors that sometimes occur together. That's all it is." All you are saying, when a child has been diagnosed with ADHD, is that a child is struggling to focus. "It doesn't tell you anything about the 'why' question." It's like being told that a child has a cough, listening to the cough, and then saying "yes, the child has a cough." If a doctor identifies a child with attention problems, that should be the first step in the process—not the last.

I was moved by Sami's experiences, but I also asked: How do we know if this kind of approach—listening to the child, and trying to solve the underlying problem—actually works, beyond these moving anecdotes? I dug deeply into this question. It turns out there's a huge number of studies investigating what happens when you give children stimulant drugs (I'll come to the results of them soon). There are some studies into what happens when you give parenting classes on how to set boundaries, give consistent feedback, and so on (the evidence is mixed, but you often see a mild improvement). But I wanted to know—is there any research into what happens when you intervene in the way Sami does?

It turned out that—so far as I could uncover—in the whole world, there seemed to be only one group of scientists who had studied something close to this question, in a remarkable long-term study, so I went to Minneapolis, where they conducted their research, to meet them. In 1973, Alan Sroufe, who became a professor of child psychology there, started a massive collective research project, which was designed to answer a really big question—what factors in your life really shape you? We met in the café of a garden center in the city's suburbs. Alan is a gentle, soft-spoken scientist who, at the end of our conversation, went to pick up his grandchildren from school. For more than forty years, Alan and his team have been studying the same two hundred people, who were all born into poor families. They have been tracked and analyzed from birth all the way into middle age. These scientists measured a huge range of factors in these people's lives—from their bodies to their home lives, from their personalities to their parents. One of the many things they wanted to figure out is: What factors in a person's life can lead to them developing attention problems?

At the start, Alan was fairly confident about the answer they would find. He believed—like most scientists at the time—that ADHD was caused entirely by some inborn biological problem in the child's brain, so he was sure one of the most important things they measured would be the child's neurological status at birth. They also measured the baby's temperament in its first few months, and then, over time, they measured all sorts of other things—like how stressful the parents' lives were, and how much social support the family got. His eye was keenly fixed on those neurological measures.

By the time the kids were three and a half, the scientists started to make predictions about which of them would develop ADHD. They wanted to see: Which factors made it more likely? Alan was startled by what they found, as the kids got older and some were indeed diagnosed with attention problems. It turned out their neurological status at birth didn't help at all in predicting which kids would develop serious attention problems. So what did? They discovered that "the surrounding context is the most important thing," Alan told me, and a crucial factor was "the amount of chaos in the environment." If a child is raised in an environment where there is a lot of stress, they are significantly more likely to then develop attention problems and be diagnosed with ADHD. It turns out that the elevated levels of stress in their parents' lives usually came first. He told me: "You could see it unfolding."

But why would a child growing up in a stressful environment be more likely to have this problem? I of course thought back to everything I had learned from Nadine Burke Harris. Alan began to offer an additional layer of explanation—one that is compatible with her findings. He explained that when you're very young, if you get upset or angry, you need an adult to soothe you and calm you down. Over time, as you grow up, if you are soothed enough, you learn to soothe yourself. You internalize the reassurance and relaxation your family gave to you. But stressed-out parents, through no fault of their own, find it harder to soothe their children—because they are so amped-up themselves. That means that their children don't learn how to calm and center themselves in the same way. Their kids are, as a result, more likely to respond to difficult situations by getting angry or distressed—feelings that wreck their focus. To give an extreme example, he said to me, try being evicted from your apartment, and then giving your child all the soothing she needs that night. It's not just poverty that causes this, he added; middle-class parents struggle with stress too. He told me: "Many parents are currently overwhelmed with their life circumstances, such that they cannot provide a stable and calm and supportive environment for their children." The worst response to this discovery is to "point fingers at the parents." That only causes more stress, and more problems for the kids, and misses the truth: "Those parents were doing the best they could. I guarantee you they loved their children." Parenting takes place in an environment—and if that environment floods parents with stress, it will inevitably affect their children.

After gathering evidence on this for decades, Alan concluded that "none of what I originally believed turned out to be true," and a "clear majority" of the kids who were later diagnosed "were not born to be ADHD. They developed these problems in reaction to their circumstances."

There was one crucial question, Alan said, that held the key to whether parents overcame these problems—one that seemed to me to tell us a lot about Sami's work: Is there somebody giving you support? The families they studied sometimes got help from people around them. It usually wasn't from a professional—they just found a supportive partner, or a group of friends. When their social support went up in this way, they found "the children are less likely to have problems at the next stage." Why would this be? Alan wrote: "Parents experiencing less stress can be more responsive to their infants; then infants can become more secure." This effect was so large that "the strongest predictor of positive change was an increase in social support available to the parents during the intervening years." Social support is, I reflected, the main thing Sami provides to families whose children struggle with attention.

∽

Yet there's a challenge here. There is no question that when you give a child a stimulant like Adderall or Ritalin, their attention will significantly improve in the short term. All the experts I interviewed, wherever they stand on this debate, agreed with this, and I've seen it for myself. I knew a little boy who was constantly running around, shouting, and bouncing off the walls, who—when given Ritalin—sat still and was able to look people in the eye with a steady gaze for the first time in his life. The evidence is clear that this effect is real, and due to the drugs. I have plenty of adult friends who use stimulants when they have to blitz a work project, and it has the same effect on them. In Los Angeles in 2019, I caught up with my friend Laurie Penny, who is a British writer on various TV shows there, and she told me she uses prescribed stimulants when she wants to do a big writing job because they help her to concentrate. This seems to me like a reasonable decision for adults to make.

But there is a reason why most doctors across the world are very cautious about prescribing stimulant drugs to children, and no country (with the solitary exception of Israel) comes close to prescribing them as freely as the U.S.

My concerns about this started to crystallize when I met with a woman named Nadine Ezard, who is the clinical director of alcohol and drug services at St. Vincent's Hospital in Sydney. She's a doctor who works with people who have addiction problems, and by the time we met in 2015, Aussies were in the middle of a severe spike in methamphetamine addiction. For a while, doctors weren't sure how to respond. With heroin, there is a drug they could legally prescribe to addicted people that's a reasonable substitute, methadone—but with meth, there didn't seem to be one. So Nadine—along with a group of other doctors—was part of a crucial experiment, licensed by the government. They started to give people addicted to meth a stimulant that is prescribed over a million times a year in the U.S. for kids with ADHD—dextroamphetamine.

At the time that I spoke with her, they had already tried it with fifty people, and the results of a bigger experiment are going to be published after this book comes out. She told me that when they are given these stimulants, the people addicted to meth seemed to feel less craving, because it scratched some of the same itch: "They say that when they first start on it, it's the first time in a long time their brain hasn't been focused completely on meth. That they suddenly feel this freedom." Speaking about one patient, she recalled: "He would be thinking about meth constantly. He'd be in the supermarket, [or] wherever, [and] his constant decision making would be— 'Am I going to have enough money left to buy crystal?' And then [giving him dextroamphetamine] relieved him from that." She compared it to giving nicotine patches to smokers.

She is not the only scientist discovering the similarities between methamphetamine and the other amphetamines the U.S. routinely prescribes to children. Later, I went to see Carl Hart, professor of psychology at Columbia University, who had conducted experiments giving Adderall to people who were addicted to meth. When Adderall and meth were given in similar ways in the lab, these people with long-standing meth addictions responded in almost identical ways.

Nadine's program is a thoughtful, compassionate way to treat people with meth addictions—but I felt unsettled to learn that the drugs we give kids turn out to be a reasonable proxy for meth. Sami told me: "It's a bit bizarre when you start realizing that we are prescribing legally the same substances that you are saying on the other hand are very dangerous to take if you take them illicitly. . . . They're chemically similar. They work in a similar way. They work on very similar neurotransmitters." But—as Nadine stressed to me—there are some important differences. They give higher doses to people recovering from meth addiction than children are given for ADHD. They give them as pills, which releases them more slowly into your brain than smoking or injecting. And street drugs—because they are banned and have to be sold by criminals—contain all sorts of contaminants that aren't in the pills you get from a pharmacist. But still, it made me resolve to research the mass prescription of this drug to children some more.

༄

For years, lots of parents were told that you could figure out if your child has ADHD in a straightforward way, related to these drugs. Many doctors told them that a normal child would become manic and high if they were given these pills, whereas an ADHD kid would slow down, focus, and pay attention. But when scientists actually gave these drugs both to kids with attention problems and kids without attention problems, this turned out to be wrong. All children—indeed, all people—given Ritalin focus and pay attention better for a while. The fact the drug works isn't evidence that you had an underlying biological problem all along—it's just proof that you are taking a stimulant. This is why, during the Second World War, radar operators were given stimulants by the army—it made it easier for them to continue to focus on the very boring job of watching a mostly unchanging screen. It's also why people who snort a line of stimulants then become very boring and go off on long monologues—they become very focused on their own train of thought, and filter out the bored-to-tears look on your face.

There is scientific evidence that there are several risks associated with giving these drugs to kids. The first risk associated with these drugs is physical—there is evidence that taking stimulants stunts a child's growth. Kids taking a standard dose are about three centimeters shorter, over a three-year period, than they would have otherwise been. Several scientists have also warned that stimulants increase the risk of a child having heart problems and dying as a result. Obviously, heart problems are rare among children—but when millions of kids are taking these drugs, even a small increase in risk means a real rise in deaths.

But James Li, assistant professor of psychology, who I went to see at the University of Wisconsin in Madison, told me about what I found to be the most worrying thing. He explained: "We simply don't know the long-term effects. That's a fact." Most people assume—I certainly did—that these drugs have been tested and found to be safe, but he explained "there hasn't been a lot of research done on long-term consequences to brain development." This is especially concerning, he says, since "we're so quick to give them to young kids. Kids are our most vulnerable population, because their brains are developing. . . . These are drugs that operate directly on the brain, right? It's not an antibiotic."

He showed me that the best long-term research we have is in animal studies—where the findings are sobering. I read them, and they show that if you give adolescent rats Ritalin for three weeks—which is the equivalent of giving it to a human for several years—you find that the striatum, a crucial part of the brain that deals with experiencing rewards, shrinks significantly. He said that you can't assume that these drugs will affect humans the same way they affect rats, and he stressed there are some benefits to taking these drugs—but we need to be aware "there's the benefit, and there's the risk. What we currently operate under is the short-term benefit."

When I interviewed other scientists, I also learned that the positive effects of these drugs—while real—are surprisingly limited. At

New York University, Xavier Castellanos, a professor of child and adolescent psychiatry, explained to me that the best research on the effects of stimulants found something important. They improve a child's behavior on tasks that require repetition, but they do *not* improve their learning. I frankly didn't believe him, but then I went and looked it up in the study that the supporters of stimulant prescription had directed me to as the gold standard on ADHD research. After fourteen months on stimulants, kids performed 1.8 percent better on academic tests. But kids who for the same amount of time were simply given guidance on their behavior improved by 1.6 percent.

Just as critically, the evidence suggests that the initial positive effects of stimulants don't last. Anyone who takes stimulants develops tolerance for the drug—your body gets used to it, so you need a higher dose to get the same effect. Eventually, you hit the maximum dose kids are allowed to take.

One of the most alarmed scientists I spoke with was Dr. Charles Czeisler, the sleep expert at Harvard Medical School, who told me that one of the main effects of taking stimulants is that you sleep less. This, he explained, has very worrying implications for the development of young people's brains—particularly all the young people he sees using them so they can study longer and longer hours. "The pushing of all these amphetamines for these kids reminds me of the opioid crisis, except nobody's talking about it," he said. "When I was a kid, if people gave me amphetamines, sold them to children, they would go to jail. But just like the opioid crisis . . . nobody does anything about it. It's a dirty little secret in our society."

Most of the scientists I interviewed in the U.S.—and I talked with a lot of the most prestigious experts on ADHD—told me that they believe prescribing stimulants is safe and provides a lot of benefits that outweigh the risks. Indeed, many U.S. scientists argue that presenting the counterarguments—as I am doing here—is actively dangerous; it will, they say, make parents less likely to bring their kids forward to be prescribed stimulants, and as a result, those children will needlessly suffer and do worse in their lives. They also believe it may make some people quit these drugs abruptly, which is dangerous—they could go through a horrible physical withdrawal. But in the rest of the world, scientific opinion is more divided, and it's more common to hear skepticism or outright opposition to this approach.

$\backsim$

There is one decisive reason why many people—like the woman I met on the Amtrak train—are persuaded that their child's attention problems are largely the result of a physical disorder. It is because they have been told that this is a problem caused primarily by their child's genetic makeup. As I mentioned before, Professor Stephen Hinshaw told me that genes explain "75 to 80 percent" of the problem, and even higher figures are often put forward. If this is a mainly biological problem, then a mainly biological solution intuitively makes sense—and the kind of interventions Sami and others argue for can only ever be additional extras. When I dug into this, I came to believe that the truth is complicated—and doesn't really fit with the strident claims of either side of this polarized debate.

I was keen to understand: Where do these statistics showing that a very high percentage of ADHD is caused by a genetic disorder come from? I was surprised to learn, from the scientists who put these statistics forward, that it does not come from any direct analysis of the human genome. Almost all of it comes from a much simpler method, known as twin studies. They take a pair of identical twins. If one of them has been diagnosed with ADHD, they ask: Has the other twin been diagnosed with it too? Then they take a pair of non-identical twins. If one of them has been diagnosed with ADHD, they ask: Has the other twin been diagnosed with it? They then repeat this many times, until they have a big enough sample, and they compare the figures.

The reason they do this is simple. All sets of twins in these studies—whether they are identical or not—grow up in the same home, with the same family, so they figure if you find a difference between the two types of twins, they reason, it can't be attributed to their environment. The difference has to be explained instead by their genes. Identical twins are much more genetically similar to each other than non-identical twins, so if you discover that something is more common among identical twins, the scientists conclude there's a genetic component. You can figure how much is determined by genes by seeing how big this gap is. This method has been used for years by all sorts of highly reputable scientists.

Whenever scientists investigate ADHD in this way, they *always* find that identical twins are much more likely to both be diagnosed than non-identical twins. Over twenty studies have found this result—it's consistent. This is where the very high odds on ADHD being genetically determined come from.

But a small group of scientists have been asking if there is a serious problem with this technique. I spoke with one of the people who has made this case in the greatest scientific detail, Dr. Jay Joseph, who is a psychologist in Oakland, California. He talked me through the facts. It has been proven—in a different set of scientific studies—that identical twins do *not* actually experience the same environments as non-identical twins. Identical twins spend more time together than non-identical twins. They are treated more alike—by their parents, friends, and schools (indeed, often people can't tell them apart). They are more likely to become confused about their identity and to feel merged with their twin. They are psychologically closer. Jay told me that in most respects, "their environment's more similar. . . . They're copying each other's behavior more. They're being treated more alike. All of these things lead to more similar behavior—whatever the behavior may be."

So, he explained, there is something *other* than genes that could explain the gap that's showing up in all these studies. It could be accounted for by the fact that "identical twins grow up in a much more similar behavior-shaping environment than non-identical twins." Their attention problems may be more alike not because their genes are more similar, but because their lives are more similar. If there are factors in the environment causing attention problems, identical twins are more likely to both experience them to the same extent than non-identical twins. So, he explains, "twin studies are unable to disentangle the potential influences of genes and environment." This means the statistics we often hear—of 75 to 80 percent of ADHD being due to genetics, for example—are built on an unreliable foundation. Such figures are, Jay says, "misleading, and misunderstood."

It seemed to me implausible that so many prominent scientists would draw on this technique if it was so flawed. I was conscious that in my previous books, I drew on evidence from twin studies myself. But when I asked some scientists who argue that ADHD is primarily genetically driven about the flaws in these studies, many of them readily conceded that these criticisms have some legitimacy, in a way that was disarming. Usually, they would then simply switch the conversation onto other reasons why we should believe this is a genetically based problem. (I'll come to them in a moment.) I came to believe that twin studies are a kind of zombie technique, which people keep referencing even though they know they can't fully defend it, because it tells us what we want to hear—that this problem is mostly in our kids' genes.

When you set aside these twin studies, Professor James Li told me, "time after time, every single study" looking at the role any individual gene plays in causing ADHD finds that "no matter how you measure [it], it is always small. The effect of the environment is always bigger." So as I absorbed all this, I began to ask myself: Does this mean genes play no role in ADHD? There are some people who get close to arguing this—and that is where I think the ADHD skeptics go too far.

James explained to me that although the twin studies overestimate the role of genes, there's a new technique called SNP heritability, which figures out how much of a characteristic is genetically driven by using a different method from twin studies. Instead of comparing types of twins, these studies compare the genetic makeup of two totally unrelated people. It could pluck, say, you and me, and see whether matchups in genes between us correlate with a problem we might both have—like (say) depression or obesity or ADHD. These studies currently find that around 20 to 30 percent of attention problems relate to your genes. James told me that this is a new way of studying the question and it only looks at common variation genes, so in the end the proportion caused by our genetics might end up being somewhat more than that. So it's wrong, he explained, to dismiss a genetic component—but it's also wrong to say it's all or most of the problem.

$\backsim$

One of the people who most helped me to understand some aspects of these questions was Professor Joel Nigg, who I interviewed at Oregon Health & Science University in Portland. He is the former president of the International Society for Research in Child and Adolescent Psychopathology, and a leading figure in this field.

He told me it used to be thought that some kids were simply wired by their genes to be different and to develop different brains. But, as he has written, now "the science has moved on." The latest research shows that "genes aren't destiny; rather they affect probability." Alan Sroufe, who did the long-term study into what factors cause ADHD, said the same: "Genes don't operate in a vacuum. That's the main thing we've learned from gene studies. . . . Genes are turned on and off in response to environmental input." As Joel puts it, "our experiences literally get under our skin" and change how our genes are expressed.

To help me think about how this works, Joel offers an analogy.

He explains: "If your child is tired and run down, she will catch a cold at school more easily in the winter. She is more susceptible." But "if there was no cold virus," then neither an exhausted kid nor a well-rested one would get a cold. Similarly, your genes might make you more vulnerable to a trigger in the environment—but there still has to be a trigger in the environment. He writes: "In some ways, the truly big news about ADHD today is that we've revived our interest in the environment."

Joel believes there is some role for stimulants. He says that in a bad situation, he believes they are better than nothing, and can give kids and parents some real relief. "I'm splinting a broken bone in a battlefield. I'm not healing it, you know? But at least the guy can walk off, even if he might have a crooked leg the rest of his life."

But if we are going to do that, he said, we crucially also need to ask: "Where is the problem located? Do we need to look at what our kids are facing?" He says that kids at the moment face many large forces that we know harm their attention—stress, poor nutrition, pollution—all things I was going to investigate more after learning about them from him. "I would say we should not accept those things. We should not accept that our kids have to grow up in a chemical soup [of pollutants], for example. We shouldn't accept that they have to grow up with grocery stores that hardly have any food in them that's really food. . . . That should change. . . . For some kids, there's actually something wrong with them because their environment has injured them. In that case, it's a bit criminal to say nothing more than, in effect, 'Let's placate them with medications so that they can cope with this damaging environment we've created.' How is that different from giving sedatives to prisoners so they can handle being in prison?" He believes you can only ethically give out drugs if you are also at the same time trying to solve the deeper problem.

He looked somber, and said: "There's the old metaphor that . . . villagers are at the river one day, and they notice a dead body come floating down the river. So they do the right thing. They take it out and they give it an appropriate burial. The next day two bodies come down the river and they do the appropriate thing and they bury the bodies. This goes on for a while, and finally they start to wonder— I wonder where these bodies are coming down the river [from], and if we should do something to stop that? So they go up the river to find out."

He leaned forward in his chair and said: "We can treat these kids—but sooner or later, we need to figure out why is this happening." I realized it was time for me to go upriver.

CHAPTER FOURTEEN

Cause Twelve: The Confinement of Our Children, Both Physically and Psychologically

A few years ago I was sitting drinking coffee at sunset in a small village at the edge of a forest in Cauca, in the southwest of Colombia. A few thousand people lived there, growing the caffeinated drinks that we glug across the world to keep ourselves alert. I watched them as they slowly unwound for the day. The adults had put tables and chairs out on the street, and they were talking and chatting in the shadow of a lush green mountain. I looked on as they wandered from table to table, when I noticed something that I rarely see in the Western world anymore. All across the village, children were playing freely, without adults watching over them. Some had a hoop they were rolling along the ground in a group. Some were chasing each other around at the edge of the forest, and daring each other to run in, only to dash out again thirty seconds later, shrieking and laughing. Even very small children—they seemed to be three or four—were running around with just other kids to look out for them. Occasionally, one of the children would fall over and run back to their mother. The rest only returned home when their parents called for them at eight in the evening, and the streets would finally empty.

It occurred to me that this is what childhood looked like for my parents, in very different places—an Alpine Swiss village, and a working-class Scottish tenement. They ran around freely without their parents for most of the day from when they were quite small, and only returned to eat and sleep. This is, in fact, what childhood looked like for all of my ancestors, so far as I can tell, going back thousands of years. There are periods when some children didn't live like this—when they were forced to work in factories, for example, or during the living nightmare of chattel slavery—but in the long human story, these are extreme exceptions.

Today, I don't know any children who live like that. In the past thirty years there have been huge changes in childhood. By 2003, in the U.S. only 10 percent of children spent any time playing freely outdoors on a regular basis. Childhood now happens, overwhelmingly, behind closed doors, and when they do get to play, it is supervised by grown-ups, or takes place on screens. The way children spend their time at school has also changed dramatically. The school systems in the U.S. and Britain have been redesigned by politicians so that teachers are forced to spend the majority of their time preparing and drilling children for tests. In the U.S., only 73 percent of elementary schools now have *any* form of recess. Free play and free inquiry have fallen off a cliff.

These changes have happened so quickly, and all at once, that it's hard to scientifically measure the effects this transformation might be having on children's ability to pay attention and focus. We can't randomly assign some kids to live freely in that village in Cauca, and some to live indoors in an American suburb, and come back to see how well they focus. But there is, I believe, a way we can begin to figure out some of the effects of this shift. We can do it if we break down this big transformation into its smaller constituent parts, and see what the science tells us about those effects.

One of the ways I did this was by following the story of a

remarkable woman I got to know named Lenore Skenazy. She's not a scientist. She's an activist. She was driven to try to understand how this transformation is affecting kids because of a shocking experience she had in her own life. It led her to start to work with some of the best social scientists studying these questions. Together with them, she has pioneered practical proposals to understand why so many more kids seem to be struggling to focus—and how to restore it.

♾

In the 1960s, in a suburb of Chicago, a five-year-old girl walked out of her house, alone. It was a fifteen-minute walk to Lenore's school, and every day she did it by herself. When she got to the road near school, she was helped to safely cross by another child, a ten-year-old boy wearing a yellow sash across his chest whose job was to stop the cars and shepherd the smaller kids across the tarmac. At the end of each school day, Lenore would walk out of the gates, again without an adult, and she would wander the neighborhood with her friends, or try to spot four-leaf clovers, which she collected. There was often a kickball game going on outside her house that the kids would spon-taneously organize, and sometimes she would join in. By the time she was nine years old, when she felt like it, she would get on her bike and ride a few miles to the library to pick out books, and then curl up reading them somewhere quiet. At other times, she'd knock on her friends' doors to see if they wanted to play. If Joel was home, they'd play Batman, and if Betsy was home, they'd play Princess and the Witch. Lenore always insisted on being the witch. Finally, when she was hungry or it started to get dark, she went home.

To many of us, this scene now seems jarring, or even shock-ing. Across the U.S. over the past decade, there have been many instances where people have seen children as old as nine walking unaccompanied in the street and they've called the police to report it as a case of parental negligence. But in the 1960s, this was the norm all over the world. Almost all children's lives looked something like this. Being a kid meant you went out into your neighborhood and you wandered around, found other kids, and made up your own games. Adults had only a vague idea where you were. A parent who kept their child indoors all the time, or walked them to school, or stood over them while they played, and intervened in their games, would have been regarded as crazy.

By the time Lenore had grown up and had her own children, in New York City in the 1990s, everything had changed. She was expected to walk her own children to school and wait while they went through the gates, and then pick them up at the end of the day. Nobody let their kids out to play unsupervised, ever. Children stayed in the home all the time, unless there was an adult to watch over them. One time, Lenore took her family to a resort in Mexico, and the kids would gather every morning on the beach and play, usually at whatever game they made up among themselves. It was the only time she had ever seen her son get up before her. He would race to the beach to find the other kids. She had never seen her son so gleeful. Lenore told me: "What I realized is that for one week, he had what I had for my entire childhood—which was the ability to go outside, meet up with friends, and play."

Lenore thought that back home, her nine-year-old son, Izzy, still needed to have some small taste of freedom if he was going to mature. So when, one day, he asked her if he could be taken to a place in New York he'd never been to before and then be left to find his own way home, it struck her as a good idea. Her husband sat on the floor with him and helped him plan out the route he would take, and one sunny Sunday, she took him to Bloomingdale's, and—with a little catch in her heart—they parted ways. An hour later, he appeared at the door of their apartment. He had taken a subway and a bus, alone. "He was very happy—I'd say he was levitating," she recalls. It seemed like such a commonsense thing to do that Lenore—who was a journalist—wrote an article telling this story, so other parents would have the confidence to do the same thing.

Then something strange happened. Lenore's article was greeted with horror and revulsion. She was denounced on many of the top news shows in the United States as "America's worst mom." She was slammed as shamefully neglectful, and she was told that she had put her own child at terrible risk. She was invited to appear on TV shows where they would put her on with a parent whose child had been kidnapped and murdered, as if it was equally likely that your child would ride the subway safely and that he would be killed. Every host would ask her a variant of: But, Lenore, how would you have felt if he never came home?

"I was always flabbergasted," Lenore told me when we sat together in her home in Jackson Heights in New York. She told them that she was simply giving her son what she—and all the adults condemning her—had taken for granted when they were kids, just a few decades before. She tried to explain to people that we live in one of the safest moments in human history. Violence against adults and children has dramatically plunged, and our children are now three times more likely to be struck by lightning than to be killed by a stranger. She asked: Would you imprison your child to prevent them from being hit by lightning? Statistically, that would make more sense. People responded with disgust to this argument. Other mothers told her that every time they turned their heads, they pictured their kids being snatched. After hearing this a lot, Lenore realized, "That was my crime. My crime was not thinking that way. I hadn't gone to the darkest place first and decided—oh my God, it's not worth it. To be a good American mom is to think that way now." She realized that somehow, we had—in a very short period of time—ended up believing only "a bad mom takes her eyes off her kids."

She noticed that when a DVD of the early episodes of *Sesame Street* from the late 1960s was released, they had put a warning on the screen at the start. Five-year-olds are shown walking the streets on their own, talking to strangers, and playing on vacant lots. The warning says: "The following is intended for adult viewing only and may not be suitable for our youngest viewers." She realized the change was so dramatic that now it was as if kids couldn't even be allowed to see what freedom might look like. Lenore was puzzled by how quickly this "gigantic shift" had happened. Children's lives have come to be dominated by ideas "that are very radical and new. The idea that kids can't play outside without this being dangerous—that has never been the case in human history. Kids have always played together, much of the time without direct adult supervision. . . . That's been the way for all of humanity. To suddenly say no, it's too dangerous—it's like saying kids should sleep upside down." It's an inversion of what every previous human society has thought.

∽

As I spent a lot of time with Lenore, I came to believe that to understand the effects of this change, we need to break it down into five different components and look at the scientific evidence behind each one. The first is the most obvious. For years, scientists have been discovering a broad body of evidence showing that when people run around—or engage in any form of exercise—their ability to pay attention improves. For example, one study that investigated this found exercise provides "an exceptional boost" to attention in children. Professor Joel Nigg, who I interviewed in Portland, has summarized the evidence clearly—he explains that "for developing children, aerobic exercise expands the growth of brain connections, the frontal cortex, and the brain chemicals that support self-regulation and executive functioning." Exercise causes changes that "make the brain grow more and get more efficient." The evidence showing this is so broad that these findings should be regarded, he writes, as "definite." The evidence couldn't be clearer: if you stop kids from acting on their natural desire to run around, on average, their attention, and the overall health of their brains, will suffer.

∽

But Lenore suspected there might be an even deeper way this is harming kids. She started to seek out the leading scientists who have studied these questions—including professor of psychology Peter Gray, evolutionary primatologist Dr. Isabel Behncke, and social psychologist Professor Jonathan Haidt. They taught her that in fact it is when children play that they learn their most important skills—the ones they need for their whole lives.

To understand this second component of the change that has taken place—the deprivation of play—picture again that scene on Lenore's street when she was a child back in that Chicago suburb, or the scene I saw in Colombia. What skills are the kids learning there, as they play freely with each other? For starters, if you're a kid and you're on your own with other kids, "you figure out how to make something happen," Lenore says. You have to use your creativity to come up with a game. You then have to persuade the other kids that your game is the best one they could play. Then "you figure out how to read people enough so that the game keeps going." You have to learn how to negotiate when it's your turn and when it's their turn—so you have to learn about other people's needs and desires, and how to meet them. You learn how to cope with being disappointed, or frustrated. You learn all this "through being excluded, through coming up with a new game, through getting lost, through climbing the tree and [then] somebody says, 'Climb higher!' and you can't decide if you will or you won't. Then you do, and it's exhilarating, and then you climb a little higher the next time—or you climb a little higher and it's so scary that you're crying. . . . And yet—now you're on top." These are all crucial forms of attention.

One of Lenore's intellectual mentors, Dr. Isabel Behncke, the Chilean expert on play, told me when we sat together in Scotland that the scientific evidence we have so far suggests "there are three main areas [of child development] where play has a major impact. One is creativity and imagination"—it's how you learn to think about problems and solve them. The second is "social bonds"—it's how you learn to interact with other people and socialize. And the third is "aliveness"—it's how you learn to experience joy and pleasure. The things we learn from play aren't trivial add-ons to becoming a functioning human being, Isabel explained. They are the core of it. Play builds the foundation of a solid personality, and everything that adults sit down and explain to the child afterward builds on this base. If you want to be a person who can pay attention fully, she told me, you need this base of free play.

Yet suddenly, we have been "taking all this out of kids' lives," Lenore says. Today, even when children do finally get to play, it's mainly supervised by adults, who set the rules and tell them what to do. On Lenore's street when she was a kid, everyone played softball and policed the rules themselves. Today, they go to organized activities where the adults intervene all the time to tell them what the rules are. Free play has been turned into supervised play, and so—like processed food—it has been drained of most of its value. This means that now, as a kid, Lenore said, "you're not getting that [chance to develop these skills]—because you're in a car being driven to a game where somebody tells you what position you're playing, and when to catch the ball, and when it's your time to hit, and who's bringing the snack, and you can't bring grapes because they have to be cut into quarters and it's your mom's job to do that. . . . That's a very different childhood, because you haven't experienced the give-and-take of life that's going to prepare you for adulthood." As a result, kids are "not having the problems and the exhilaration of getting there on their own." One day, Barbara Sarnecka, an associate professor of cognitive sciences at the University of California, Irvine, told Lenore that today "adults are saying: 'Here's the environment. I've already mapped it. Stop exploring.' But that's the opposite of what childhood is."

Lenore wanted to know: Now that they are effectively under house arrest, what are kids doing with the time they used to spend playing? One study of this found that this time is now overwhelmingly spent on homework (which exploded by 145 percent between 1981 and 1997), screens, and shopping with their parents. A 2004 study found that U.S. kids spent 7.5 hours more each week on academics than they had twenty years before.

Isabel told me the schools squeezing out play are "making a huge mistake." She said: "I would first ask them—what is their objective? What are you trying to achieve?" Presumably, they want children to learn. "I just can't see where these people get their insights from, because all the evidence shows it's the other way round: our brains are more supple, more plastic, more creative" when we have had the chance to "learn through play. The *primary* technology for learning is play. You learn to learn in play. And in a world where information is always changing, why do you want to fill their heads with information? We have no idea what the world will be in twenty years. Surely we want to be creating brains that are adaptable, and have the capacity to assess context, and can be thinking critically. All these things are trained through play. So it's so misguided, it's unbelievable."

~

This led Lenore to explore the third component of this change. Professor Jonathan Haidt—a leading social psychologist—has argued that there has been a big rise in anxiety among children and teens, in part because of this play deprivation. When a child plays, he learns the skills that make it possible to cope with the unexpected. If you deprive children of those challenges, as they grow up they will feel panicked and unable to cope a lot of the time. They don't feel they are competent, or can make things happen without older people guiding them. Haidt argues this is one reason why anxiety is skyrocketing— and there is strong scientific evidence that if you are anxious, your attention will suffer.

~

Lenore believes there is also a fourth factor at work. To understand it, you have to grasp a discovery that was made by the scientist Ed Deci, a professor of psychology who I interviewed in Rochester in upstate New York, and his colleague Richard Ryan, who I also spoke with.

Their research uncovered that all human beings have within us two different kinds of motivation for why we do anything. Imagine you are a runner. If you go running in the morning because you love how it feels—the wind in your hair, the sense that your body is powerful and it's carrying you forward—that's an "intrinsic" motive. You're not doing it to get some other reward farther down the line; you're doing it because you love it. Now imagine you go running not because you love it, but because you have a drill-sergeant dad who forces you to get up and run with him. Or imagine you go running in order to post the videos of you shirtless on Instagram and you're hooked on getting the hearts and "yum, you're so hot" comments you receive. That would be an "extrinsic" motive to run. You're not doing it because the act itself gives you a sense of pleasure or fulfillment— you are doing it because you have been forced to, or to get something out of it at a later point.

Richard and Ed discovered that it's easier to focus on something, and stick with it, if your motives are intrinsic—if you are doing something because it's meaningful to you—than if your motives are extrinsic, and you're doing it because you are forced to, or to get something out of it afterward. The more intrinsic your motivation, the easier it will be to sustain your attention.

Lenore came to suspect that children—in this new and radically different model of childhood—are being deprived of the chance to develop intrinsic motives. Most people, she said, "learn focus by doing something that is either very important or very interesting to them." You "learn the habit of focus by being interested in something enough that you notice what's going on, and you process it. . . . The way you learn to focus is automatic if there's something that interests you . . . or absorbs you, or thrills you." But if you are a kid today, you live almost all of your life according to what adults tell you to do. She asked me: "How do you find meaning when your day is filled, from seven in the morning to nine at night when you go to bed, with somebody else's idea of what is important? . . . If you don't have any free time to figure out what [emotionally] turns you on, I'm not sure you're going to find meaning. You're not given any *time* to find meaning."

As a child, wandering around her neighborhood, Lenore had the freedom to figure out what excited her—reading, writing, playing dress-up—and to pursue these things when she wanted to. Other kids learned they loved soccer, or climbing, or little scientific experiments. That was at least one way they learned attention and focus. That route is largely being cut off for kids now. She asked me: If your attention is constantly managed by other people, how can it develop? How do you learn what fascinates you? How do you find your intrinsic motives, the ones that are so important to developing attention?

After learning all this, Lenore was so worried about what we are doing to our kids that she started to tour the country, urging parents to let their children play in a free, unstructured, unsupervised way some of the time. She set up a group named Let Grow, designed to promote free play and freedom to explore for kids. She would say to the parents: "I want everybody to think back to your own childhood" and to describe "something that you loved—absolutely loved—to do, that you don't let your own children do." Their eyes would light up with memories. They would tell her: "We built forts. We played manhunt." Lenore added: "I met a guy the other day who played marbles. I said, 'What was your favorite marble?' He said, 'Oh, it was burgundy, and it was a swirl.' You could just see this love of something from so long ago. It infused him with joy." The parents admitted that "they all rode their bikes. They all climbed trees. They all went to town and got candy." But then they said it was much too dangerous today to allow their kids to do the same.

Lenore would explain how absolutely minuscule the risk of kidnapping is—and that violence is lower now than when they were young. This is not, she added, *because* we hide our kids away—we know that because violence against adults has also massively fallen, and they still move around freely. Parents would nod, and keep their kids indoors nonetheless. She would explain the clear benefits of free play. Parents would nod, and still they wouldn't let their kids out. Nothing seemed to work. She became more and more frustrated. She began to conclude that "even the people who are on our side, or who wonder what happened . . . they can't let go." She realized "you can't be the only people [doing it]—because then you're the crazy person sending your kid" out alone.

So she asked herself: What if we did this differently? What if we stopped trying to change parents' minds, and started trying to change their behavior instead—and what if we tried to change them not as isolated individuals, but as a group? With those thoughts, Lenore became a part of a crucial experiment.

One day, Roanoke Avenue Elementary, a school on Long Island, decided to take part in something called Global Play Day, where for one day a year, kids are allowed to play freely and create their own fun. The teachers filled four of their classrooms with empty boxes and Lego and some old toys, and they said, Go play. You get to choose what you do. Donna Verbeck, who had been a teacher at the school for more than twenty years, watched the kids, expecting to see glee and laughter—but she quickly realized something was wrong. Some of the kids plunged in and started playing right away, as she'd expected—but a large number of the children just stood there. They stared at the boxes and the Lego and the handful of children who were starting to improvise games, but they didn't move. They watched, inert, for a long time. Finally one of the kids, puzzled by the experience and unsure what to do, lay down in a corner and went to sleep.

Suddenly Donna realized, as she explained to me later: "They don't know what to do. They don't know how to get involved when somebody else is playing, or how to just start free play by themselves. They just did not know how to do it." Thomas Payton, who was the principal, added: "And we're not talking one or two kids. There were a *lot* of kids like that." Donna felt shaken, and sad. She realized that these kids had never been set free to play before. Their attention had been constantly managed for them by adults for their whole lives.

So Roanoke Avenue Elementary decided to become one of the

first schools to sign up for the program that Lenore leads. Let Grow is based on the idea that if children are going to become adults who can make their own decisions and pay attention, they need to experience increasing levels of freedom and independence throughout their childhood. When a school signs up, they commit that one day a week, or once a month, a child's "homework" will be to go home and do something new, independently, without adult supervision, and then report back on it. They choose their own mission. Every child, when they go out into the world, is given a card to show to any adult who stops them to ask where their parents are. It says: "I'm not lost or neglected. If you think it's wrong for me to be on my own, please read *Huckleberry Finn* and visit letgrow.org. Remember your own childhood. Was your parent with you every second? And with today's crime rate back to what it was in 1963, it is safer to play outside now than when you were at my age. Let me grow."

I went to meet the kids who had been taking part in this program at Roanoke for over a year. It's in a poor neighborhood with a lot of parents who are financially struggling, and many who are recent immigrants. The first group I met were nine years old, and they jostled to tell me about what they had done as part of their project with a gleeful energy. One of them set up a lemonade stand on his street. Another walked down to the local river and collected the trash that had built up there, because she said this would "save the turtles." (A few of the other kids joined in when she said this and shouted, "Save the turtles! Save them!") A little girl told me that, before this project: "Well, I'd literally sit in front of a TV all day. It doesn't really pop into your head to do stuff." But for Let Grow, the first thing she did was cook something for her mother on her own. She waved her hands excitedly as she described it. It seemed to have blown her mind—to discover that she could *do* something.

I also wanted to talk with the kids who didn't immediately volunteer their stories, so I spoke with a pale, rather serious-faced boy. He told me quietly: "We have a rope [in our backyard] that's connected to a tree." It had never crossed his mind to try to climb it. "But I finally said, well, I could at least try to do it." He managed to get a little way up. He offered a sly little beam of a smile as he described how it felt to be climbing for the first time.

Some of the kids discovered new ambitions. In Donna's class, there was a boy I'll call L.B., who wasn't particularly academic, and had often been distracted or bored in lessons. There was a constant struggle between him and his mom to get him to read or do his home-work. He chose as his Let Grow project to build a replica of a boat. He assembled a piece of wood, a foam core, a hot-glue gun, and toothpicks and thread, and he sat night after night, intensely working on it. He tried one set of techniques, and the boat fell apart—so he tried again, and again. Once he had successfully built this small boat and showed it to his friends, he decided he was going to build some-thing bigger—a life-size wagon that he could sleep in, in his yard. He took an old door that was in his garage, and his dad's wrenches and screwdrivers, and he started to read about how to put all this together. He persuaded his neighbors to give him some old bamboo they had lying around in their garden, to use for the frame. Before long, L.B. had a wagon.

Then he decided he wanted to do something even more ambitious—to build an amphibious wagon, one he could push out onto the ocean. So he started to read about how to build things that float. When I talked with L.B., he described the process of building it in detail. He told me he was going to build another wagon next: "I have to figure out how I'm going to cut the hula hoops to go on it, and then I got to lay shrink-wrap over it." I asked him how this project made him feel. "It's different because I'm actually using my hands on materials. . . . I think it's cool to just have your hands on something instead of seeing it on a screen, not really being able to touch it." I went to meet his mother, who worked in medical billing, and she told me: "I don't think, as a parent, I realized how much he could do on his own." She saw him change: "I could see the confidence—and him wanting to do more and more and figure it out his way." She glowed with pride. Her struggles to get him to read had ended, because now he was reading all the time about how to build stuff.

It struck me: When L.B. was being told what to do constantly—when he was being forced to act on extrinsic motivations—he couldn't focus, and he was bored all the time. But when he was given the chance, through play, to find out what interested him—to develop an intrinsic motivation—his ability to focus flourished, and he worked for hours and hours without a break, building his boats and wagons.

His teacher, Donna, told me L.B. changed in class after that. His reading hugely improved, and "he didn't consider it to be 'reading,' because it was his hobby. It was something he really, really liked." He started to gain status among the other kids—whenever they wanted to build anything, the cry would go up to find L.B., because he knew how to do it. She told me that—like with all the deepest learning—"nobody taught him. His mom and dad just let him do it. . . . He just used his own head and really taught himself." Gary Karlson, another teacher there, told me: "That learning is going to do more for that kid than anything academic that we could've brought to him through his time here."

As I talked with L.B., I thought about another aspect of attention that I had been taught about by scientists—one that is, I think, the fifth way in which we are currently hobbling our children's attention. In Aarhus in Denmark, Jan Tonnesvang, a professor of psychology there, had told me that we all need to have a sense of what he called "mastery"—that we are good at something. It's a basic human psychological need. When you feel you are good at something, you will find it much easier to focus on it, and if you feel incompetent, your attention will shrivel like a salted snail. When I listened to L.B., I realized that we have a school system right now that is so narrow that it makes a lot of kids (especially boys, I think) feel that they aren't good at anything. Their experience of school is contantly being made to feel incompetent. But once L.B. started to feel that he could master something—that he could become *good* at it—his focus began to form.

I went to see another aspect of the program, half an hour's drive away at a local middle school, in a wealthier part of Long Island. The teacher, Jodi Maurici, told me she realized her students needed a Let Grow program when thirty-nine out of her two hundred students—aged twelve and thirteen—were diagnosed with anxiety problems in a single year, way more than she'd ever had before. Yet when Jodi explained that their thirteen-year-olds should do something—anything—independently, lots of parents became angry. "I had one child tell me they wanted to do the laundry, and [her] mom said, 'Absolutely not. You're not doing the laundry. You may ruin it.' The child was so defeated at that point. . . . When I say defeated, I mean defeated." They told Jodi: "They don't even trust me to try on my own." She said: "[The kids] get no confidence, because the small things build confidence."

When I talked with Jodi's students, it was startling to hear how terrified they had been at the start of the program. A tall, strapping fourteen-year-old boy told me he had always been too frightened of kidnapping and "all the ransom calls that happen" to walk into town. He lives in a place where the French bakery is across the street from the olive oil store, but he had anxiety levels that would have been appropriate to living in a war zone. The Let Grow program gave him a taste of independence in small steps. First, he did his own laundry. Then, a month later, his parents let him go for a run around the block. Within a year, he had teamed up with his friends and they had built a fort in their local woods, where they now spend a lot of their time hanging out. He told me: "We sit there and talk, or we have little competitions. We don't have our moms. We can't say, 'Hey, Mom—can you get us this?' It doesn't work like that. It's different." As I spoke with him, I thought about something the writer Neale Donald Walsch wrote: "Life begins at the edge of your comfort zone."

Lenore met this boy with me, and afterward she said: "Think of history, and prehuman history. We have to chase things to eat. We have to hide from things that want to eat us, and [we have to] seek. We need to build shelter. Everybody does that for a million years, and just this generation, we've taken it all away. Kids don't get to build their shelter, or hide, or seek with a bunch of other kids on their own. . . . And that boy, given the chance, went into the woods and built a shelter."

One day, after a year of growing, and building, and focusing, L.B. and his mom walked down to the ocean, and placed the amphibious wagon he had built onto the water. They pushed it out to sea. They watched it float for a moment—and then it sank. They went home.

"I felt disappointment, but I was kind of determined to get it afloat. So I siliconed it," L.B. told me. They went back to the ocean. This time, the wagon floated, and L.B. and his mother watched it drift away. "I felt kind of proud," L.B. told me. "I was happy to see it float."

And then they went home, and he started to focus on the next thing he wanted to build.

At first, a lot of parents were very nervous about letting their kids take part in the Let Grow experiment. But, Lenore said, "when the kid comes through the door proud, and happy, and excited, and maybe a little sweaty or hungry, and they met a squirrel, or they ran into a friend, or they found a quarter," the parents see that "their kid rose to the occasion." Once this happens, "they are so proud that the parents are rewired. The parents are like—'That's my boy. Look at him.' That's what changes them. Not me telling them this is what is going to be good for your kid. . . . The only thing that actually changes the parents is seeing their own kids do something without them watching or helping. . . . People have to see it to believe it. See their kid blossom. And afterward they can't understand why they didn't trust their kids sooner. You have to change the picture in people's heads."

~

After everything I had learned from Lenore and the scientists she works with, I began to wonder if our kids are not only more confined at home, but also more confined at school too. I started to ask myself: Is the way our schools are structured today helping our kids develop a healthy sense of focus, or in fact hindering it?

I thought about my own education. When I was eleven years old, I was sitting at a wooden desk in a chilly classroom on my first day at secondary school, which is roughly equivalent to middle school in the U.S. A teacher placed a piece of paper in front of every kid in the class. I looked down and saw that on this sheet of paper, there was a grid, full of little boxes. "This is your timetable," I remember him saying. "It says where you have to be, and at what time, every day." I looked at it. It said that on Wednesday at 9 a.m. I would be learning woodwork; at 10 a.m. history; at 11 a.m. geography; and so on. I felt a flush of anger, and looked around me. I thought, Wait, what's happening here? Who are these people to tell me what I will be doing at 9 a.m. on a Wednesday morning? I haven't committed any crime. Why am I being treated like a prisoner?

I put up my hand and asked the teacher why I had to do these lessons, and not, say, learn about things I found interesting. "Because you have to," he said. This didn't seem to me to be a satisfying answer, so I asked him what he meant. "Because I say so," he said, flustered. In every lesson after that, I asked why we were learning these things. The answers were always the same: because you'll have a test on it; because you have to; because I tell you so. After a week, I was told to "shut up and learn." When I was at home, choosing my own material, I could read for days on end. At school, I could barely read for five minutes. (This was before the notion of ADHD had spread to Britain, so I was not given stimulants, though I suspect that if I was at school today I would be.)

I always loved learning, and I always hated school. For a long time I thought this was a paradox, until I got to know Lenore. Because it consisted mostly of fragmented rote-learning, very little in my education was meaningful to me, and since I was at school twenty-five years ago, education has been stripped of meaning even more. Across most of the Western world, the school system has been radically restructured by politicians to prioritize testing children much more. Almost everything else has been steadily squeezed out—from play, to music, to breaks. There was never a golden age when most schools were progressive, but there has been a swing toward a school system built around a narrow vision of efficiency. In 2002, George W. Bush signed into law the No Child Left Behind Act, which massively increased standardized testing across the U.S. In the four years that followed, diagnoses of severe attention problems in children rose by 22 percent.

I thought back over all the factors that I had learned make it possible for kids to develop attention. Our schools allow kids less exercise. They allow kids less play. They create more anxiety, because of the frenzy of tests. They don't create conditions where kids can find their intrinsic motivations. And for many kids, we don't give them opportunities to develop mastery—the sense they are good at something. All along, many teachers warned that dragging schools in this direction was a bad idea, but politicians tied financial support for schools to it nonetheless.

I wondered if there was a better way—so I decided to visit places that take a radically different approach to education, to see what I could learn from them. In the late 1960s, a group of Massachusetts parents who were unhappy with their kids' schooling decided to do something that sounds, at first glance, quite mad. They opened a school that would have no teachers, no classes, no curriculum, no homework, and no tests. One of the founders told me their goal was to create a completely new model, from scratch, of how a school could be. It left out almost everything we think of as schooling. More than fifty years later, I arrived at their creation. It is named Sudbury Valley School, and from the outside, it looks like a raddled Downton Abbey—a big, roomy, old-fashioned mansion, surrounded by woods and barns and creeks. It feels like you are stepping into a clearing in a forest, with the scent of pine trees filling every space you enter.

An eighteen-year-old student named Hannah offered to show me around and explain how the school works. We stood at first by the piano room, with kids milling freely around us, and she explained that before she came here, she went to a standard American high school. "I just dreaded it. I didn't want to get up. I was so anxious, and then I'd just go to school, and I'd get through it, and then I'd just get home as fast as I could," she said. "It was really hard for me to have to sit still and learn stuff that I didn't think was any good to me." So, she told me, when she arrived here, four years before I met her, "it was shocking." It was explained to her that there is no structure at Sudbury except for the one you create with your fellow students. There's no timetable or lessons. You learn what you want. You choose how to spend your time. You can ask the staff—who mill around and talk to the kids—to teach you things if you want, but there's no pressure to do that.

So, I asked, what do the kids do all day? From age four to eleven, the kids spend most of their time playing extraordinarily elaborate games they have created, which go on for months, and build up into an epic mythology, like a children's version of *Game of Thrones*. They have clans and fight goblins and dragons, and in the school's extensive grounds, they build forts. Waving toward the rocks, Hannah says that through all these games, "I think they're learning problem-solving, because they're building these forts, and then there could be a conflict within the group, and they have to figure that out. They're learning how to be creative and think about things in a different way."

The older students tend to form groups and ask to learn things together—whether it's cooking, or pottery, or music. People go on learning jags, she says. "I'll find this topic that I'm really interested in, and I'll just latch onto it, and I'll research it or I'll read about it for a week or a few days, and then I move on to the next thing. . . . I'm really interested in medicine, so there's one specialty of medicine [where] I would read about it intensively and learn everything I could. Then I would go to lizards—lizards are my favorite animal, so I read a lot about lizards. Right now, there's a bunch of people who have been doing origami all day, which is really cool." Hannah had been spending the past year teaching herself Hebrew, with the help of a staff member.

The fact that you have to create order for yourself doesn't mean there's no order at all, she told me as we walked through the grounds. On the contrary: all the school's rules are created and voted on by a daily meeting. Anyone can turn up and make a proposal, and anyone can vote on it. Everyone—from a four-year-old to the adult staff—has the same say, a single vote. There's an elaborate legal code that the school has built up over the years. If you are caught breaking the rules, you get tried by a jury that represents the whole age range of kids at the school, and they decide on the punishment. For example, if you break a tree branch, they might decree that you aren't allowed on the trees for a few weeks. The school is so democratic that the kids even vote on whether the individual staff members get rehired every year.

We walked through the dance room, the computer room, and past many walls covered with books. At this school, it became clear, kids only do things that are meaningful to them. "I think if you're not getting to use your imagination and be creative, then it's really putting you in a box," Hannah told me. "I don't feel as much pressure to learn every single fact, and I trust that the main idea or the most important things will just stay in my brain, and not having tests also gives me the freedom to take my time learning things." Because I—and everyone I know—was raised in such a different system, I found this, at first glance, overwhelmingly weird. Given the freedom to do nothing, wouldn't most kids go crazy and indulge themselves? There aren't even formal lessons in reading at Sudbury, though kids can ask the staff, or each other, to show them how reading works. Surely, I thought at first, this produces semiliterates?

I wanted to know what the outcome of this kind of education is, so I went to interview Professor Peter Gray, a research psychologist

at Boston College who tracked down the alumni of Sudbury Valley School to see how they turned out. Were they undisciplined
wrecks who couldn't function in the modern world? It turned out
that over 50 percent went on to higher education, and almost all of
them, he has written, have been "remarkably successful in finding
employment that interested them and earned them a living. They
had gone on, successfully, to a wide range of occupations, including business, arts, science, medicine, other service professions, and
skilled trades." There have been similar results for other kids like
them in other places. Peter's research found that kids who have been
"unschooled" like this were more likely to go on to higher education
than other kids.

How can that be? Peter explained to me that in fact for most
of human history, children have learned in the way they do at Sudbury. He studied the evidence that's been gathered about children
in hunter-gatherer societies—the way humans lived until, in evolutionary terms, the day before yesterday. At Sudbury, kids will play,
mill around, imitate adults, ask lots of questions, and slowly, over
time, they become competent, without being formally instructed
very much. The anomaly isn't Sudbury, he explained—it's the modern school, which was designed very recently, in the 1870s, to train
children to sit still, shut up, and do what they are told, to prepare
them to work in factories. He told me that children evolved to be
curious and to explore their environment. They naturally want to
learn, and they'll do it spontaneously when they can pursue things
that seem interesting to them. They learn primarily by playing freely.
His research found that Sudbury was particularly effective with kids
who had been told that they had learning problems. Of the eleven
students he studied who had been judged to have "serious learning
difficulties" before they arrived at Sudbury, four went on to receive
college degrees and a fifth was enrolled to get one.

These findings are important but need to be handled with a bit of
caution. Sudbury Valley charges fees between $7,500 and $10,000
a year—so the parents who send their kids there already have more

financial advantages than the rest of the population. That means their kids would already—in any circumstances—be more likely to go on to higher education, and the parents themselves are also quite likely to teach their kids some stuff at home. So the success of the kids at Sudbury Valley can't be attributed solely to the school.

But Peter argues this model is doing something that does boost real learning, in a way conventional schools don't. To understand why, he says, we should look at the evidence for what happens when animals are deprived of play. For example, he told me he started to study this subject after he was struck by a typical study—which I later read myself—that compared two groups of rats. The first were prevented from playing with other rats at all. The second were allowed to play with other rats for one hour a day. The scientists then watched as they grew up, to see if there were any differences. By the time they became adults, the play-deprived rats experienced much more fear and anxiety, and they were much less able to deal with unexpected events. The rats who got to play were braver, more likely to explore, and better able to cope with new situations. They tested both sets of rats for their ability to solve new problems—they set it up so that in order to get food, the rats would have to figure out a new sequence. It turned out the rats who had been allowed to play when they were young were significantly smarter.

At Sudbury, Hannah told me that once she was free from the mindless and meaningless grilling of standardized schooling, she found, "I really appreciate education more, and I'm excited to learn, and I want to pursue different things. Since I don't feel like I'm being forced to, I'm motivated to do that." This fits with a wider body of scientific evidence—the more something is meaningful, the easier it is to pay attention to and learn, for adults and kids. Standardized schooling too often drains learning of meaning, while progressive schooling tries to infuse it into everything. This is why the best research on this question shows that kids at more progressive schools are more likely to retain what they've learned in the long run, more likely to want to carry on learning, and more likely to be able to apply what they've learned to new problems. These, it seems to me, are among the most precious forms of attention.

Standing outside Sudbury, Hannah told me she used to long for the school day to end, but now, "I don't want to go home." The other kids I spoke with told me they had a similar point of view, before they ran off to join some collective activity with other children. I found it startling to discover that you can throw out almost everything we regard as schooling—all the testing, all the assessments, even formal teaching—and still produce people who can read, write, and function in society. This tells you how much of what we are neurotically putting our kids through is pointless (at best).

Personally, my instinct is that Sudbury goes too far. I went to other progressive schools to see if there's a way you can mix much greater freedom with some adult guidance. One I particularly liked was in Berlin, named the Evangelische Schule Berlin Zentrum. There, the kids decide collectively on a topic they want to investigate—when I visited, it was whether humans can live in space. Then, for a whole term, half of all their lessons are built around investigating this question—they investigate the physics of how to build rockets, the history of going to the moon, the geography of what would grow on other planets. It builds to a big collective project—they were literally building a rocket in their classroom. In this way, subjects that seem dry and boring when they are broken up and rote-learned were infused for these kids with meaning, and they wanted to know more about them.

Because I had grown up in such a different system, I kept having doubts about these alternatives. But I kept coming back to one key fact: The country that is often judged by international league tables to have the most successful schools in the world, Finland, is closer to these progressive models than anything we would recognize. Their children don't go to school at all until they are seven years old—before then, they just play. Between the ages of seven and sixteen, kids arrive at school at 9 a.m. and leave at 2 p.m. They are given almost no homework, and they take almost no tests until they graduate from high school. Free play is at the beating heart of Finnish kids' lives: by law, teachers have to give kids fifteen minutes of free play for every forty-five minutes of instruction. What's the outcome? Only 0.1 percent of their kids are diagnosed with attention problems, and Finns are among the most literate, numerate, and happy people in the world.

Hannah told me as I was leaving that when she remembers her time at a conventional high school, "I see myself sitting at a desk, and it's all gray. It's this weird image." She told me she worries about her friends still stuck in that system. "They hate it, and I feel bad they don't have the opportunity to do something else."

∽

When adults notice that children and teens seem to be struggling to focus and pay attention today, we often say it with a weary and exasperated superiority. The implication is: Look at this degraded younger generation! Aren't we better than them? Why can't they be like us? But after learning all this, I think about it very differently. Children have needs—and it's our job, as adults, to create an environment that meets those needs. In many cases, in this culture, we aren't meeting those needs. We don't let them play freely; we imprison them in their homes, with little to do except interact via screens; and our school system largely deadens and bores them. We feed them food that causes energy crashes, contains drug-like additives that can make them hyper, and doesn't contain the nutrients they need. We expose them to brain-disrupting chemicals in the atmosphere. It's not a flaw in them that causes children to struggle to pay attention. It's a flaw in the world we built for them.

∽

Now, when Lenore speaks to parents, she still gets them to talk about the happiest moments in their own childhoods. It's almost always a moment when they were free—building a fort, walking through the woods with friends, playing out in the street. She says to them:

"We're scrimping and saving to send them to the dance class," but when it comes down to it, "you're not giving them the thing you loved the most." We don't have to continue like this, she tells them. There's a different childhood waiting for our kids, if we commit, together, to rebuild it—one where they can learn, like L.B. building his boats, to focus deeply again.

Attention Rebellion

I f this was a self-help book, I would be able to serve up a delight-fully simple conclusion to this story. Those books have a very sat-isfying structure. The author identifies a problem—usually one he's had himself—and he talks you through how he personally solved it. Then he says: And now, dear reader, you can do what I have done, and it will set you free. But this is not a self-help book, and what I have to say to you is more complex, and it means starting with an admission: I have not entirely solved this problem in myself. In fact, at this moment, as I write this in lockdown, my attention has never been worse.

For me, the collapse came in a strange dreamlike month. In February 2020, I walked into Heathrow Airport to board a flight to Moscow. I was on my way to interview James Williams, the former Google strategist who you've seen quoted throughout this book. As I hurried through the alienating yellow light of the airport toward my gate, I noticed something strange. Some of the staff were wearing face masks. I had, of course, read in the news about the new virus that had emerged in Wuhan in China, but I assumed—as so many of us did—that like the swine flu or Ebola crises a few years before, this problem would be contained at source before it could become a pandemic. I felt a flicker of irritation at what I saw as their paranoia, and I boarded my flight.

I landed into a freakishly warm Russian winter. There was no snow on the ground, and people were wearing T-shirts and selling off their fur coats for a pittance. As I strolled through the eerily snowless streets, I felt tiny and disorientated. Everything in Moscow is massive—people live in enormous concrete lumps of apartment blocks, and they work in ugly fortresses, and they trudge between them across eight-lane highways. The city is designed to make the collective seem vast and to make you, the individual, feel like a speck on the wind. James was living in a nineteenth-century Moscow apartment block, and as we sat in front of a huge bookcase filled with Russian classics, I felt like I had stumbled into a Tolstoy novel. He was living there partly because his wife worked for the World Health Organization, and partly because he loved Russian culture and philosophy.

He told me that after years of studying focus, he has come to believe that attention takes three different forms—all of which are now being stolen. When we went through them, it clarified for me a lot of what I had learned so far.

The first layer of your attention, he said, is your *spotlight*. This is when you focus on "immediate actions," like, "I'm going to walk into the kitchen and make a coffee." You want to find your glasses. You want to see what's in the fridge. You want to finish reading this chapter of my book. It's called the spotlight because—as I explained earlier—it involves narrowing down your focus. If your spotlight gets distracted or disrupted, you are prevented from carrying out near-term actions like these.

The second layer of your attention is your *starlight*. This is, he says, the focus you can apply to your "longer-term goals—projects over time." You want to write a book. You want to set up a business.

You want to be a good parent. It's called the starlight because when you feel lost, you look up to the stars, and you remember the direction you are traveling in. If you become distracted from your starlight, he said, you "lose sight of the longer-term goals." You start to forget where you are headed.

The third layer of your attention is your *daylight*. This is the form of focus that makes it possible for you to know what your longer-term goals are in the first place. How do you know you want to write a book? How do you know you want to set up a business? How do you know what it means to be a good parent? Without being able to reflect and think clearly, you won't be able to figure these things out. He gave it this name because it's only when a scene is flooded with daylight that you can see the things around you most clearly. If you get so distracted that you lose your sense of the daylight, James says, "In many ways you may not even be able to figure out who you are, what you wanted to do, [or] where you want to go."

He believes that losing your daylight is "the deepest form of distraction," and you may even begin "decohering." This is when you stop making sense to yourself, because you don't have the mental space to create a story about who you are. You become obsessed with petty goals, or dependent on simplistic signals from the outside world like retweets. You lose yourself in a cascade of distractions. You can only find your starlight and your daylight if you have sustained periods of reflection, mind-wandering, and deep thought. James has come to believe that our attention crisis is depriving us of all three of these forms of focus. We are losing our light.

He also said a different metaphor might further help us to understand this. Sometimes, hackers decide to attack a website in a very specific way. They get an enormous number of computers to try to connect to a website all at once—and by doing this, they "overwhelm its capacity for managing traffic, to the point where it can't be accessed by anyone else, and it goes down." It crashes. This is called a "denial-of-service attack." James thinks we are all living through something like a denial-of-service attack on our minds. "We're that server, and there's all these things trying to grab our attention by throwing information at us. . . . It undermines our capacity for responding to anything. It leaves us in a state of either distraction, or paralysis." We are so inundated "that it fills up your world, and you can't find a place to get a view on all of it and realize that you're so distracted and figure out what to do about it. It can just colonize your entire world," he said. You are left so depleted that "you don't get the space to push back against it."

I left James's apartment and walked the streets of the Russian capital, and I began to wonder if there is, in fact, a fourth form of attention. I would call it our *stadium lights*—it's our ability to see each other, to hear each other, and to work together to formulate and fight for collective goals. I could see a creepy example of what happens when this is lost unfolding all around me. I was in Moscow in winter, and people were walking around outside in T-shirts because it was so warm. A heat wave was just starting in Siberia— a sentence I never thought I would write. The climate crisis couldn't be clearer—Moscow itself, ten years before, had been choked by the smoke from severe wildfires. But there is very little climate activism in Russia, nor—given the scale of the crisis—anywhere in the world. Our attention is occupied with other, less important things. I knew I was more guilty of this than most—I thought about my own horrendous carbon emissions.

As I flew back to London, I felt like on this long journey I had learned a huge amount about attention—and I felt I could fix mine a little, step by step. When I landed, I noticed that everyone who worked at the airport was now wearing a mask, and the newspaper stands were full of images of hospitals in Italy where people were dying on the floor or in the corridors. I didn't know it then, but these were the last days before air travel all but ceased across the world. Soon after, Heathrow would be empty and echoing.

A few days later, I was walking home when I noticed that my teeth were chattering. It was a mild winter in London too, and I assumed I was caught in a cold draft, but by the time I got home half an hour later, I was shivering and shaking. I crawled into bed, and I didn't get out again, except to go to the bathroom, for three weeks. I had a raging temperature, and I became feverish and almost delusional. By the time I was able to understand what was going on, British prime minister Boris Johnson was appearing on television telling everyone that they must not leave their homes, and then, soon after, he was in the hospital himself, almost dead. It was like a stress dream, where the walls of reality start to collapse.

$\backsim$

Up to this point, I had been applying what I'd learned on this journey steadily, step by step, to improve my own attention. I'd made six big changes in my life.

One: I used pre-commitment to stop switching tasks so much. Pre-commitment is when you realize that if you want to change your behavior, you have to take steps now that will lock in that desire and make it harder for you to crack later. One key step for me was buying a kSafe, which—as I mentioned briefly before—is a large plastic safe with a removable lid. You put your phone in it, put the lid back on, and turn the dial at the top for however long you want—from fifteen minutes to two weeks—and then it locks your phone away for as long as you selected. Before I went on this journey, my use of it was patchy. Now I use it every day without exception, and that buys me long stretches of focus. I also use on my laptop a program called Freedom, which cuts it off from the internet for as long as I select. (As I write this sentence, it's counting down from three hours.)

Two: I have changed the way I respond to my own sense of distraction. I used to reproach myself, and say: You're lazy. You're not good enough. What's wrong with you? I tried to shame myself into focusing harder. Now, based on what Mihaly Csikszentmihalyi taught me, instead I have a very different conversation with myself. I ask: What could you do now to get into a flow state, and access your mind's own ability to focus deeply? I remember what Mihaly taught me are the main components of flow, and I say to myself:

What would be something meaningful to me that I could do now? What is at the edge of my abilities? How can I do something that matches these criteria now? Seeking out flow, I learned, is far more effective than self-punishing shame.

Three: based on what I learned about the way social media is designed to hack our attention spans, I now take six months of the year totally off it. (This time is divided into chunks, usually of a few months.) To make sure I stick to it, I always announce publicly when I am going off—I'll tweet that I am leaving the site for a certain amount of time, so that I will feel like a fool if I suddenly crack and go back a week later. I also get my friend Lizzie to change my passwords.

Four: I acted on what I learned about the importance of mind-wandering. I realized that letting your mind wander is not a crumbling of attention, but in fact a crucial form of attention in its own right. It is when you let your mind drift away from your immediate surroundings that it starts to think over the past, and starts to game out the future, and makes connections between different things you have learned. Now I make it a point to go for a walk for an hour every day without my phone or anything else that could distract me. I let my thoughts float and find unexpected connections. I found that, precisely because I give my attention space to roam, my thinking is sharper, and I have better ideas.

Five: I used to see sleep as a luxury, or—worse—as an enemy. Now I am strict with myself about getting eight hours every night. I have a little ritual where I make myself unwind: I don't look at screens for two hours before I go to bed, and I light a scented candle and try to set aside the stresses of the day. I bought a FitBit device to measure my sleep, and if I get less than eight hours, I make myself go back to bed. This has made a really big difference.

Six: I'm not a parent, but I am very involved in the lives of my godchildren and my young relatives. I used to spend a lot of my time with them deliberately doing things—busy, educational activities I would plan out in advance. Now I spend most of my time with them just playing freely, or letting them play on their own without being managed or oversupervised or imprisoned. I learned that the more free play they get, the more sound a foundation they will have for their focus and attention. I try to give them as much of that as I can.

I would like to be able to tell you that I also do other things I learned I should do to improve my focus—cut out processed foods, meditate every day, build in other slow practices like yoga, and take an extra day off work each week. The truth is I struggle with this—so much of how I deal with ordinary anxiety is tied up with comfort eating and overworking.

But I would estimate that by making these six changes, I had—by the time I went to Moscow—improved my own focus by about 15 to 20 percent, which is a fair whack. It made a real and marked difference to my life. All of these changes are worth trying, and there will probably be other tweaks to your life that you are considering based on what you've read in this book. I am strongly in favor of individuals making the changes they can in their personal lives. I am also in favor of being honest about the fact there are limits to how far that can take you.

$\backsim$

As I was recovering from Covid-19, I found myself in a weird mirror image of where I started this journey. I began by going to Provincetown for three months to escape the internet and cellphones. Now I was shut away for three months in my apartment with almost nothing but the internet and cellphones. Provincetown had liberated my focus and attention; the Covid-19 crisis brought it lower than it had ever been. For months, I couldn't focus on anything. I skipped from news channel to news channel, seeing fear and fever spread across the world. I took to spending hours listlessly watching live webcams of all the places I had been to research this book. It didn't matter where they were—Memphis or Melbourne, Fifth Avenue in New York or Commercial Street in Provincetown—they were all the same; the streets were almost empty, except for short sightings of masked people scuttling. I was not alone in finding it impossible to focus. Some of what I experienced was likely a biological aftereffect of the virus—but many people who hadn't been infected were reporting a similar problem. There was a 300 percent increase in people googling "how to get your brain to focus." All over social media, people were saying they couldn't get their minds to work.

But now, I felt, I had the tools to understand why this was happening to us. Your individual efforts to improve your attention can be dwarfed by an environment full of things that wreck it. This had been true for years leading up to Covid-19—and it was even more true during it. Stress shatters attention, and we were all more stressed. There was a virus we couldn't see and didn't fully understand and it was threatening all of us. The economy was tanking and many of us were suddenly even more financially insecure. On top of this, our political leaders often seemed dangerously incompetent, which ramped up the stress further. For all these reasons, many of us were suddenly hypervigilant.

And how did we cope? We turned more heavily than ever before to our Silicon Valley–controlled screens, which were waiting for us, offering connection, or a least a hologram of it. As we used them more, our attention seemed to get worse. In the U.S., in April 2020, the average citizen spent thirteen hours a day looking at a screen. The number of children looking at screens for more than six hours a day increased sixfold, and traffic to kids' apps trebled.

In this respect, Covid gave us a glimpse of the future we were already skidding toward. My friend Naomi Klein, a political writer who has made many strikingly accurate predictions about the future for twenty years, explained to me: "We were on a gradual slide into a world in which every one of our relationships was mediated by platforms and screens, and because of Covid, that gradual process went into hyper-speed." The tech companies were planning for us to be immersed in their world to such an extreme extent in a decade's time, not now. "The plan was not for it to leap in this way," she said. "That leaping is an opportunity, really—because when you do something that quickly, it comes as a shock to your system." We didn't slowly acclimatize to it, and get hooked on its increasing patterns of reinforcements. Instead, we got slammed headfirst into a vision of the future—and we realized "we hate it. It's not good for our well-being. We desperately miss each other." Under Covid, even more than before, we were living in simulations of social life, not the real thing. It was better than nothing, to be sure—but it felt thinner. And all the while, the algorithms of surveillance capitalism were altering us—tracking and changing us—for many more hours a day.

I could see that in the pandemic, the environment changed—and this wrecked our ability to focus. For many of us, the pandemic didn't create new factors that ruined our attention—it supercharged the factors that had already been corroding our attention for years. I saw this when I talked with my godson Adam, whom I had taken to Memphis. His attention, which had been deteriorating for some time, was now shattered. He was on his phone almost every waking hour, seeing the world mainly through TikTok, a new app that made Snapchat look like a Henry James novel.

Naomi told me that the way we felt when we were spending all day in lockdown on Zoom and Facebook was awful but "also kind of a gift," because it showed us the road we were headed down with such clarity. More screens. More stress. More collapse of the middle class. More insecurity for the working class. More invasive technology. She calls this vision of the future the "Screen New Deal." She told me: "The ray of hope in all of this is that we are in touch with how much we dislike this vision of the future that we have just trial run. . . . We weren't going to have a trial run. We were going to have a gradual rollout. But we got a crash course."

One thing was now very clear to me. If we continue to be a society of people who are severely under-slept and overworked; who switch tasks every three minutes; who are tracked and monitored by social-media sites designed to figure out our weaknesses and manipulate them to make us scroll and scroll and scroll; who are so stressed that we become hypervigilant; who eat diets that cause our energy to spike and crash; who are breathing in a chemical soup of brain-inflaming toxins every day—then, yes, we will continue to be a society with serious attention problems. But there is an alternative. It's to organize and fight back—to take on the forces that are setting fire to our attention, and replace them with forces that will help us to heal.

I started thinking about why we need to do this with an analogy that seemed to tie together a lot of what I had learned. Imagine you bought a plant and you wanted to help it grow. What would you do? You would make sure certain things were present: sunlight, and water, and soil with the right nutrients. And you would protect it from the things that could damage or kill it: you would plant it far from the trampling feet of other people, and from pests and diseases. Your ability to develop deep focus is, I have come to believe, like a plant. To grow and flourish to its full potential, your focus needs certain things to be present: play for children and flow states for adults, to read books, to discover meaningful activities that you want to focus on, to have space to let your mind wander so you can make sense of your life, to exercise, to sleep properly, to eat nutritious food that makes it possible for you to develop a healthy brain, and to have a sense of safety. And there are certain things you need to protect your attention from, because they will sicken or stunt it: too much speed, too much switching, too many stimuli, intrusive technology designed to hack and hook you, stress, exhaustion, processed food pumped with dyes that amp you up, polluted air.

For a long time we took our attention for granted, as if it was a cactus that would grow in even the most desiccated climate. Now we know it's more like an orchid, a plant that requires great care or it will wither.

With this image in mind, I now had a sense of what a movement to reclaim our attention might look like. I would start with three big, bold goals. One: ban surveillance capitalism, because people who are being hacked and deliberately hooked can't focus. Two: introduce a four-day week, because people who are chronically exhausted can't pay attention. Three: rebuild childhood around letting kids play freely—in their neighborhoods and at school—because children who are imprisoned in their homes won't be able to develop a healthy ability to pay attention. If we achieve these goals, the ability of people to pay attention would, over time, dramatically improve. Then we will have a solid core of focus that we could use to take the fight further and deeper.

The idea of building a movement sometimes seemed to me still to be quite hard to picture concretely—so I wanted to talk to people who had built movements around really big, impossible-seeming goals, and actually achieved them. My friend Ben Stewart was the head of communications at Greenpeace U.K. for years, and when I first met him more than fifteen years ago, he told me about a plan he was drawing up with other environmentalist activists. He explained that Britain was the birthplace of the Industrial Revolution, and this revolution had been powered by one thing: coal. Because coal contributes more than any other fuel to global warming, his team was drawing up a plan to force the government to end all new coal mines and new power stations in Britain, and move rapidly to leaving all the country's existing coal in the ground to ensure it will never be burned. When he explained it, I literally laughed out loud. Good luck to you, I said. I'm on your side, but you're being a dreamer.

Within five years, the development of every single new coal mine and new coal power plant in Britain was stopped, and the government had been forced to set in stone plans to close down all the ones that already existed. As a result of their campaign, the place that launched the world on the road to global warming had begun to seek out a path beyond it.

I wanted to talk to Ben about our attention crisis, and how we could learn from other movements that have succeeded in the past. He said: "I agree with you it's a crisis. It's a crisis for the human species. But I don't think it's being identified [like that] in the same way that structural racism or climate change [are]. I don't think we're at that point yet. . . . I don't think that it's understood that it's a societal problem, and that it's caused by decisions by corporate actors, and that it can change." So Ben told me the very first step to building a movement is to create a "consciousness-raising breakthrough cultural moment, where people go—'Shit, my brain's been frazzled by this stuff. It's why I don't have some of the pleasures in life I used to have.'" How do we do that? The ideal tool, he said, is what he calls "a site battle." This is where you choose a place that symbolizes the wider struggle, and begin a nonviolent fight there. An obvious example is Rosa Parks taking her seat on a bus in Montgomery, Alabama.

Think, he said, about how we did it with coal. Man-made global warming is a rapidly unfolding disaster, but—like our attention crisis—it can easily seem pretty abstract, and far away, and hard to get a handle on. Even once you do understand it, it can seem so huge and overwhelming that you are often left feeling powerless to do anything. When Ben first drew up his plans, there was a coal-fired power station in Britain named Kingsnorth, and the government was planning to authorize the construction of another coal station right next to it. This, Ben realized, was the whole global problem in microcosm. So after a lot of planning with his allies, he broke into the power station and rappelled down its side, painting onto the side of the building a warning about the extreme weather events that coal unleashes across the world.

They were all arrested and put on trial—which was part of their plan. They intended to use the justice process—in a jujitsu move—as a perfect opportunity to put coal itself on trial. They called some of the leading scientific experts from all over the world to testify, to explain what the burning of coal is doing to the ecosystem. In Britain there's a law that says that in an emergency, you can break some rules—you don't get charged with trespassing, for example, if you break into a burning building to save people. Ben and his legal team argued that this was an emergency: they were trying to prevent the planet from being set on fire. Twelve ordinary British jurors considered the facts—and they acquitted Ben and the other activists on all counts. It was a sensational story, reported all over the world. In the wake of the negative publicity around coal that emerged out of the trial, the British government abandoned all plans to build new coal-powered stations—and began to shutter the ones that remained.

Ben explained that a site battle makes it possible to "tell the story about the wider problem," and when you do this, "it speeds up the national conversation" by waking up a lot of people to what's really going on. For this first stage, Ben said, "you don't need millions of people. You need a small group of people that get [what] the problems [are], and know about creative confrontation—to create drama around it, to begin the consciousness-raising. . . . You capture people's attention, and then enough people feel that it's a vital issue that they want to give their time and their energy [to], and that there's a clear direction."

So Ben asked: Should people be surrounding Facebook HQ? Twitter? What's the site battle here? What's the issue we start on? This is something activists need to debate and decide on. As I write this, I know one group is considering projecting a video of Holocaust survivors talking about the dangers of supercharging far-right ideas onto the side of Facebook's HQ. Ben stressed that site battles alone don't deliver victory—what they do is establish the crisis clearly in the public's mind, and draw more people into a movement. Their participation after that will take many different forms. On attention, Ben said, a site battle is an opportunity to explain to people this is a fight "about personal liberation"—about "liberating ourselves from people who are controlling our minds without our consent." That is "something that people can coalesce around—and it's highly motivating as well." That then becomes a movement millions of people can join—and that movement can then begin to fight at lots of different levels. Some of it will be inside the political system, organizing within political parties, or lobbying the government. Some of it will continue to be outside the political system, with direct action and persuading other citizens. To succeed, you need both.

As I talked with Ben, I wondered if a movement to achieve these goals should be named Attention Rebellion. He smiled when I suggested it. "It *is* an attention rebellion," he said. I realized this will require a shift in how we think about ourselves. We are not medieval peasants begging at the court of King Zuckerberg for crumbs of attention. We are the free citizens of democracies, and we own our own minds and our own society, and together, we are going to take them back.

At times it seemed to me that this would be a hard movement to get off the ground—but then I remembered that all the movements that have changed your life and my life were hard to get off the ground. For example, when gay people first started organizing in the 1890s, they could be put in prison just for saying who they loved. When labor unions started fighting for the weekend, they were beaten by the police and their leaders were shot or hanged. What we face is, in many ways, vastly less challenging than the cliff they had to scale. Often, when a person argues for social change, they are called "naive." The exact opposite is the truth. It's naive to think we as citizens can do nothing, and leave the powerful to do whatever they want, and somehow our attention will survive. There's nothing naive about believing that concerted democratic campaigning can change the world. As the anthropologist Margaret Mead said: "It's the only thing that ever has."

I realized that we have to decide now: Do we value attention and focus? Does being able to think deeply matter to us? Do we want it for our children? If we do, then we have to fight for it. As one politician said: "You don't get what you don't fight for."

∽

Even as it became clearer to me what we need to do now, there were some unresolved thoughts that kept nagging at me. Lying beneath so many of the causes of this crisis that I had learned about, there seemed to be one big cause—but I was reluctant to reckon with it because it is so big, and, to be honest, I hesitate to write about it now, in case it daunts you too. Back in Denmark, Sune Lehmann had shown me the evidence that the world is speeding up, and that process is shrinking our collective attention span. He showed that social media is a major accelerant. But he made it clear that this has been happening for a very long time. His study started analyzing data from the 1880s, and it showed that every decade since, the way we experience the world has been getting faster, and we have been focusing on any one topic less and less.

I kept puzzling away at this question. Why? Why has this been happening so long? This trend far precedes Facebook, or most of the factors I have written about here. What's the underlying cause stretching back to the 1880s? I discussed it with many people, and the most persuasive answer came from the Norwegian scientist Thomas Hylland Eriksen, who is a professor of social anthropology. Ever since the Industrial Revolution, he said, our economies have been built around a new and radical idea—economic growth. This is the belief that every year, the economy—and each individual company in it—should get bigger and bigger. That's how we now define success. If a country's economy grows, its politicians are likely to be reelected. If a company grows, its CEOs are likely garlanded. If a country's economy or a company's share price shrinks, politicians or CEOs face a greater risk of being booted out. Economic growth is the central organizing principle of our society. It is at the heart of how we see the world.

Thomas explained that growth can happen in one of two ways. The first is that a corporation can find new markets—by inventing something new, or exporting something to a part of the world that doesn't have it yet. The second is that a corporation can persuade existing consumers to consume more. If you can get people to eat more, or to sleep less, then you have found a source of economic growth. Mostly, he believes, we achieve growth today primarily through this second option. Corporations are constantly finding ways to cram more stuff into the same amount of time. To give one example: they want you to watch TV *and* follow the show on social media. Then you see twice as many ads. This inevitably speeds up life. If the economy has to grow every year, in the absence of new markets it has to get you and me to do more and more in the same amount of time.

As I read Thomas's work more deeply, I realized this is one of the crucial reasons why life has accelerated every decade since the 1880s: we are living in an economic machine that requires greater speed to keep going—and that inevitably degrades our attention over time. In fact, when I reflected on it, this need for economic growth seemed to be the underlying force that was driving so many of the causes of poor attention that I had learned about—our increasing stress, our swelling work hours, our more invasive technologies, our lack of sleep, our bad diets.

I thought about what Dr. Charles Czeisler had told me back at Harvard Medical School. If we all went back to sleeping as much as our brains and our bodies need, he said, "it would be an earthquake for our economic system, because our economic system has become dependent on sleep-depriving people. The attentional failures are just roadkill. That's just the cost of doing business." This is true of sleep—and it's true of much more than sleep.

It was intimidating to realize that something so deeply ingrained in our way of life is—over time—an acid on our attention. But I already knew we don't have to live like this. My friend Dr. Jason Hickel, who is an economic anthropologist at the University of London, is perhaps the leading critic of the concept of economic growth in the world—and he has been explaining for a long time that there is an alternative. When I went to see him, he explained that we need to move beyond the idea of growth, to something called a "steady-state economy." We would abandon economic growth as the driving principle of the economy and instead choose a different set of goals. At the moment we think we're prosperous if we are working ourselves ragged to buy things—most of which don't even make us happy. He said we could redefine prosperity to mean having time to spend with our children, or to be in nature, or to sleep, or to dream, or to have secure work. Most people don't want a fast life—they want a good life. Nobody lies on their deathbed and thinks about all that they contributed to economic growth. A steady-state economy can allow us to choose goals that don't raid our attention, and don't raid the planet's resources.

As Jason and I talked, in a public park in London in the middle of the Covid-19 crisis, I looked around us, where people were sitting in the middle of a workday under the trees, enjoying nature. This was, I realized, the only time in my life the world had truly slowed down. A terrible tragedy had forced us to do it—but there was also, for many of us, a hint of relief. It was the first time in centuries that the world chose, together, to stop racing, and pause. We decided as a society to value something other than speed and growth. We literally looked up and saw the trees.

I suspect that, in the long run, it will ultimately not be possible to rescue attention and focus in a world that is dominated by the belief that we need to keep growing and speeding up every year. I can't tell you I have all the answers to how we do that—but I believe that if an Attention Rebellion begins, we will, sooner or later, have to take on this very deep issue: the growth machine itself.

But we will have to do this in any event—for another reason. The growth machine has pushed humans beyond the limits of our minds—but it is also pushing the planet beyond its ecological limits. And these two crises, I was coming to believe, are intertwined.

∽

There is one particularly large reason why we need an Attention Rebellion today. It's stark. Human beings have never needed our ability to focus—our superpower as a species—more than we do at this moment, because we face an unprecedented crisis.

As I write these words, I am looking at a webcam of San Francisco, showing the streets where I walked with Tristan Harris. He told me there—just over a year before—that his biggest worry about the destruction of our attention is that it will prevent us from dealing with global warming. Right now, on those streets, it's midday, but you can't see the sun—it has been blacked out by ash from the massive wildfires ripping across California. One in every thirty-three acres in the state has burned. The house Tristan grew up in, not far away, has been consumed by the flames, and most of his belongings have been destroyed. The streets where I had this conversation about the climate crisis with him have ash flecked across them, and the sky is glowing a low, dark orange.

The three years I've worked on this book have been years of fire. Several of the cities I've spent time in have been choked by the smoke from huge and unprecedented wildfires—Sydney, São Paulo, and San Francisco. Like a lot of people, I read about the fires, but only a little—I began to feel quickly overwhelmed. The moment when it became real to me—when I felt it in my gut—was a moment that might seem small when I describe it.

Starting in 2019, Australia experienced what became known as its Black Summer, a series of wildfires so vast that they are hard to describe. Three billion animals had to flee or were burned to death, and so many species were lost that Professor Kingsley Dixon, a botanist, called it a "biological Armageddon." Some Australians had to huddle on the beaches, surrounded by a ring of flames, as they wondered if they should try to scramble onto boats to escape. They could hear the fires getting closer. It sounded like a raging waterfall, witnesses said, and it was broken only by the sound of bottles smashing as their houses burned up, one by one. The smoke from the fires was visible 1,200 miles away in New Zealand, where the skies over the South Island turned orange.

About three weeks or so into the fires, I was on the phone to a friend in Sydney when I heard a loud shrieking sound. It was the fire alarm in his apartment. All over the city, in offices and homes, these alarms had started to sound. This was because there was so much smoke in the air traveling in from the wildfires that the smoke alarms believed each individual building was on fire. This meant that one by one, many people in Sydney turned off their smoke alarms, and they sat in the silence and the smoke. I only realized why I found this so disturbing when I talked it over with my friend Bruno Giussani, a Swiss writer. He said to me that we were turning off the warning systems in our homes that are designed to protect us, because the bigger warning systems that are meant to protect us all—our society's ability to focus on what scientists are telling us, and act on what they say—are not working.

The climate crisis can be solved. We need to rapidly transition away from fossil fuels and toward powering our societies by clean, green sources of energy. But to do that we will need to be able to focus, to have sane conversations with each other, and to think clearly. These solutions are not going to be achieved by an addled population who are switching tasks every three minutes and screaming at each other all the time in algorithm-pumped fury. We can only solve the climate crisis if we solve our attention crisis. As I contemplated this, I began to think again about something that James Williams wrote: "I used to think there were no great political struggles left. . . . How wrong I was. The liberation of human attention may be the defining moral and political struggle of our time. Its success is the prerequisite for the success of virtually all other struggles."

When I look now at the orange, fire-scarred skies over San Francisco on this grainy webcam, I keep thinking about the light in Provincetown in the summer I spent there without my phone or the internet, and how pure and perfect it seemed. James Williams was right: our attention is a kind of light, one that clarifies the world and makes it visible to us. In Provincetown I could see more clearly than I ever had before in my life—my own thoughts, my own goals, my own dreams. I want to live in that light—the light of knowing, of achieving our ambitions, of being fully alive—and not in the menacing orange light of it all burning down.

When I hung up on my friend in Sydney so he could unscrew his fire alarm and switch it off, I thought, if our attention continues to shatter, the ecosystem won't wait patiently for us to regain our focus.

It will fall and it will burn. At the start of the Second World War, the English poet W. H. Auden—when he looked out over the new technologies of destruction that had been created by humans—warned: "We must love one another, or die." I believe that now we must focus together—or face the fires alone.

Acknowledgments

I was only able to write this book with the help and support of a large number of people. First and foremost, I want to thank the brilliant Sarah Punshon, who helped me with additional research and fact-checking, but much more than that—her insights and thoughts were central to the shaping of what you've just read. I am deeply in her debt.

I owe a huge amount to the social scientists and other experts who gave so much of their time to explain their research to me. The social sciences have been having a rough time lately, but they are an essential tool for how we understand the world, and I'm really grateful to them.

My totally brilliant editors, Kevin Doughten at Crown and Alexis Kirschbaum at Bloomsbury, both made this a much better book, as did my agents, Natasha Fairweather at Rogers, Coleridge & White (RCW) in London, and Richard Pine at Inkwell in New York. Lydia Morgan at Crown also made really helpful suggestions that reshaped

the text. Thanks also to Tristan Kendrick, Matthew Marland, Sam
Coates, Laurence Laluyaux, Stephen Edwards, and Katharina Volck-
mer at RCW.

Conversations with my friends Naomi Klein and V, formerly
known as Eve Ensler, really transformed this book and I owe them
a lot, for this, and for so much more. My friend Lizzie Davidson
helped me to track down lots of the people I talked with, using her
sinister NSA-like powers of detection.

In Provincetown, I am really grateful to Andrew Sullivan, James
Barraford, Dave Grossman, Stefan Piscitelli, Denise Gaylord, Chris
Bodenner, Doug Belford, Pat Schultz, Jeff Peters, and everyone at
Café Heaven. If you want to learn yoga from Stefan, go to outer
mostyoga.com.

On my travels, I was helped by so many people—Jake Hess
in Washington, D.C.; Anthony Bansie, Jeremy Heimans, Kasia
Malinowska, and Sarah Evans in New York; Colleen Haikes and
Christopher Rogers in San Francisco; Elizabeth Flood and Mario
Burrell in L.A.; Stephen Hollis in Ohio; Jim Cates in Indiana; Sam
Loetscher and John Holder in Miami; Hermione Davis (the queen of
publicists) and Andy Leonard in Australia; Alex Romain, Ben Birks
Ang, and everyone at the NZ Drug Foundation in New Zealand;
Sarah Kay, Adam Biles, Katy Lee, and everyone at Shakespeare and
Company in Paris; Rosanne Kropman in the Netherlands; Christian
Lerch, Kate McNaughton, and Jacinda Nandi in Berlin; Halldor
Arnason and everyone at Snarotin in Iceland; Sturla Haugsgyerd and
Oda Bergli in Norway; Kim Norager in Denmark; Rebekah Lehrer,
Ricardo Teperman, Julita Lemgruber, and Stefano Nunes in Brazil;
Alnoor Lahda in Costa Rica; and Joe Daniels and Beatriz Vejarano
in Colombia.

Thank you to James Brown for explaining magic to me. If you
want to hire him in the U.K. go to www.powa.academy. Thank you
to Ayesha Lyn-Birkets at YouGov, and to everyone at the Council
for Evidence-Based Psychiatry, particularly Dr. James Davies. Thank
you to Kate Quarry for her copyediting.

My transcriptions were all done by the team at CLK Transcription. Thank you to CarolLee Streeter Kidd and everyone there. If you need good transcripts, contact them at CLKtranscripts@gmail.com.

And thank you to the people who discussed this topic with me for years: Decca Aitkenhead, Stephen Grosz, Dorothy Byrne, Alex Higgins, Lucy Johnstone, Jess Luxembourg, Ronan McCrea, Patrick Strudwick, Jacquie Grice, Jay Johnson, Barbara Bateman, Jemima Khan, Tom Costello, Rob Blackhurst, Amy Pollard, Harry Woodlock, Andrew Gow, Josepha Jacobson, Natalie Carpenter, Deborah Friedell, Imtiaz Shams, Bruno Giussani, Felicity McMahon, Patricia Clark, Ammie al-Whatey, Jake and Joe Wilkinson, Max Jeffrey, Peter Marshall, Anna Powell-Smith, Ben Stewart, Joss Garman, Joe Ferris, Tim Dixon, Ben Ramm, Harry Quilter-Pinner, Jamie Janson, and Elisa Hari.

The reference to W. H. Auden at the end of this book is thanks to David Kinder, my brilliant former English teacher, who taught me to love his poetry. Thank you also to two other brilliant English teachers I had: Sue Roach and Sidney McMinn.

I am really grateful to all my Patreon supporters, particularly Pam Roy, Robert King, Martin Mander, Lewis Black, Lynn McFarland, Deandra Christianson, Fiona Houslip, Pam Roy, Roby Abeles, Rachel Bomgaar, Roger Cox, and Susie Robinson. To find out more about my Patreon—and get regular updates on what I'm working on next—go to patreon.com/johannhari.

Any errors in this book are entirely mine. If you spot anything that you think might be wrong, please do reach out to me so I can correct it on the website and in future editions of the book at chasingthescream@gmail.com. To see any corrections I've already issued, go to stolenfocusbook.com/corrections.

Groups Already Fighting to Improve Attention

The fight to heal and restore our attention has already begun. This is a list of groups you can join today that have started the work. It's an early and provisional index—I believe more groups will be formed as we become more informed about the attention crisis. If there isn't a group doing what you believe needs to be done, set it up and email me at chasingthescream@gmail.com, and I'll add it to the book's website and to future editions of this book.

ON FIGHTING TO CHANGE HOW THE INTERNET WORKS

Center for Humane Technology: humanetech.com
The Avaaz campaign to detoxify the algorithms: secure.avaaz.org/campaign/en/detox_the_algorithm_loc
Stop Hate for Profit: stophateforprofit.org/backup-week-of-action-toolkit

ON FIGHTING FOR A FOUR-DAY WEEK

Andrew Barnes and Charlotte Lockhart have co-founded this
    group: 4dayweek.com

In Europe, the New Economics Foundation is fighting for this:
    neweconomics.org/campaigns/euro-working-time

Four Day Week Ireland: fourdayweek.ie

ON CHILDREN BEING ALLOWED TO PLAY

Let Grow: letgrow.org

Let Our Kids Be Kids: letthekidsbekids.wordpress.com

The Daily Mile: thedailymile.co.uk

The Less Testing, More Learning Campaign:
    citizensforpublicschools.org/less-testing-more-learning-ma
    -campaign/sign-the-less-testing-more-learning-petition-today

More Than a Score (opposing overtesting in the
    U.K.): morethanascore.org.uk; www.facebook.com/
    parentssupportteachers

Keeping Early Years Unique: keyu.co.uk

Upstart Scotland: upstart.scot

ON PROTECTING KIDS FROM GETTING HOOKED ON TECH WHEN THEY ARE YOUNG

Turning Life On: turninglifeon.org

ON CHANGING OUR FOOD SUPPLY

Alliance for a Healthier Generation: healthiergeneration.org

Healthy Food America: healthyfoodamerica.org

Healthy Schools Campaign: healthyschoolscampaign.org/issues/
    school-food

Better Food Britain, and the Children's Food Campaign:
    sustainweb.org/projectsandcampaigns; sustainweb.org/
    childrensfoodcampaign

School Food Matters: schoolfoodmatters.org/campaigns

Henry: henry.org.uk

ON RESISTING POLLUTANTS THAT CAN DAMAGE ATTENTION

Little Things Matter: littlethingsmatter.ca

Client Earth: clientearth.org

BreatheLife Campaign: ccacoalition.org/en/activity/breathelife
   -campaign; breathelife2030.org

Healthy Air Campaign: healthyair.org.uk

Endocrine Society (ES): endocrine.org

European Society of Endocrinology (ESE): ese-hormones.org

Health and Environmental Alliance (HEAL): env-health.org

ON A UNIVERSAL BASIC INCOME

Citizen's Basic Income Trust: citizensincome.org

Basic Income: basicincome.org.uk

∽

If you'd like to be very occasionally kept up to date on developments
in the movement to reclaim our attention by me, you can sign up to
my mailing list: www.stolenfocusbook.com/mailinglist

Notes

Please note these are partial endnotes. There's more references, background, and extra explanatory material—as well as audio of the quotes in the book—at www.stolenfocusbook.com/endnotes.

INTRODUCTION: WALKING IN MEMPHIS

10   **For example, a small study investigated how often an average American college student** L. Yeykelis, J. J. Cummings, and B. Reeves, "Multitasking on a Single Device: Arousal and the Frequency, Anticipation, and Prediction of Switching Between Media Content on a Computer," *Journal of Communications* 64 (2014): 167–92, doi:10:1111/jcom.12070, cited in J. Twenge, *iGen: Why Today's Super-Connected Kids Are Growing Up Less Rebellious, More Tolerant, Less Happy—and Completely Unprepared for Adulthood—and What That Means for the Rest of Us* (New York: Atria Books, 2017), 64. See also Adam Gazzaley and Larry D. Rosen, *The Distracted Mind: Ancient Brains in a High-Tech World* (Cambridge, Mass.: MIT Press, 2017), 165–67.

10   **A different study by Gloria Mark, professor of informatics at the University of California, Irvine** V. M. González and G. Mark, "Constant, Constant, Multi-tasking Craziness: Managing Multiple Working Spheres," in *CHI '04: Proceedings of the SIGCHI Conference on Human Factors in Computing Systems, April 2004* (New York: Association for Computing Machinery, 2004), 113–20.

Professor Mark described this in this interview with *Business Journal,* and elucidated further in my subsequent interview with her years later: "Too Many Interruptions at Work?," *Business Journal,* June 8, 2006, https://news.gallup.com/businessjournal/23146/too-many-interruptions-work.aspx. See also C. Marci, "A (Biometric) Day in the Life: Engaging Across Media," paper presented at Re:Think 2012, New York, March 28, 2012.

For a study with similar (not identical) results, see: L. D. Rosen et al., "Facebook and Texting Made Me Do It: Media-Induced Task-Switching While Studying," *Computers in Human Behavior* 29, no. 3 (2013): 948–58.

13   **A study by Professor Michael Posner at the University of Oregon** G. Mark et al., "Focused, Aroused, but So Distractible," in *CSCW '15: Proceedings of the 18th ACM Conference on Computer Supported Cooperative Work and Social Computing* (2015): 903–16, doi:10:1145/2675133:2675221; and J. Williams, *Stand out of Our Light* (Cambridge, U.K.: Cambridge University Press, 2018), 51.

See also L. Dabbish, G. Mark, and V. González, "Why Do I Keep Interrupting Myself? Environment, Habit and Self-Interruption," in *Proceedings of ACM CHI 2011 Annual Conference on Human Factors in Computing Systems* (New York: Association for Computing Machinery, 2011), 3127–30; and K. Pattison, "Worker, Interrupted: The Cost of Task-Switching," *Fast Company,* July 28, 2008, https://www.fastcompany.com/944128/worker-interrupted-cost-task-switching.

13   **A different study of office workers in the U.S.** J. MacKay, "The Myth of Multitasking: The Ultimate Guide to Getting More Done by Doing Less," *RescueTime* (blog), January 17, 2019, https://blog.rescuetime.com/multitasking/#at-work; and J. MacKay, "Communication Overload: Our Research Shows Most Workers Can't Go 6 Minutes Without Checking Email or

IM," *RescueTime* (blog), July 11, 2018, https://blog.rescuetime
.com/communication-multitasking-switches/.

15 **"nothing can be changed until it is faced"** D. Charles
William, *Forever a Father, Always a Son* (New York: Victor Books,
1991), 112.

CHAPTER ONE: CAUSE ONE

20 **For the average American, it's three hours and fifteen
minutes** J. MacKay, "Screen Time Stats 2019: Here's How
Much You Use Your Phone During the Work Day," *RescueTime*
(blog), March 21, 2019, https://blog.rescuetime.com/screen-time
-stats-2018/.

20 **We touch our phones 2,617 times every twenty-four hours**
J. Naftulin, "Here's How Many Times We Touch Our Phones
Every Day," *Insider,* July 13, 2016, https://www.businessinsider
.com/dscout-research-people-touch-cell-phones-2617-times-a-day
-2016-7?r=US&IR=T.

21 **something the Spanish writer José Ortega y Gasset said**
Original: *"La vida no puede esperar a que las ciencias expliquen
científicamente el Universo. No se puede vivir ad kalendas graecas.
El atributo más esencial de la existencia es su perentoriedad: la
vida es siempre urgente. Se vive aquí y ahora sin posible demora ni
traspaso. La vida nos es disparada a quemarropa. Ya la cultura, que
no es sino su interpretación, no puede tampoco esperar."* J. Ortega
y Gasset, *Mission of the University* (1930), trans. H. L. Nostrand
(Princeton: Princeton University Press, 1944), 73.

22 **It turned out pre-commitment was strikingly successful**
Molly J. Crockett et al., "Restricting Temptations: Neural
Mechanisms of Precommitment," *Neuron* 79, no. 2 (2013):
391, doi:10:1016/j.neuron.2013:05.028. For a good summary of
the issue and current thinking, see Z. Kurth-Nelson and A. D.
Redish, "Don't Let Me Do That!—Models of Precommitment,"
Frontiers in Neuroscience 6 (2012): 138.

22 **scientists have shown the same effect in a broad range
of experiments** T. Dubowitz et al., "Using a Grocery List
Is Associated with a Healthier Diet and Lower BMI Among
Very High-Risk Adults," *Journal of Nutrition Education and
Behavior* 47, no. 3 (2015): 259–64; J. Schwartz et al., "Healthier
by Precommitment," *Psychological Science* 25, no. 2 (2015):

538–46, doi:10:1177/0956797613510950; and R. Ladouceur, A. Blaszczynski, and D. R. Lalande, "Pre-Commitment in Gambling: A Review of the Empirical Evidence," *International Gambling Studies* 12, no. 2 (2012): 215–30.

30 **the largest scientific study yet conducted to answer a key question** P. Lorenz-Spreen et al., "Accelerating Dynamics of Collective Attention," *Nature Communications* 10, no. 1 (2019), doi:10:1038/s41467-019-09311-w.

32 **The raw figures on this have been analyzed** M. Hilbert and P. López, "The World's Technological Capacity to Store, Communicate and Compute Information," *Science* 332, no. 6025 (2011): 60–65.

34 **They found that you can—but it always comes at a cost** M. E. J. Masson, "Cognitive Processes in Skimming Stories," *Journal of Experimental Psychology: Learning, Memory, and Cognition* 8, no. 5 (1982): 400–17; M. L. Slowiaczek and C. Clifton, "Subvocalization and Reading for Meaning," *Journal of Verbal Learning and Verbal Behavior* 19, no. 5 (1980): 573–82; T. Calef, M. Pieper, and B. Coffey, "Comparisons of Eye Movements Before and After a Speed-Reading Course," *Journal of the American Optometric Association* 70, no. 3 (1999): 171–81; M. Just, M. Masson, and P. Carpenter, "The Differences Between Speed Reading and Skimming," *Bulletin of the Psychonomic Society* 16 (1980): 171; and M. C. Dyson and M. Haselgrove, "The Effects of Reading Speed and Reading Patterns on the Understanding of Text Read from Screen," *Journal of Research in Reading* 23, no. 2 (2000): 210–23.

35 **Scientists then studied professional speed-readers** K. Rayner et al., "So Much to Read, So Little Time: How Do We Read, and Can Speed Reading Help?," *Psychological Science in the Public Interest* 17, no. 1 (2016): 4–34.

35 **The scientists investigating this also discovered that if you make people read quickly** S. C. Wilkinson, W. Reader, and S. J. Payne, "Adaptive Browsing: Sensitivity to Time Pressure and Task Difficulty," *International Journal of Human-Computer Studies* 70, no. 1 (2012): 14–25; and G. B. Duggan and S. J. Payne, "Text Skimming: The Process and Effectiveness of Foraging Through Text Under Time Pressure," *Journal of Experimental Psychology: Applied* 15, no. 3 (2009): 228–42.

35   **people talk significantly faster now than they did in the
      1950s** Ulf Torgersen: "Taletempo," *Nytt norsk tidsskrift* 16
      (1999): 3–5, cited in T. H. Eriksen, *Tyranny of the Moment*
      (London: Pluto Press, 2001), 71. See also M. Toft, "Med eit
      muntert blikk på styre og stell," *Uni Forum,* June 29, 2005,
      https://www.uniforum.uio.no/nyheter/2005/06/med-eit-muntert
      -blikk-paa-styre-og-stell.html; and the interesting discussion in
      M. Liberman, "Norwegian Speed: Fact or Factoid?," *Language
      Log* (blog), September 13, 2010, https://languagelog.ldc.upenn
      .edu/nll/?p=2628.

35   **people have started to walk 10 percent faster in cities**
      R. Levine, *A Geography of Time* (New York: Basic Books, 1997),
      cited in R. Colville, *The Great Acceleration: How the World Is
      Getting Faster, Faster* (London: Bloomsbury, 2016), 2–3; and
      Richard Wiseman, *Pace of Life,* www.richardwiseman.com/
      quirkology/pace_home.htm.

35   **"Anything worth doing is worth doing faster"** Colville, *Great
      Acceleration*, 11.

35   **"If you're not fast, you're fucked"** Ibid., 20.

36   **He has analyzed what happens to a person's focus if
      they engage in deliberately slow practices** G. Claxton,
      Intelligence in the Flesh (New Haven, Conn.: Yale University
      Press, 2016), 260–61; P. Wayne et al., "Effects of Tai Chi on
      Cognitive Performance in Older Adults: Systematic Review and
      Meta-Analysis," *Journal of the American Geriatric Society* 62, no. 1
      (2014): 25–39; N. Gothe et al., "The Effect of Acute Yoga on
      Executive Function," *Journal of Physical Activity and Health* 10,
      no. 4 (2013): 488–95; P. Lovatt, "Dance Psychology," *Psychology
      Review* 19, no. 1 (2013): 18–21; and C. Lewis and P. Lovatt,
      "Breaking Away from Set Patterns of Thinking: Improvisation and
      Divergent Thinking," *Thinking Skills and Creativity* 9 (2013):
      46–58.

37   **when I went to interview Professor Earl Miller** A good
      primer on his positions on this is E. Miller, "Multitasking: Why
      Your Brain Can't Do It and What You Should Do About It"
      (seminar recording and presentation slides), *Radius,* April 11,
      2017, https://radius.mit.edu/programs/multitasking-why-your
      -brain-cant-do-it-and-what-you-should-do-about-it.

38   **The first is called the "switch cost effect"** Switch costs

are very firmly established in the academic literature. Here is a typical example: R. D. Rogers and S. Monsell, "The Cost of a Predictable Switch Between Simple Cognitive Tasks," *Journal of Experimental Psychology: General* 124, no. 2 (1995): 207–31. This is also a good summary: "Multitasking: Switching Costs," American Psychological Association, March 20, 2006, https://www.apa.org/research/action/multitask.

39 **To give you a sense of how big that is** J. Williams, *Stand out of Our Light* (Cambridge, U.K.: Cambridge University Press, 2018), 69. The study by Dr. Glenn Wilson was not published because it was commissioned by a private company. You can read Dr. Wilson discussing the study at this link, if you select the section marked "Infomania": http://drglennwilson.com/links.html. See also P. Hemp, "Death by Information Overload," *Harvard Business Review,* September 2009, https://hbr.org/2009/09/death-by-information-overload. Dr. Wilson has been uncomfortable with how some journalists have written about this study, and I have tried to absorb his criticisms in the text here. He says that the comparison with cannabis is only true in the short term—in the longer term, cannabis may harm your IQ more. I have worded the sentence here to reflect this fact.

40 **It turned out that afterward they couldn't remember** E. Hoffman, *Time* (London: Profile Books, 2010), 80–81; and W. Kirn, "The Autumn of the Multitaskers," *Atlantic,* November 2017.

40 **Professor Gloria Mark, at the Department of Informatics at the University of California, Irvine** V. M. González and G. Mark, "Constant, Constant, Multi-tasking Craziness: Managing Multiple Working Spheres," in *CHI '04: Proceedings of the SIGCHI Conference on Human Factors in Computing Systems* (New York: Association for Computing Machinery, 2004), 113–20. See also L. Dabbish, G. Mark, and V. González, "Why Do I Keep Interrupting Myself? Environment, Habit and Self-Interruption," in *Proceedings of the 2011 Annual Conference in Human Factors in Computing Systems* (New York: Association for Computing Machinery, 2011), 3127–30; T. Klingberg, *The Overflowing Brain* (Oxford, U.K.: Oxford University Press, 2009), 4; and Colville, *Great Acceleration*, 47.

40 **Several other studies have shown a large chunk of**

Americans T. Harris, "Pardon the Interruptions," *Your Undivided Attention* (podcast), August 14, 2019, https://www.humanetech .com/podcast; and C. Thompson, "Meet the Life Hackers," *New York Times Magazine,* October 16, 2005.

41   **most office workers *never* get an hour to themselves without being interrupted** J. MacKay, "The Myth of Multi-tasking: The Ultimate Guide to Getting More Done by Doing Less," *RescueTime* (blog), January 17, 2019, https:// blog.rescuetime.com/multitasking/#at-work; and J. MacKay, "Communication Overload: Our Research Shows Most Workers Can't Go 6 Minutes Without Checking Email or IM," *RescueTime* (blog), July 11, 2018, https://blog.rescuetime.com/ communication-multitasking-switches/.

41   **the average CEO of a Fortune 500 company** Colville, *Great Acceleration,* 47.

41   **The students who received messages performed, on average, 20 percent worse** B. Sullivan, "Students Can't Resist Distraction for Two Minutes . . . and Neither Can You," NBC News, May 18, 2013, https://www.nbcnews.com/technolog/ students-cant-resist-distraction-two-minutes-neither-can-you -1C9984270. This study was not published.

41   **Other studies in similar scenarios have found even worse outcomes** Adam Gazzaley and Larry D. Rosen, *The Distracted Mind: Ancient Brains in a High-Tech World* (Cambridge, Mass.: MIT Press, 2017), 127.

41   **It turned out their level of impairment was "very similar"** D. L. Strayer, "Is the Technology in Your Car Driving You to Distraction?," *Policy Insights from the Behavioral and Brain Sciences* 2, no. 1 (2015): 157–65. The phrase "very similar" was used by him here: K. Ferebee, "Drivers on Cell Phones Are as Bad as Drunks," *UNews Archive* (University of Utah), March 25, 2011, https://archive.unews.utah.edu/news_releases/ drivers-on-cell-phones-are-as-bad-as-drunks/.

42   **around one in five car accidents** S. P. McEvoy, M. R. Stevenson, and M. Woodward, "The Impact of Driver Distraction on Road Safety: Results from a Representative Survey in Two Australian States," *Injury Prevention* 12, no. 4 (2006): 242–47.

42   **genuinely believes they can follow six or seven forms of media at once** Gazzaley and Rosen, *Distracted Mind,* 11;

and L. M. Carrier et al., "Multitasking Across Generations: Multitasking Choices and Difficulty Ratings in Three Generations of Americans," *Computers in Human Behavior* 25, no. 2 (2009): 483–89.

44   **For example, children in noisy classrooms** A. Kahkashan and V. Shivakumar, "Effects of Traffic Noise Around Schools on Attention and Memory in Primary School Children," *International Journal of Clinical and Experimental Physiology* 2, no. 3 (2015): 176–79.

CHAPTER TWO: CAUSE TWO

51   **"By the time I was ten years old"** K. S. Beard, "Theoretically Speaking: An Interview with Mihaly Csikszentmihalyi on Flow Theory Development and Its Usefulness in Addressing Contemporary Challenges in Education," *Educational Psychology Review* 27 (2015): 353–64.

52   **Take a pigeon. Put it in a cage** See B. F. Skinner, "'Superstition' in the Pigeon," *Journal of Experimental Psychology* 38, no. 2 (1948): 168–72.

54   **"When they finished"** Beard, "Theoretically Speaking," 353–64.

54   **something about "the process of painting itself"** R. Kegan, *The Evolving Self: Problem and Process in Human Development* (Cambridge, Mass.: Harvard University Press, 1983), xii.

54   **"I was carried on by the flow"** M. Csikszentmihalyi, *Flow: The Psychology of Optimal Experience* (New York: Harper, 2008), 40.

54   **"The mystique of rock-climbing is climbing"** Ibid., 54.

57   **They have also shown that the more flow you experience, the better you feel** Ibid., 158–59.

59   **He wrote: "Many forces, both within ourselves and in the environment, stand in the way" of flow** Ibid., 7. See also Brigid Schulte, *Overwhelmed: Work, Love and Play When No One Has the Time* (London: Bloomsbury Press, 2014), 66–67.

59   **In the late 1980s, he discovered that staring at a screen** R. Kubey and M. Csikszentmihalyi, *Television and the Quality of Life: How Viewing Shapes Everyday Experience* (Abingdon-on-Thames, U.K.: Routledge, 1990).

59   **He warned that "surrounded by an astonishing panoply of recreational gadgets"** Csikszentmihalyi, *Flow*, 83.

59   **"To have a good life, it is not enough to remove what
        is wrong with it"** M. Csikszenmihalyi, *Creativity: Flow and
        the Psychology of Discovery and Invention* (New York: Harper
        Perennial, 2013), 11.

CHAPTER THREE: CAUSE THREE

66   **Over the past century, the average child has lost eighty-
        five minutes of sleep every night** L. Matricciani, T. Olds, and
        J. Petkov, "In Search of Lost Sleep: Secular Trends in the Sleep
        Time of School-Aged Children and Adolescents," *Sleep Medicine
        Reviews* 16, no. 3 (2012): 203–11.

68   **She discovered that on average, a typical student has
        the same sleep quality** H. G. Lund et al., "Sleep Patterns and
        Predictors of Disturbed Sleep in a Large Population of College
        Students," *Journal of Adolescent Health* 46, no. 2 (2010): 124–32.

69   **"'Raise your blood pressure'"** J. E. Gangwisch, "A Review
        of Evidence for the Link Between Sleep Duration and
        Hypertension," *American Journal of Hypertension* 27, no. 10
        (2014): 1235–42.

69   **"'I'm going to make you want more fast food'"** E. C. Hanlon
        and E. Van Cauter, "Quantification of Sleep Behavior and of
        Its Impact on the Cross-Talk Between the Brain and Peripheral
        Metabolism," *Proceedings of the National Academy of Sciences*
        108, suppl. 3 (2011): 15609–16; and M. Walker, *Why We Sleep*
        (London: Penguin, 2018), 3.

69   **it's why narcoleptic people, who sleep a lot, are
        significantly more creative** J. Hamzelou, "People with
        Narcolepsy May Be More Creative Because of How They Sleep,"
        New Scientist, June 18, 2019.

69   **your mind will start to transfer the things you have
        learned during the day into your long-term memory** Sleep
        doubles your chances of remembering previously unremembered
        material. See the University of Essex study, N. Dumay, "Sleep
        Not Just Protects Memories Against Forgetting, It Also Makes
        Them More Accessible," *Cortex* 74 (2016): 289–96.

70   **you can get rats to learn a maze, and that night, you
        can monitor what happens in their brains as they sleep**
        The landmark study is K. Louie and M. A. Wilson, "Temporally

Structured Replay of Awake Hippocampal Ensemble Activity During Rapid Eye Movement Sleep," *Neuron* 29, no. 1 (2001): 145–56.

70   **If you deprive kids of sleep, they begin to show attention problems rapidly** A. Hvolby. "Associations of Sleep Disturbance with ADHD: Implications for Treatment," *Attention Deficit and Hyperactivity Disorders* 7, no. 1 (2015): 1–18; E. J. Paavonen et al., "Short Sleep Duration and Behavioral Symptoms of Attention-Deficit/Hyperactivity Disorder in Healthy 7- to 8-Year-Old Children," *Pediatrics* 123, no. 5 (2009): e857–64; A. Pesonen et al., "Sleep Duration and Regularity Are Associated with Behavioral Problems in 8-Year-Old Children," *International Journal of Behavioral Medicine* 17, no. 4 (2010): 298–305; and R. Gruber et al., "Short Sleep Duration Is Associated with Teacher-Reported Inattention and Cognitive Problems in Healthy School-Aged Children," *Nature and Science of Sleep* 4 (2012): 33–40.

72   **Dr. Maiken Nedergaard, at the University of Rochester, told one interviewer** A. Huffington, *The Sleep Revolution: Transforming Your Life, One Night at a Time* (New York: Harmony, 2016), 103–4.

74   **you're more likely to get into a car accident, for example** K. Janto, J. R. Prichard, and S. Pusalavidyasagar, "An Update on Dual Orexin Receptor Antagonists and Their Potential Role in Insomnia Therapeutics," *Journal of Clinical Sleep Medicine* 14, no. 8 (2018): 1399–408.

75   **Charles believes that—as he said to another interviewer** S. R. D. Morales, "Dreaming with the Zeitgeber, Part I: A Lecture on Moderns and Their Night," *Peninsula* 2, no. 1 (2012), https://journals.uvic.ca/index.php/peninsula/article/view/11518/3217.

76   **We are now exposed to ten times the amount of artificial light** T. Farragher, "Sleep, the Final Frontier. This Guy Studies It. Here's What He Has to Say," *Boston Globe*, August 18, 2018.

CHAPTER FOUR: CAUSE FOUR

80   **men reading for pleasure had fallen by 40 percent, while for women, it was down by 29 percent** C. Ingraham, "Leisure Reading in the U.S. Is at an All-Time Low," *Washington Post,* June 29, 2018.

80   **the proportion of Americans who never read a book in any given year tripled between 1978 and 2014**. D. W. Moore, "About Half of Amerians Reading a Book," Gallup News Service, June 3, 2005, https://news.gallup.com/poll/16582/about-half -americans-reading-book.aspx.

80   **This has escalated to the point that by 2017, the average American spent seventeen minutes a day reading books** C. Ingraham, "The Long, Steady Decline of Literary Reading," *Washington Post,* September 7, 2016. Pew found it was slightly higher: A. Perrin, "Who Doesn't Read Books in America?," Pew Research Center, September 26, 2019, https://www.pewresearch .org/fact-tank/2019/09/26/who-doesnt-read-books-in-america/.

80   **5.4 hours on their phone** E. Brown, "Americans Spend Far More Time on Their Smartphones Than They Think," *ZDNet,* April 28, 2019, https://www.zdnet.com/article/americans-spend -far-more-time-on-their-smartphones-than-they-think/.

80   **less than half of Americans read literature for pleasure** National Endowment for the Arts, *Reading at Risk: A Survey of Literary Reading in America* (2002), https://www.arts.gov/sites/ default/files/RaRExec_0.pdf.

80   **similar trends in Britain and other countries** A. Flood, "Literary Fiction in Crisis as Sales Drop Dramatically, Arts Council England Reports," *Guardian,* December 15, 2017, https://www.theguardian.com/books/2017/dec/15/literary-fiction -in-crisis-as-sale-drop-dramatically-arts-council-england-reports.

80   **In one single year—2011** W. Self, "The Printed Word in Peril," *Harper's,* October 2018.

82   **Anne has conducted studies that split people into two groups** A. Mangen, G. Olivier, and J. Velay, "Comparing Comprehension of a Long Text Read in Print Book and on Kindle: Where in the Text and When in the Story?," *Frontiers in Psychology* 10 (2019): 38.

82   **There's broad scientific evidence for this now, emerging from fifty-four studies** P. Delgado et al., "Don't Throw Away Your Printed Books: A Meta-Analysis on the Effects of Reading Media on Reading Comprehension," *Educational Research and Reviews* 25 (2018): 23–38.

82   **in elementary-school children, it's the equivalent of two-thirds of a year's growth in reading comprehension** Ibid.

83   **one that was also mulled, in a different way, by Nicholas**
        Carr in his book N. Carr, *The Shallows: How the Internet Is*
        Changing the Way We Think, Read and Remember (London:
        Atlantic Books, 2010), 6.

83   **"the medium is the message"** Gerald Emanuel Stern, ed.,
        McLuhan: Hot & Cool (New York: Dial Press, 1967), 20, 23, 65,
        212–13, 215.

89   **one of his studies found that the more a child is read**
        storybooks R. A. Mar et al., "Exposure to Media and Theory-of-
        Mind Development in Preschoolers," *Cognitive Development* 25,
        no. 1 (2010): 69–78.

89   **One of his studies showed that children are more**
        empathetic if they read storybooks or watch movies, but
        not if they watch shorter shows Ibid.

CHAPTER FIVE: CAUSE FIVE

91   **"everyone knows what attention is"** W. James, *The Principles*
        of Psychology (1890), chap. 11, available at https://psychclassics
        .yorku.ca/James/Principles/prin11.htm.

94   **a teenage boy named Marcus Raichle** M. E. Raichle et al.,
        "A Default Mode of Brain Function," *Proceedings of the National*
        Academy of Sciences 98, no. 2 (2001): 676–82. I first learned
        about his work in Leonard Mlodinow's excellent book *Elastic:*
        Flexible Thinking in a Constantly Changing World (London:
        Penguin, 2018), 110–21. See also G. Watson, *Attention: Beyond*
        Mindfulness (London: Reaktion Books, 2017), 90.

95   **This isn't a flaw in your reading. This *is* reading**
        J. Smallwood, D. Fishman, and J. Schooler, "Counting the
        Cost of an Absent Mind," *Psychonomic Bulletin and Review* 14
        (2007): 230–36. I first learned about this from W. Galagher, *Rapt:*
        Attention and the Focused Life (London: Penguin, 2009), 149.

96   **Some mind-wandering is essential for things to make**
        sense Y. Citton, *The Ecology of Attention* (Cambridge, Mass.:
        Polity, 2016), 116–17.

96   **the better you are at having organized personal goals**
        B. Medea et al., "How Do We Decide What to Do? Resting-
        State Connectivity Patterns and Components of Self-Generated
        Thought Linked to the Development of More Concrete

Personal Goals," *Experimental Brain Research* 236 (2018): 2469–81.

96   **being creative** B. Baird et al., "Inspired by Distraction: Mind Wandering Facilitates Creative Incubation," *Psychological Science* 23, no. 10 (2012): 1117–22.

96   **making patient, long-term decisions** J. Smallwood, F. J. M. Ruby, and T. Singer, "Letting Go of the Present: Mind-Wandering Is Associated with Reduced Delay Discounting," *Consciousness and Cognition* 22, no. 1 (2013): 1–7. Jonathan added via email: "It might also be important to note that many of these features may be most obvious in people who can control when they mind wander (i.e., who can avoid doing it when the external world demands their attention)."

100   **"A wandering mind is an unhappy mind"** M. Killingsworth and D. Gilbert, "A Wandering Mind Is an Unhappy Mind," *Science,* November 12, 2010. See also Watson, *Attention*, 15, 70.

CHAPTER SIX: CAUSE SIX (PART ONE)

106   **"It's really about the limits of attention"** T. Ferriss, "The Tim Ferriss Show Transcripts—Fighting Skynet and Firewalling Attention," *Tim.Blog* (blog), September 24, 2019, https://tim .blog/2019/09/24/the-tim-ferriss-show-transcripts-tristan-harris -fighting-skynet-and-firewalling-attention-387/.

107   **"It's about something more subtle," he said later** Ibid.

109   **"be more persistent than human beings, offer greater anonymity"** B. J. Fogg, *Persuasive Technology: Using Computers to Change What We Think and Do* (San Francisco: Morgan Kaufmann, 2002), 7–8.

109   **He had previously worked on a course dedicated to "the psychology of mind control"** In 1996, B. J. Fogg was a teaching assistant in Professor Philip Zimbardo's popular course on the psychology of mind control that primarily focused on how to personally protect yourself from mind control.

109   **In the fall of 2006, B.J. testified before the Federal Trade Commission (FTC), warning that there was a "potential dark side" looming, where it will be hard for you to tell "when you are being persuaded and when you are not"** You can watch Professor Fogg's important testimony about the

dangers of what he saw as persuasion profiling and sounding the alarm bells here: https://vimeo.com/117427520. And you can read it here: https://www.ftc.gov/sites/default/files/documents/public_events/protecting-consumers-next-tech-ade/transcript_061107.pdf. (Both as accessed May 20, 2022.)

110 **As part of the class, he was paired with a young man named Mike Krieger** There was a third partner on this class project in addition to Mike Krieger and Tristan Harris.

110 **If you want to shape the user's behavior, make sure he gets hearts and likes right away** Professor Fogg, commenting on what he considers to be the key to Instagram's early success, writes: "My opinion: The key to Instagram's early success came from two things: (1) Super easy to use. (2) Filters (Oh, I'm an artist!). I don't believe hearts and likes were the key at the early stages."

110 **"the millionaire maker"** I. Leslie, "The Scientists Who Make Apps Addictive," *1843 Magazine,* October 20, 2016, https://www.1843magazine.com/features/the-scientists-who-make-apps-addictive.

110 **He had learned at Stanford and elsewhere how to use technology to change people's behavior** Tristan was learning insights B.J. had gathered in his lab at Stanford, but was never a researcher in or learning in the Persuasive Technology Lab itself.

111 **"What if in the future you had a profile of every single person on earth?"** Ferriss, "Show Transcripts—Fighting Skynet and Firewalling Attention."

112 **"I want you to imagine walking into a room. A control room, with a bunch of people, a hundred people"** T. Harris, "How a Handful of Tech Companies Control Billions of Minds Every Day" (TED talk), *TED2017,* https://www.ted.com/talks/tristan_harris_how_a_handful_of_tech_companies_control_billions_of_minds_every_day?language=en.

113 **"Why don't we make it buzz your phone every time we get an email?"** C. Newton, "Google's New Focus on Well-Being Started Five Years Ago with This Presentation," *Verge,* May 10, 2018, https://www.theverge.com/2018/5/10/17333574/google-android-p-update-tristan-harris-design-ethics.

114 **"How can we make this more engaging?"** A. Marantz, "Silicon Valley's Crisis of Conscience," *New Yorker,* August 19, 2019.

115   **"on a treadmill of continuous checking"** You can read the full
       presentation at minimizedistraction.com.

118   **"This is hard, it's confusing, and it's often at odds with
       our bottom line"** N. Thompson, "Tristan Harris: Tech Is
       Downgrading Humans," *Wired,* April 23, 2019; and N. Hiltzik,
       "Ex-Google Manager Leads a Drive to Rein in Pernicious Impact
       of Social Media," *Los Angeles Times,* May 10, 2019.

119   **"You don't even really get to make that ethical decision"** to
       improve people's attention spans Ferriss, "Show Transcripts—
       Fighting Skynet and Firewalling Attention."

119   **"I failed because companies don't [currently] have the
       right incentive to change"** T. Harris, testimony to the Senate
       Commerce Committee, June 25, 2019, https://www.commerce
       .senate.gov/services/files/96E3A739-DC8D-45F1-87D7
       -EC70A368371D.

119   **"I felt completely hopeless"** P. Marsden, "Humane: A New
       Agenda for Tech," *Digital Wellbeing,* April 25, 2019, https://
       digitalwellbeing.org/humane-a-new-agenda-for-tech-speed
       -summary-and-video/.

119   **"It's about making us extra-human"** This is as recalled by Aza
       in his interview with me.

120   **At a conservative estimate, infinite scroll makes you
       spend 50 percent more of your time** There's a debate about
       the precise numbers for this, because it's inherently hard to
       measure. One way of measuring it is what's called the "bounce
       rate" (the number of people who arrive on a site and immediately
       leave without going to any other page on the website). For
       example, *Time*'s bounce rate apparently dropped by 15 percent
       when it introduced infinite scroll in 2014; *Quartz* readers view
       about 50 percent more stories than they would without infinite
       scroll. Both of these figures come from S. Kirkland, "Time
       .com's Bounce Rate Down 15 Percentage Points Since Adopting
       Continuous Scroll," *Poynter,* July 20, 2014, https://web.archive
       .org/web/20150207201902/http://www.poynter.org:80/news/
       mediawire/257466/time-coms-bounce-rate-down-15-percentage
       -points-since-adopting-continuous-scroll/.

123   **"God only knows what it's doing to our children's brains"**
       T. Ong, "Sean Parker on Facebook," *Verge,* November 9, 2017,
       https://www.theverge.com/2017/11/9/16627724/sean-parker

-facebook-childrens-brains-feedback-loop. For more such quotes from tech figures, see A. Alter, *Irresistible: The Rise of Addictive Technology and the Business of Keeping Us Hooked* (London: Penguin, 2017), 1.

123   **"aren't allowed to use that shit"** Roger McNamee, *Zucked: Waking Up to the Facebook Catastrophe* (New York: Penguin Press, 2019), 146–47; and R. Seymour, *The Twittering Machine* (London: Indigo Press, 2019), 26–27.

123   **"I wake up in cold sweats every so often thinking, what did we bring to the world?"** J. Williams, *Stand out of Our Light* (Cambridge, U.K.: Cambridge University Press, 2018), 102.

123   **"Unless the forms of technological progress that produced these things are subject to different laws"** N. Eyal, *Hooked: How to Build Habit-Forming Products* (London: Penguin, 2014), 11; and P. Graham, "The Acceleration of Addictiveness," *Paul Graham* (blog), July 2010, http://www.paulgraham.com/addiction.html?viewfullsite=1.

CHAPTER SEVEN: CAUSE SIX (PART TWO)

127   **"surveillance capitalism"** S. Zuboff, *The Age of Surveillance Capitalism* (New York: Public Affairs, 2019). Visit www.shoshana zuboff.com for more on Professor Zuboff's fight for "a human future."

131   **On average, we will stare at something negative and outrageous for a lot longer than we will stare at something positive and calm** C. H. Hansen and R. D. Hansen, "Finding the Face in the Crowd: An Anger Superiority Effect," *Journal of Personality and Social Psychology* 54, no. 6 (1988): 917–24, cited in P. M. Litvak et al., "Fuel in the Fire: How Anger Affects Decision-Making," in *International Handbook of Anger*, ed. M. Potegal, G. Stemmler, and C. Spielberger (New York: Springer, 2010), 287–310; R. C. Solomon, *A Passion for Justice* (Reading, Mass.: Addison-Wesley, 1990); and C. Tavris, *Anger: The Misunderstood Emotion* (New York: Simon & Schuster, 1989).

131   **Even ten-week-old babies respond differently to angry faces** J. M. Haviland and M. Lelwica, "The Induced Affect Response: 10-Week-Old Infants' Responses to Three Emotion Expressions," *Developmental Psychology* 23, no. 1 (1987): 97–104, cited in Litvak et al., "Fuel in the Fire."

131 **It's called "negativity bias"** For a good summary, see
M. Jaworski, "The Negativity Bias: Why the Bad Stuff
Sticks," *PsyCom,* February 19, 2020, https://www.psycom.net/
negativity-bias.

131 **"hates," "obliterates," "slams," "destroys"** See algotransparency
.org, a website that tracks words that trend on YouTube.

131 **your retweet rate will go up by 20 percent on average, and
the words that will increase your retweet rate most are
"attack," "bad," and "blame"** William J. Brady et al., "Emotion
Shapes the Diffusion of Moralized Content in Social Networks,"
Proceedings of the National Academy of Sciences 114, no. 28
(2017): 7313–18.

131 **A study by the Pew Research Center** "Partisan Conflict
and Congressional Outreach," Pew Research Center,
February 23, 2017, https://www.pewresearch.org/politics/
2017/02/23/partisan-conflict-and-congressional-outreach/
pdl-02-23-17_antipathy-new-00-02/.

132 **"to condemn a little more, and understand a little less"**
John Major made these remarks in 1993 in an interview with the
Mail on Sunday, which was widely reported.

132 **In 2015 a researcher named Motahhare Eslami** N. Gertz,
Nihilism and Technology (London: Rowman & Littlefield
International, 2018), 97; A. Madrigal, "Many Many Facebook
Users Still Don't Know That Their Feed Is Filtered by an
Algorithm," *Splinter,* March 27, 2015, https://splinternews.
com/many-many-facebook-users-still-dont-know-that-their
-ne-1793846682; and M. Eslami et al., "'I Always Assumed That
I Wasn't Really That Close to [Her]': Reasoning About Invisible
Algorithms in News Feeds," *Proceedings of the 33rd Annual ACM
Conference on Human Factors in Computing Systems* (New York:
Association for Computing Machinery, 2015), 153–62, available
at http://www-personal.umich.edu/~csandvig/research/Eslami
_Algorithms_CHI15.pdf.

133 **"it's very hard to be with reality, the physical world, the
built world"** Tristan said this to Decca Aitkenhead, the chief
interviewer of the *Sunday Times*. She gave me the unpublished
transcript of their full conversation, which helped to inform this
part of the book.

133 **They have discovered that if I make you angry, you will**

pay less attention to the quality of arguments around you
G. V. Bodenhausen et al., "Happiness and Stereotypic Thinking
in Social Judgment," *Journal of Personality and Social Psychology*
66, no. 4 (1994): 621–36, cited in Litvak et al., "Fuel in the
Fire"; and D. DeSteno et al., "Beyond Valence in the Perception
of Likelihood: The Role of Emotion Specificity," *Journal of
Personality and Social Psychology* 78, no. 3 (2000): 397–416.

133   **"decreased depth of processing"** Litvak et al., "Fuel in the
Fire," 299.

135   **A study by the Massachusetts Institute of Technology
found that fake news travels six times faster on Twitter
than real news** S. Vosoughi, D. Roy, and S. Aral, "The Spread
of True and False News Online," *Science* 359 (2018): 1146–51.

135   **during the 2016 U.S. presidential election, flat-out
falsehoods on Facebook outperformed the top stories at
nineteen mainstream news sites put together** C. Silverman,
"This Analysis Shows How Viral Fake Election News Stories
Outperformed Real News on Facebook," *BuzzFeed,* November
16, 2016.

136   **"Let's compare that—what is the aggregate traffic of the
New York Times"** Tristan to Decca Aitkenhead. The *Guardian*
had approximately 286 million visits in the six months before
September 2020; the *New York Times* nearly 354 million; the
Washington Post just over 185 million, according to SimilarWeb
.com. The 15 billion figure comes from M. Hiltzik, "Column: Ex-
Google Manager Leads a Drive to Rein in the Pernicious Impact
of Social Media," *Los Angeles Times,* May 10, 2019.

136   **A major study asked white nationalists** A. Jones, "From
Memes to Infowars: How 75 Fascist Activists Were 'Red-Pilled,'"
Bellingcat, October 11, 2018.

137   **A separate study of far-right people on Twitter found
that YouTube was by far the website they turned to the
most** J. M. Berger, "The Alt-Right Twitter Census: Defining
and Describing the Audience for Alt-Right Content on Twitter,"
VOX-Pol Network of Excellence, 2018, https://www.voxpol.eu/
download/vox-pol_publication/AltRightTwitterCensus.pdf.

137   **"Do we have a system that is systematically, as you turn
the crank every day, pumping out more radicalization?"**
Tristan to Decca Aitkenhead.

138 **that they weren't "worthy" of it** C. Alter, "Brazilian Politician tells Congresswoman She's 'Not Worthy' of Sexual Assault," *Time,* December 11, 2014.

138 **"are not even good for breeding"** A. Forrest, "Jair Bolsonaro: The Worst Quotes from Brazil's Far-Right Presidential Frontrunner," *Independent,* October 8, 2018.

139 **"Facebook! Facebook! Facebook!"** C. Doctorow, "Fans of Brazil's New Fascist President Chant 'Facebook! Facebook! Whatsapp! Whatsapp!' at Inauguration," *BoingBoing,* January 3, 2019.

141 **"the collective downgrading of humans and the upgrading of machines"** Tristan to Decca Aitkenhead.

142 **"How can we solve the world's most urgent problems if we've downgraded our attention spans"** T. Harris, testimony to the Senate Commerce Committee, June 25, 2019, https://www.commerce.senate.gov/services/files/96E3A739-DC8D-45F1-87D7-EC70A368371D.

CHAPTER EIGHT: CAUSE SEVEN

144 **Like Tristan, he had learned from B. J. Fogg, attending a retreat at his home and sitting in on some of his lectures, and then he went on to work with some of the most influential companies in Silicon Valley, helping them figure out how to get their users "hooked"** Professor Fogg stresses that Nir Eyal was never his student at Stanford and was not involved in the Persuasive Technology Lab at Stanford.

144 **"iPad time! iPad time!"** N. Eyal, *Indistractible: How to Control Your Attention and Choose Your Life* (London: Bloomsbury, 2020), 213.

146 **"ten-minute rule"** Ibid., 41–42.

146 **"time-box"** Ibid., 62.

146 **"office hours"** Ibid., 113.

148 **"cookbook"** Ibid., 1.

148 **"Let's admit it: we are all in the persuasion business"** N. Eyal, *Hooked: How to Build Habit-Forming Products* (London: Penguin, 2014), 164. When I later read this quote to Nir, he said: "Well, you have to read the book, right? So if you just take it out of context, and just say that one sentence, of course you can make me say anything you want me to say." But I did read

it in context, and I urge other people to. Nothing in the context surrounding this sentence or the wider book mitigates the clear meaning of this sentence.

148   **which he describes as "mind manipulation"** Ibid., 2.

148   **"Want to Hook Your Users? Drive Them Crazy"** N. Eyal, "Want to Hook Your Users? Drive Them Crazy," *TechCrunch* (blog), March 26, 2012, https://techcrunch.com/2012/03/25/want-to-hook-your-users-drive-them-crazy/.

148   **The goal of the designer is to create an "internal trigger"** Eyal, *Hooked*, 47.

148   **he says they should imagine a user he names Julie, who "fears being out of the loop"** Ibid., 57.

149   **Once you have succeeded in playing on feelings like this, "a habit is formed"** Ibid.,18.

149   **"to repeat behaviors for long periods, ideally for the rest of their lives"** Ibid., 25.

149   **"Habits can be very good for the bottom line"** Ibid., 17.

149   **Nir says there should be some ethical limits to this** He also lists some healthy uses of these techniques—for example, to design fitness apps that encourage people to go to the gym, or apps that help you learn another language.

150   **"Stress isn't something imposed on us. It's something we impose on ourselves"** R. E. Purser, *McMindfulness: How Mindfulness Became the New Capitalist Spirituality* (London: Repeater, 2019), 138.

150   **the top causes of stress in the U.S. have been identified by scientists at Stanford Graduate School of Business in a major study** D. Becker, *One Nation Under Stress: The Trouble with Stress as an Idea* (Oxford, U.K.: Oxford University Press, 2013), cited in Purser, *McMindfulness*, 139.

153   **The average weight gain for an adult between 1960 and 2002 was twenty-four pounds** Mark Bittman, "Why Your New Year's Diet Is Doomed," *New York Times*, January 9, 2021.

153   **The scientists who have studied this have discovered that 95 percent of people in our culture who lose weight on a diet regain it within one to five years** The original study finding that 95 percent of diets fail was with one hundred obese patients: A. Stunkard and M. McLaren-Hume, "The Results of Treatment for Obesity," *AMA Archives of Internal Medicine* 103,

no. 1 (1959): 79–85. Other, more recent studies have found very similar outcomes—in this one, only 2 percent of people maintained a greater than twenty-kilogram weight loss two years later: J. Kassirer and M. Angell, "Losing Weight—An Ill-Fated New Year's Resolution," *New England Journal of Medicine* 338 (1998): 52–54.

Some scientists argue this is too pessimistic or defining success too demandingly. See, for example, R. R. Wing and S. Phelan, "Long-Term Weight Loss Maintenance," *American Journal of Clinical Nutrition* 82, no. 1 (2005): 222S–25S. They argue we should define success as maintaining a 10 percent weight loss one year after the diet. But even using this redefinition, only about 20 percent of dieters can manage it, and 80 percent fail.

This article covers the 1959 study and argues it's too negative: J. Fritsch, "95% Regain Lost Weight. Or Do They?," *New York Times,* May 25, 1999. See also T. Mann, *Secrets from the Eating Lab* (New York: Harper Wave, 2017). The author reviewed sixty years of diet literature and found that on average dieters lose 10 percent of their starting weight, and that within two years they've on average regained all but about two of those pounds.

154 **like the U.S. and U.K., have very high levels of obesity** More than 42 percent of U.S. adults and 18.5 percent of U.S. children were obese in 2018. There have been twenty years of steady increase: "Overweight and Obesity Data and Statistics," Centers for Disease Control and Prevention, https://www.cdc.gov/obesity/data/index.html.

In 2018, 15 percent of Dutch adults were obese—much less, but they still (rightly) consider this to be a major public health crisis. See C. Stewart, "Share of the Population with Overweight in the Netherlands," *Statista,* November 16, 2020, https://www.statista.com/statistics/544060/share-of-the-population-with-overweight-in-the-netherlands/.

CHAPTER NINE: THE FIRST GLIMPSES OF THE DEEPER SOLUTION

158 **this model works so well that it is the most respected media organization in the world** D. Marshall, "BBC Most

Trusted News Source 2020," *Ipsos Mori,* May 22, 2020, https://
www.ipsos.com/ipsos-mori/en-uk/bbc-most-trusted-news-source
-2020; and W. Turvill, "Survey: Americans Trust the BBC More
Than the New York Times, Wall Street Journal, ABC or CBS,"
Press Gazette, June 16, 2020, https://www.pressgazette.co.uk/
survey-americans-trust-the-bbc-more-than-new-york-times-wall
-street-journal-abc-or-cbs/.

160   **"Just turn it off. They can turn it off in a heartbeat"** Tristan
        to Decca Aitkenhead.

160   **Amazon found that even one hundred milliseconds of
        delay** G. Linden, "Marissa Mayer at Web.20," *Glinden* (blog),
        November 9, 2006, http://glinden.blogspot.com/2006/11/
        marissa-mayer-at-web-20.html. See also A. Price, "Infographic:
        Web Performance Impacts Conversion Rates," *LoadStorm,*
        April 9, 2014, http://loadstorm.com/2014/04/infographic-web
        -performance-impacts-conversion-rates/; and R. Colville,
        The Great Acceleration: How the World Is Getting Faster, Faster
        (London: Bloomsbury, 2016), 27.

162   **Nir responds by pointing to a recent study by the coder
        Mark Ledwich** M. Ledwich and A. Zaitsev, "Algorithmic
        Extremism: Examining YouTube's Rabbit Hole of Radicalization,"
        Cornell University (2019), arXiv:1912:11211. See also
        A. Kantrowitz, "Does YouTube Radicalize?" *OneZero,* January 7,
        2020, https://onezero.medium.com/does-youtube-radicalize-a
        -debate-between-kevin-roose-and-mark-ledwich-1b99651c7bb;
        and W. Feuer, "Critics Slam Study Claiming YouTube's
        Algorithm Doesn't Lead to Radicalization," CNBC, December
        31, 2019.

162   **Tristan, in response, directs people toward the Princeton
        academic Professor Arvind Narayanan** A. Narayanan, Twitter
        post, December 29, 2019, https://twitter.com/random_walker/
        status/1211264254109765634?lang=en.

164   **One day, in the spring of 2020, it was revealed what
        Facebook actually thinks about these questions** J. Horwitz
        and D. Seetharaman, "Facebook Executives Shut Down Efforts to
        Make the Site Less Divisive," *Wall Street Journal,* May 26, 2020.

167   **"But if you can't rape your wife, who can you rape?"**
        A. Dworkin, *Life and Death: Unapologetic Writings on the*

Continuing War Against Women (London: Simon & Schuster, 1997), 210.

CHAPTER TEN: CAUSE EIGHT

172   **"The problem was"** N. Burke Harris, *The Deepest Well: Healing the Long-Term Effects of Childhood Adversity* (London: Bluebird, 2018), 215.

175   **It's named the Adverse Childhood Experiences Study** V. J. Felitti et al., "Relationship of Childhood Abuse and Household Dysfunction to Many of the Leading Causes of Death in Adults: The Adverse Childhood Experiences (ACE) Study," *American Journal of Preventive Medicine* 14, no. 4 (1998): 245–58. I have also been informed here by my interviews with Dr. Vincent Felitti, Dr. Robert Anda, and Dr. Gabor Maté. See G. Maté, *In the Realm of Hungry Ghosts: Close Encounters with Addiction* (London: Vermilion, 2018).

176   **Children who had experienced four or more types of trauma were 32.6 times more likely** Burke Harris, *Deepest Well,* 59.

176   **Dr. Nicole Brown, in a separate body of research, found that childhood trauma tripled the development of ADHD symptoms** R. Ruiz, "How Childhood Trauma Could Be Mistaken for ADHD," *Atlantic,* July 7, 2014; N. M. Brown et al., "Associations Between Adverse Childhood Experiences and ADHD Diagnosis and Severity," *Academic Pediatrics* 17, no. 4 (2017): 349–55; "Researchers Link ADHD with Childhood Trauma," Children's Hospital Association, August 9, 2017, https://www.childrenshospitals.org/Newsroom/Childrens-Hospitals-Today/Articles/2017/08/Researchers-Link-ADHD-with-Childhood-Trauma; K. Szymanski, L. Sapanski, and F. Conway, "Trauma and ADHD—Association or Diagnostic Confusion? A Clinical Perspective," *Journal of Infant, Child, and Adolescent Psychotherapy* 10, no. 1 (2011): 51–59; and R. C. Kessler et al., "The Prevalence and Correlates of Adult ADHD in the United States: Results from the National Comorbidity Survey Replication," *American Journal of Psychiatry* 163, no. 4 (2006): 716–23.

Kids raised in Romanian orphanages (where they were

severely neglected) were found to be four times more likely to later have serious attention problems. See M. Kennedy et al., "Early Severe Institutional Deprivation Is Associated with a Persistent Variant of Adult-Deficit Hyperactivity Disorder," *Journal of Child Psychology and Psychiatry* 57, no. 10 (2016): 1113–25.

See also J. Nigg, *Getting Ahead of ADHD: What Next-Generation Science Says About Treatments That Work* (New York: Guilford Press, 2017), 161–62.

See also W. Gallagher, *Rapt: Attention and the Focused Life* (London: Penguin, 2009), 167; and R. C. Herrenkohl, B. P. Egolf, and E. C. Herrenkohl, "Preschool Antecedents of Adolescent Assaultive Behavior: A Longitudinal Study," *American Journal of Orthopsychiatry* 67 (1997): 422–32.

176 **A large study by the British Office of National Statistics** H. Green et al., *Mental Health of Children and Young People in Great Britain, 2004* (Basingstoke, U.K.: Palgrave Macmillan, 2005). The stats are on page 161 and are summarized in tables 7:20 and 7:21. My attention was brought to these statistics by N. Hart and L. Benassaya, "Social Deprivation or Brain Dysfunction? Data and the Discourse of ADHD in Britain and North America," in *Rethinking ADHD: From Brain to Culture,* ed. S. Timimi and J. Leo (London: Palgrave Macmillan, 2009).

177 **One study compared children who had been sexually abused with a group of children the same age who hadn't been abused** S. N. Merry and L. K. Andrews, "Psychiatric Status of Sexually Abused Children 12 Months After Disclosure of Abuse," *Journal of the American Academy of Child and Adolescent Psychiatry* 33, no. 7 (1994): 939–44. See also T. Endo, T. Sugiyama, and T. Someya, "Attention-Deficit/Hyperactivity Disorder and Dissociative Disorder Among Abused Children," *Psychiatry and Clinical Neurosciences* 60, no. 4 (2006): 434–38, doi:10:1111/j.1440-1819:2006:01528.x.

180 **The evidence in labs shows if you are put under mild to moderate stress, you will perform *better* on some tasks that require attention in the short term** A helpful guide to the best research on this—and one I have drawn on for many of the studies in the next few paragraphs—is C. Andreotti, "Effects

of Acute and Chronic Stress on Attention and Psychobiological
Stress Reactivity in Women," Ph.D. diss., Vanderbilt University,
2013. See also E. Chajut and D. Algom, "Selective Attention
Improves Under Stress: Implications for Theories of Social
Cognition," *Journal of Personality and Social Psychology* 85 (2003):
231–48; and P. D. Skosnik et al., "Modulation of Attentional
Inhibition by Norepinephrine and Cortisol After Psychological
Stress," *International Journal of Psychophysiology* 36, no. 1 (2000):
59–68.

180   **even mild levels of stress "can significantly alter
        attentional processes"** Skosnik et al., "Modulation of
        Attentional Inhibition." See also C. Liston, B. S. McEwen, and
        B. J. Casey, "Psychosocial Stress Reversibly Disrupts Prefrontal
        Processing and Attentional Control," *Proceedings of the National
        Academy of Sciences* 106, no. 3 (2009): 912–17.

180   **"It is now obvious that stress can cause structural changes
        in the brain with long-term effects"** H. Yaribeygi et al., "The
        Impact of Stress on Body Function: A Review," *EXCLI Journal* 16
        (2017): 1057–72.

180   **Professor Charles Nunn—a leading evolutionary
        anthropologist—investigated the rise of insomnia** C. Nunn
        et al., "Shining Evolutionary Light on Human Sleep and Sleep
        Disorders," *Evolution, Medicine and Public Health,* no. 1 (2016):
        234, 238.

180   **"an adaptive trait, under circumstances of perceived
        threat"** Z. Heller, "Why We Sleep—and Why We Often Can't,"
        New Yorker, December 3, 2018.

180   **I learned that this has been studied carefully by Sendhil
        Mullainathan** A. Mani et al., "Poverty Impedes Cognitive
        Function," *Science* 341, no. 6149 (2013): 976-80, doi:10.1126/
        science.1238041. See also R. Putnam, *Our Kids: The American
        Dream in Crisis* (New York: Simon & Schuster, 2015), 130.

181   **when they had the financial security that came at the end
        of the harvest, they were on average thirteen IQ points
        smarter** Mani et al., "Poverty Impedes Cognitive Function."
            This is a great interview with Professor Mullainathan:
        C. Feinberg, "The Science of Scarcity: A Behavioral Economist's
        Fresh Perspectives on Poverty," *Harvard Magazine,* May–June

2015, https://www.harvardmagazine.com/2015/05/the-science
-of-scarcity. S. Mullainathan and E. Shafir, *Scarcity: Why Having
Too Little Means So Much* (London: Penguin, 2014), goes through
this science in great detail.

181   **Finland decided to stop talking and actually try it**
J. Howego, "Universal Income Study Finds Money for Nothing
Won't Make Us Work Less," *New Scientist,* February 8, 2019,
https://www.newscientist.com/article/2193136-universal-income
-study-finds-money-for-nothing-wont-make-us-work-less/.

184   **Ed Deci, a professor of psychology who I interviewed
at the University of Rochester in upstate New York, has
shown that** G. Maté, *Scattered Minds: The Origins and Healing
of Attention Deficit Disorder* (London: Vermilion, 2019), 175;
E. Deci, *Why We Do What We Do: Understanding Self-Motivation*
(London: Penguin, 1996), 28; and W. C. Dement, *The Promise of
Sleep: A Pioneer in Sleep Medicine Explores the Vital Connection
Between Health, Happiness, and a Good Night's Sleep* (New York:
Bantam Doubleday Dell, 1999), 218.

184   **They explained that as work hours swell and swell**
R. Colville, *The Great Acceleration: How the World Is Getting
Faster, Faster* (London: Bloomsbury, 2016), 59.

184   **"These workloads are not sustainable"** L. Duxbury and
C. Higgins, *Work-Life Conflict in Canada in the New Millennium:
Key Findings and Recommendations from the 2001 National Work-
Life Conflict Study,* Report 6 (Health Canada, January 2009),
cited in B. Schulte, *Overwhelmed: Work, Love and Play When
No One Has the Time* (London: Bloomsbury, 2014), 22. See also
L. Duxbury and C. Higgins, *Work-Life Conflict in Canada in the
New Millennium: A Status Report*, Final Report (Health Canada,
October 2003), http://publications.gc.ca/collections/Collection/
H72-21-186-2003E.pdf. See table F1 for role-overload stats.

CHAPTER ELEVEN: THE PLACES THAT FIGURED
OUT HOW TO REVERSE THE SURGE IN SPEED AND
EXHAUSTION

186   **The average British worker, the research had found, was
only actually engaged** B. Cotton, "British Employees Work
for Just Three Hours a Day," *Business Leader,* February 6, 2019,

https://www.businessleader.co.uk/british-employees-work-for-just
-three-hours-a-day/59742/.

188 **All signs of distraction, they found, were radically down**
Helen Delaney from the University of Auckland kindly gave
me their next paper on this subject, which was still under peer
review, and I have drawn on the evidence in there.

189 **In 1920s Britain, W. G. Kellogg** A. Coote et al., *The Case for
a Four Day Week* (London: Polity, 2021), 6.

189 **In 2019 in Japan, Microsoft moved to a four-day week**
K. Paul, "Microsoft Japan Tested a Four-Day Work Week and
Productivity Jumped by 40%," *Guardian,* November 4, 2019; and
Coote et al., *Case for a Four Day Week,* 89.

189 **In Gothenberg in Sweden around the same time** Coote
et al., *Case for a Four Day Week,* 68–71.

190 **In the same city, Toyota cut two hours per day** Ibid., 17–18.

192 **WORKING 90 HOURS A WEEK AND LOVING IT!** K. Onstad, *The
Weekend Effect* (New York: HarperOne, 2017), 49.

193 **the average U.S. worker clocked in three extra hours a day**
M. F. Davis and J. Green, "Three Hours Longer, the Pandemic
Workday Has Obliterated Work-Life Balance," *Bloomberg,* April
23, 2020.

193 **people worked two hours more a day on average** A. Webber,
"Working at Home Has Led to Longer Hours," *Personnel Today,*
August 13, 2020, https://www.personneltoday.com/hr/longer
-hours-and-loss-of-creative-discussions-among-home-working
-side-effects/; "People Are Working Longer Hours During the
Pandemic," *Economist,* November 24, 2020; and A. Friedman,
"Proof Our Work-Life Balance Is in Danger (But There's Hope),"
Atlassian, November 5, 2020, https://www.atlassian.com/blog/
teamwork/data-analysis-length-of-workday-covid.

194 **a third of French professionals felt they could never
unplug** F. Jauréguiberry, "Déconnexion volontaire aux
technologies de l'information et de la communication," Agence
Nationale de la Recherche (2014), hal-00925309, https://hal
.archives-ouvertes.fr/hal-00925309/document.

194 **Another study found that just the expectation that you
should be on call causes workers anxiety** W. J. Becker,
L. Belkin, and S. Tuskey, "Killing Me Softly: Electronic

Communications Monitoring and Employee and Spouse Well-Being," *Academy of Management* (2018), cited in R. Haridy, "The Right to Disconnect: The New Laws Banning After-Hours Work Emails," *New Atlas,* August 14, 2018, https://newatlas.com/right-to-disconnect-after-hours-work-emails/55879/.

CHAPTER TWELVE: CAUSES NINE AND TEN

199   **the British National Health Service's carefully fact-checked official website warns about it** "Sleep and Tiredness," NHS, March 25, 2021, https://www.nhs.uk/live-well/sleep-and-tiredness/eight-energy-stealers/.

199   **most of us now eat in a way that deprives us of the nutrients we need for our brains to develop and function fully** M. Pollan, *In Defense of Food* (London: Penguin, 2008), 85–89.

200   **in 2009 a team of Dutch scientists** L. Pelsser et al., "Effect of a Restricted Elimination Diet on the Behavior of Children with Attention-Deficit Hyperactivity Disorder (INCA Study): A Randomized Controlled Trial," *Lancet* 377, no. 9764 (2011): 494–503; and J. K. Ghuman, "Restricted Elimination Diet for ADHD: The INCA Study," *Lancet* 377, no. 9764 (2011): 446–48. See also J. Nigg, *Getting Ahead of ADHD: What Next-Generation Science Says About Treatments That Work* (New York: Guilford Press, 2017), 79–82.

201   **For example, in 2007 a group of scientists in Southampton in Britain got 297 normal kids** Donna McCann et al., "Food Additives and Hyperactive Behavior in 3-Year-Old and 8/9-Year-Old Children in the Community: A Randomized, Double-Blinded, Placebo-Controlled Trial," *Lancet* 370, no. 9598 (2007): 1560–67; B. Bateman et al., "The Effects of a Double Blind, Placebo Controlled, Artificial Food Colorings and Benzoate Preservative Challenge on Hyperactivity in a General Population Sample of Preschool Children," *Archives of Disease in Childhood* 89, no. 6 (2004): 506–11; and M. Wedge, *A Disease Called Childhood: Why ADHD Became an American Epidemic* (New York: Avery, 2016), 148–59.

202   **"A sea change is under way"** Nigg, *Getting Ahead of ADHD*, 59.

204   **has been carrying out potentially game-changing research on how it is affecting our brains** B. A. Maher,

"Airborne Magnetite- and Iron-Rich Pollution Nanoparticles: Potential Neurotoxicants and Environmental Risk Factors for Neurodegenerative Disease, Including Alzheimer's Disease," *Journal of Alzheimer's Disease* 71, no. 2 (2019): 361–75; and B. A. Maher et al., "Magnetite Pollution Nanoparticles in the Human Brain," *Proceedings of the National Academy of Sciences* 113, no. 39 (2016): 10797–801.

205 **"Depending on the dose [i.e., how bad the pollution is], depending on your genetic susceptibility, eventually, over time, your brain cells will be damaged"** F. Perera et al., "Benefits of Reducing Prenatal Exposure to Coal-Burning Pollutants to Children's Neurodevelopment in China," *Environmental Health Perspectives* 116, no. 10 (2008): 1396–400. See also M. Guxens et al., "Air Pollution During Pregnancy and Childhood Cognitive and Psychomotor Development: Six European Birth Cohorts," *Epidemiology* 25 (2014): 636–47; P. Wang et al., "Socioeconomic Disparities and Sexual Dimorphism in Neurotoxic Effects of Ambient Fine Particles on Youth IQ: A Longitudinal Analysis," *PLoS One* 12, no. 12 (2017), e0188731; Xin Zhanga et al., "The Impact of Exposure to Air Pollution on Cognitive Performance," *Procedures of the National Academy of Science* 115, no. 37 (2018): 9193–97; F. Perera et al., "Polycyclic Aromatic Hydrocarbons-Aromatic DNA Adducts in Cord Blood and Behavior Scores in New York City Children," *Environmental Health Perspectives* 119, no. 8 (2011): 1176–81; and N. Newman et al., "Traffic-Related Air Pollution Exposure in the First Year of Life and Behavioral Scores at 7 Years of Age," *Environmental Health Perspectives* 121, no. 6 (2013): 731–36.

205 **In Canada, a study found that people who lived within fifty meters of a major road** W. Yuchi et al., "Road Proximity, Air Pollution, Noise, Green Space and Neurologic Disease Incidence: A Population-Based Cohort Study," *Environmental Health* 19, no. 8 (2020).

205 **The evidence is especially worrying when it comes to children's brains** N. Rees, "Danger in the Air: How Air Pollution Can Affect Brain Development in Young Children," UNICEF Division of Data, Research and Policy Working Paper (New York: UNICEF, 2017); and Y.-H. M. Chiu et al.,

"Associations Between Traffic-Related Black Carbon Exposure and Attention in a Prospective Birth Cohort of Urban Children," *Environmental Health Perspectives* 121, no. 7 (2013): 859–64.

205 **"My colleague in Mexico [has] been doing MRI scans"** L. Calderón-Garcidueñas et al., "Exposure to Severe Urban Air Pollution Influences Cognitive Outcomes, Brain Volume and Systemic Inflammation in Clinically Healthy Children," *Brain and Cognition* 77, no. 3 (2011): 345–55.

205 **A scientist in Barcelona, Professor Jordi Sunyer, tested schoolchildren's ability to pay attention** J. Sunyer et al., "Traffic-Related Air Pollution and Attention in Primary School Children: Short-Term Association," *Epidemiology* 28, no. 2 (2017): 181–89.

206 **"Where there is lead"** T. Harford, "Why Did We Use Leaded Petrol for So Long?," BBC News, August 28, 2017.

206 **When Bruce saw the results, he was taken aback** M. V. Maffini et al., "No Brainer: The Impact of Chemicals on Children's Brain Development: A Cause for Concern and a Need for Action," CHEMTrust report, March 2017, https://www.chemtrust.org/wp-content/uploads/chemtrust-nobrainer-mar17.pdf. See also House of Commons, Environmental Audit Committee, "Toxic Chemicals in Everyday Life," Twentieth Report of Session 2017–19 (London: House of Commons, 2019), https://publications.parliament.uk/pa/cm201719/cmselect/cmenvaud/1805/1805.pdf.

207 **For example, if your mother was exposed to lead during pregnancy and she smoked** T. E. Froehlich et al., "Association of Tobacco and Lead Exposures with Attention-Deficit/Hyperactivity Disorder," *Pediatrics* 124, no. 6 (2009): e1054.

A meta-analysis of eighteen studies found that sixteen of them showed that lead played a role in the ADHD in the children they studied. See M. Daneshparvar et al., "The Role of Lead Exposure on Attention-Deficit/Hyperactivity Disorder in Children: A Systematic Review," *Iranian Journal of Psychiatry* 11, no. 1 (2016): 1–14.

Bruce Lanphear discusses this issue in "Shifting the Curve: Small Changes with a Big Impact," available at https://vimeo.com/154266125.

207   **"uneducable Negro and Puerto Rican" parents** D. Rosner
       and G. Markowitz, "Why It Took Decades of Blaming Parents
       Before We Banned Lead Paint," *Atlantic,* April 22, 2013. For
       more on the racism of this policy, see this excellent piece:
       L. Bliss, "The Long, Ugly History of the Politics of Lead
       Poisoning," *Bloomberg City Lab,* February 9, 2016. See also
       M. Segarra, "Lead Poisoning: A Doctor's Lifelong Crusade to Save
       Children from It," NPR, June 5, 2016.

207   **all this dusting and handwashing made no difference
       at all** B. Yeoh et al., "Household Interventions for Preventing
       Domestic Lead Exposure in Children," *Cochrane Database of
       Systematic Reviews,* no. 4 (2012), https://core.ac.uk/download/
       pdf/143864237.pdf.

209   **The IQ of the average preschooler** S. D. Grosse et al.,
       "Economic Gains Resulting from the Reduction in Children's
       Exposure to Lead in the United States," *Environmental Health
       Perspectives* 110, no. 6 (2002): 563–69.

209   **When monkeys are exposed to the same level of the
       common pollutant polychlorinated biphenyls (PCBs)**
       J. Nigg, *Getting Ahead of ADHD: What Next-Generation Science
       Says About Treatments That Work* (London: Guilford Press, 2017),
       152–53. For a chilling summary of the animal experiments, see
       H. J. K. Sable and S. L. Schantz, "Executive Function Following
       Developmental Exposure to Polychlorinated Biphenyls (PCBs):
       What Animal Models Have Told Us," in *Animal Models of
       Cognitive Impairment,* ed. E. D. Levin and J. J. Buccafusco (Boca
       Raton, Fla.: CRC Press, 2006), chap. 8, available at https://www
       .ncbi.nlm.nih.gov/books/NBK2531/. Barbara Demeneix discusses
       PCBs and the evidence around them in *Toxic Cocktail: How
       Chemical Pollution Is Poisoning Our Brains* (Oxford, U.K.: Oxford
       University Press, 2017), 55–56.

210   **a pollutant named bisphenol A, or BPA** Nigg, *Getting Ahead
       of ADHD,* 146, 155; "BPA Rules in European Union Now in Force:
       Limit Strengthened 12 Fold," *Food Safety News,* September 16,
       2018, https://www.foodsafetynews.com/2018/09/bpa-rules-in
       -european-union-now-in-force-limit-strengthened-12-fold/.

210   **So she began to research whether these chemicals
       have any effect on these endocrine signals** B. Demeneix,

"Endocrine Disruptors: From Scientific Evidence to Human Health Protection," Policy Department for Citizens' Rights and Constitutional Affairs, Directorate General for Internal Policies of the Union, PE 608.866 (2019).

210 **She warns that all children today are being born "precontaminated"** B. Demeneix, "Letter: Chemical Pollution Is Another 'Asteroid Threat,'" *Financial Times,* January 11, 2020; B. Demeneix, "Environmental Factors Contribute to Loss of IQ," *Financial Times,* July 18, 2017; and Demeneix, *Toxic Cocktail,* 5.

210 **This group has been funded by chemical companies** A. Kroll and J. Schulman, "Leaked Documents Reveal the Secret Finances of a Pro-Industry Science Group," *Mother Jones,* October 28, 2013.

CHAPTER THIRTEEN: CAUSE ELEVEN

216 **genetics account for "75 to 80 percent" of ADHD** When I asked him for a citation, he replied that an authoritative one is S. V. Faraone and H. Larsson, "Genetics of Attention Deficit Hyperactivity Disorder," *Molecular Psychiatry* 24, no. 4 (2019): 562–75. "They estimate heritability at 74 percent, slightly more conservative than 75 to 80 percent," he told me.

217 **he's been called the "Pied Piper" of drugging animals for psychiatric problems** L. Braitman, *Animal Madness: Inside Their Minds* (New York: Simon & Schuster, 2015), 211.

218 **One of the staff at the Toledo Zoo told a reporter** Ibid., 196.

225 **For more than forty years, Alan and his team have been studying the same two hundred people** A huge number of studies have emerged from this research. The most salient here are D. Jacobvitz and L. A. Sroufe, "The Early Caregiver-Child Relationship and Attention Deficit Disorder with Hyperactivity in Kindergarten: A Prospective Study," *Child Development* 58 (1987): 1496–504; and E. Carlson, D. Jacobvitz, and L. A. Sroufe, "A Developmental Investigation of Inattentiveness and Hyperactivity," *Child Development* 66 (1995): 37–54. See also L. A. Sroufe, "Ritalin Gone Wrong," *New York Times,* January 28, 2012.

225 **One of the many things they wanted to figure out is: What factors in a person's life** See Alan Sroufe's brilliant *A*

Compelling Idea: How We Become the Persons We Are (Brandon, Vt.: Safer Society Press, 2020), 60–65. See also Sroufe's *The Development of the Person: The Minnesota Study of Risk and Adaptation from Birth to Adulthood* (New York: Guilford Press, 2009).

226 **After gathering evidence on this for decades, Alan concluded** Sroufe, *Compelling Idea*, 63.

227 **This effect was so large that** Ibid., 64.

227 **their attention will significantly improve in the short term** L. Furman, "ADHD: What Do We Really Know?," in *Rethinking ADHD: From Brain to Culture,* ed. S. Timimi and J. Leo (London: Palgrave Macmillan, 2009), 57.

228 **part of a crucial experiment, licensed by the government** N. Ezard et al., "LiMA: A Study Protocol for a Randomised, Double-Blind, Placebo Controlled Trial of Lisdexamfetamine for the Treatment of Methamphetamine Dependence," *BMJ Open* 8, no. 7 (2018): 8:e020723.

228 **who had conducted experiments giving Adderall to people who were addicted to meth** M. G. Kirkpatrick et al., "Comparison of Intranasal Methamphetamine and D-Amphetamine Self-Administration by Humans," *Addiction* 107, no. 4 (2012): 783–91.

229 **All children—indeed, all people—given Ritalin focus and pay attention better for a while** The classic research was done by Judith Rapoport: J. L. Rapoport et al., "Dextroamphetamine: Its Cognitive and Behavioral Effects in Normal Prepubertal Boys," *Science* 199 (1978): 560–63; J. L. Rapoport et al., "Dextroamphetamine: Its Cognitive and Behavioral Effects in Normal and Hyperactive Boys and Normal Men," *Archives of General Psychiatry* 37, no. 8 (1980): 933–43; M. Donnelly and J. Rapoport, "Attention Deficit Disorders," in *Diagnosis and Psychopharmacology of Childhood and Adolescent Disorders,* ed. J. M. Wiener (New York: Wiley, 1985); and S. W. Garber, *Beyond Ritalin: Facts About Medication and Other Strategies for Helping Children* (New York: HarperPerennial, 1996).

230 **there is evidence that taking stimulants stunts a child's growth** D. Rabiner, "Consistent Use of ADHD Medication May Stunt Growth by 2 Inches, Large Study Finds," *Sharp*

Brains (blog), March 16, 2013, https://sharpbrains.com/blog/ 2018/03/16/consistent-use-of-adhd-medication-may-stun-growth -by-2-inches-large-study-finds/; and A. Poulton, "Growth on Stimulant Medication: Clarifying the Confusion: A Review," *Archives of Disease in Childhood* 90, no. 8 (2005): 801–6. See also G. E. Jackson, "The Case Against Stimulants," in Timimi and Leo, *Rethinking ADHD*, 255–86.

230 **Kids taking a standard dose are about three centimeters shorter** J. M. Swanson et al., "Effects of Stimulant Medication on Growth Rates Across 3 Years in the MTA Follow-Up," *Journal of the American Academy of Child and Adolescent Psychiatry* 46, no. 8 (2007): 1015–27, cited in J. Moncrieff, *The Myth of the Chemical Cure: A Critique of Psychiatric Drug Treatment* (London: Palgrave Macmillan, 2009), 217.

230 **stimulants increase the risk of a child having heart problems** A. Sinha et al., "Adult ADHD Medications and Their Cardiovascular Implications," *Case Reports in Cardiology* (2016), 2343691; J.-Y. Shin et al., "Cardiovascular Safety of Methylphenidate Among Children and Young People with Attention-Deficit/Hyperactivity Disorder (ADHD): Nationwide Self-Controlled Case Series Study," *British Medical Journal* (2016): 353.

230 **if you give adolescent rats Ritalin for three weeks** K. van der Marel et al., "Long-Term Oral Methylphenidate Treatment in Adolescent and Adult Rats: Differential Effects on Brain Morphology and Function," *Neuropsychopharmacology* 39 (2014): 263–73. Curiously, the same study found that in adults, the striatum had grown.

231 **the study that the supporters of stimulant prescription had directed me to** See MTA Cooperative Group, "A 14-Month Randomized Clinical Trial of Treatment Strategies for Attention-Deficit/Hyperactivity Disorder," *Archives of General Psychiatry* 56, no. 12 (1999): 1073–86, table 4.

233 **so if you discover that something is more common among identical twins** J. Joseph, *The Trouble with Twin Studies: A Reassessment of Twin Research in the Social and Behavioral Sciences* (Abingdon-on-Thames, U.K.: Routledge, 2016), 153–78.

233 **Over twenty studies have found this result—it's consistent** See, for example, P. Heiser et al., "Twin Study on Heritability of

Activity, Attention, and Impulsivity and Assessed by Objective Measures," *Journal of Attention Disorders* 9, no. 4 (2006): 575–81; R. E. Lopez, "Hyperactivity in Twins," *Canadian Psychiatric Association Journal* 10 (1965): 421–26; D. K. Sherman et al., "Attention-Deficit Hyperactivity Disorder Dimensions: A Twin Study of Inattention and Impulsivity-Hyperactivity," *Journal of the American Academy of Child and Adolescent Psychiatry* 36, no. 6 (1997): 745–53; and A. Thapar et al., "Genetic Basis of Attention-Deficit and Hyperactivity," *British Journal of Psychiatry* 174, no. 2 (1999): 105–11.

233   **It has been proven—in a different set of scientific studies—that identical twins do *not* actually experience the same environments** Joseph, *Trouble with Twin Studies*, 153–78. Jay has compiled all the studies that show this: J. Joseph, "Levels of Identity Confusion and Attachment Among Reared-Together MZ and DZ Twin Pairs," *Gene Illusion* (blog), April 21, 2020, https://thegeneillusion.blogspot.com/2020/04/levels -of-identity-confusion-and_21.html. For a typical example, see A. Morris-Yates et al., "Twins: A Test of the Equal Environments Assumption," *Acta Psychiatrica Scandinavica* 81 (1990): 322–26. See also J. Joseph, "Not in Their Genes: A Critical View of the Genetics of Attention-Deficit Hyperactivity Disorder," *Developmental Review* 20, no. 4 (2000): 539–67.

234   **are built on an unreliable foundation** There has been a very long debate about this. Jay's response to the most common defenses of twin studies and his rebuttals are here—I find them persuasive: "It's Time to Abandon the 'Classical Twin Method' in Behavioral Research," *Gene Illusion* (blog), June 21, 2020, https://thegeneillusion.blogspot.com/2020/06/its-time-to-abandon -classical-twin_21.html.

235   **These studies currently find that around 20 to 30 percent of attention problems relate to your genes** D. Demontis et al., "Discovery of the First Genome-Wide Significant Risk Loci for Attention Deficit/Hyperactivity Disorder," *Nature Genetics* 51, no. 1 (2019): 63–75.

235   **But, as he has written, now "the science has moved on"** J. Nigg, *Getting Ahead of ADHD: What Next-Generation Science Says About Treatments That Work* (London: Guilford Press, 2017), 6–7.

235   **"genes aren't destiny; rather they affect probability"** Ibid., 45.
235   **"our experiences literally get under our skin"** Ibid., 41.
236   **"If your child is tired and run down"** Ibid., 39.
236   **"In some ways, the truly big news about ADHD today"**
       Ibid., 2.

CHAPTER FOURTEEN: CAUSE TWELVE

239   **By 2003, in the U.S. only 10 percent of children spent
       any time playing freely outdoors on a regular basis** S. L.
       Hofferth, "Changes in American Children's Time—1997 to
       2003," *Electronic International Journal of Time-Use Research* 6,
       no. 1 (2009): 26–47. See also B. Schulte, *Overwhelmed: Work,
       Love and Play When No One Has the Time* (London: Bloomsbury,
       2014), 207–8; P. Gray, "The Decline of Play and the Rise of
       Psychopathology in Children and Adolescents," *American
       Journal of Play* 3, no. 4 (2011): 443–63; and R. Clements, "An
       Investigation of the Status of Outdoor Play," *Contemporary Issues
       in Early Childhood* 5 no. 1 (2004): 68–80.

       For more striking figures demonstrating a similar point, see
       C. Steiner-Adair, *The Big Disconnect: Protecting Childhood and
       Family Relationships in the Digital Age* (New York: HarperCollins,
       2013), 88: "In America, half of kids walked or cycled to school
       in 1969, and only 12 percent drove; by 2009, those proportions
       were almost exactly reversed. In Britain, the proportion of seven-
       or eight-year-olds walking to school dropped from 80 percent in
       1971 to just 9 percent in 1990."

       See also L. Skenazy, *Free-Range Kids: How to Raise Safe, Self-
       Reliant Children (Without Going Nuts with Worry)* (Hoboken,
       N.J.: Jossey-Bass, 2010), 126.

243   **a broad body of evidence showing that when people run
       around—or engage in any form of exercise—their ability
       to pay attention improves** L. Verburgh et al., "Physical
       Exercise and Executive Functions in Preadolescent Children,
       Adolescents and Young Adults: A Meta-Analysis," *British Journal
       of Sports Medicine* 48 (2014): 973–79; Y. K. Chang et al., "The
       Effects of Acute Exercise on Cognitive Performance: A Meta-
       Analysis," *Brain Research* 1453 (2012): 87–101; S. Colcombe and
       A. F. Kramer, "Fitness Effects on the Cognitive Function of Older

Adults: A Meta-Analytic Study," *Psychological Science* 14, no. 2 (2003): 125–30; and P. D. Tomporowski et al., "Exercise and Children's Intelligence, Cognition, and Academic Achievement," *Educational Psychology Review* 20, no. 2 (2008): 111–31.

243   **one study that investigated this found exercise provides "an exceptional boost" to attention in children** M. T. Tine and A. G. Butler, "Acute Aerobic Exercise Impacts Selective Attention: An Exceptional Boost in Lower-Income Children," *Educational Psychology* 32, no. 7 (2012): 821–34. This particular study looked at low-income children who struggled with attention, but as Joel Nigg explains, this effect can be seen more widely.

243   **"for developing children, aerobic exercise expands the growth"** J. Nigg, *Getting Ahead of ADHD: What Next-Generation Science Says About Treatments That Work* (London: Guilford Press, 2017), 90.

243   **"definite"** Ibid., 92.

244   **Play builds the foundation of a solid personality, and everything that adults sit down and explain to the child afterward builds on this base** For further evidence of Isabel's arguments here, see A. Pellegrini et al., "A Short-Term Longitudinal Study of Children's Playground Games Across the First Year of School: Implications for Social Competence and Adjustment to School," *American Educational Research Journal* 39, no. 4 (2002): 991–1015; C. L. Ramstetter, R. Murray, and A. S. Garner, "The Crucial Role of Recess in Schools," *Journal of School Health* 80, no. 11 (2010): 517–26; National Association of Early Childhood Specialists in State Departments of Education, *Recess and the Importance of Play: A Position Statement on Young Children and Recess* (Washington, D.C.: National Association of Early Childhood Specialists in State Departments of Education, 2002); and O. Jarrett, "Recess in Elementary School: What Does the Research Say?," *ERIC Digest*, ERIC Clearinghouse on Elementary and Early Childhood Education, July 1, 2002, www .eric.ed.gov/PDFS/ED466331.pdf.

245   **One day, Barbara Sarnecka, an associate professor of cognitive sciences** L. Skenazy, "To Help Kids Find Their Passion, Give Them Free Time," *Reason,*

December 2020, https://reason.com/2020/11/26/
to-help-kids-find-their-passion-give-them-free-time/.

245 **One study of this found that this time is now
overwhelmingly spent on homework** S. L. Hofferth and J. F.
Sandberg, "Changes in American Children's Time, 1981–1997,"
in *Children at the Millennium: Where Have We Come From?
Where Are We Going?*, ed. T. Owens and S. L. Hofferth (Oxford,
U.K.: Elsevier Science, 2001), 193–229, cited in P. Gray, "The
Decline of Play and the Rise of Psychopathology in Children and
Adolescents," *American Journal of Play* 3, no. 4 (2011): 443–63.

245 **A 2004 study found that U.S. kids spent 7.5 hours more
each week on academics** Skenazy, "To Help Kids Find Their
Passion"; F. T. Juster, H. Ono, and F. P. Stafford, "Changing
Times of American Youth, 1981–2003," *Child Development
Supplement* (University of Michigan, 2004), http://ns.umich.edu/
Releases/2004/Nov04/teen_time_report.pdf.

246 **all human beings have within us two different kinds of
motivation** R. J. Vallerand et al., "The Academic Motivation
Scale: A Measure of Intrinsic, Extrinsic, and Amotivation in
Education," *Educational and Psychological Measurement* 52, no. 4
(1992): 1003–17.

256 **In the four years that followed, diagnoses** M. Wedge,
*A Disease Called Childhood: Why ADHD Became an American
Epidemic* (New York: Avery, 2016), 144. See also J. Henley et al.,
"Robbing Elementary Students of Their Childhood: The Perils of
No Child Left Behind," *Education* 128, no. 1 (2007): 56–63.

259 **"remarkably successful in finding employment"** P. Gray,
*Free to Learn: Why Unleashing the Instinct to Play Will Make Our
Children Happier, More Self-Reliant, and Better Students for Life*
(New York: Basic Books, 2013), 93; and P. Gray and D. Chanoff,
"Democratic Schooling: What Happens to Young People Who
Have Charge of Their Own Education?," *American Journal of
Education* 94, no. 2 (1986): 182–213.

259 **Peter's research found that kids** G. Riley and P. Gray,
"Grown Unschoolers' Experiences with Higher Education
and Employment: Report II on a Survey of 75 Unschooled
Adults," *Other Education* 4, no. 2 (2015): 33–53; M. F. Cogan,
"Exploring Academic Outcomes of Homeschooled Students,"
Journal of College Admission, no. 208 (2010): 18–25; and G. W.

Gloeckner and P. Jones, "Reflections on a Decade of Changes in Homeschooling," *Peabody Journal of Education* 88, no. 3 (2013): 309–23.

259 **He studied the evidence that's been gathered about children in hunter-gatherer societies** P. Gray, "Play as a Foundation for Hunter-Gatherer Social Existence," *American Journal of Play* 1, no. 4 (2009): 476–522; P. Gray, "The Value of a Play-Filled Childhood in Development of the Hunter-Gatherer Individual," in *Evolution, Early Experience and Human Development: From Research to Practice and Policy,* ed. D. Narvaez et al. (New York: Oxford University Press, 2012).

260 **To understand why, he says, we should look at the evidence for what happens when animals are deprived of play** P. Gray, "Evolutionary Functions of Play: Practice, Resilience, Innovation, and Cooperation," in *The Cambridge Handbook of Play: Developmental and Disciplinary Perspectives,* ed. P. K. Smith and J. Roopnarine (Cambridge, U.K.: Cambridge University Press, 2019), 84–102.

260 **It turned out the rats who had been allowed to play** D. Einon, M. J. Morgan, and C. C. Kibbler, "Brief Periods of Socialization and Later Behavior in the Rat," *Developmental Psychobiology* 11, no. 3 (1978): 213–25.

CONCLUSION: ATTENTION REBELLION

281 **"biological Armageddon"** L. Albeck-Ripka, "Koala Mittens and Baby Bottles: Saving Australia's Animals After Fires," *New York Times,* January 7, 2020. For more cautious estimates, see, for example, "Australia's Fires Killed or Harmed Three Billion Animals," BBC News, July 28, 2020.

282 **"I used to think there were no great political struggles left"** J. Williams, *Stand out of Our Light* (Cambridge, U.K.: Cambridge University Press, 2018), xii.

Index

JOHANN HARI is a British writer who has authored two *New York Times* bestselling books, which have been translated into thirty-seven languages and praised by a broad range of people, from Oprah Winfrey to Noam Chomsky, from Elton John to Naomi Klein.

His first book, *Chasing the Scream: The First and Last Days of the War on Drugs,* was adapted into the Oscar-nominated film *The United States vs. Billie Holiday*—on which Hari served as executive producer—and a separate eight-part documentary series narrated by Samuel L. Jackson, entitled *The Fix.*

His second book, *Lost Connections: Uncovering the Real Causes of Depression—and the Unexpected Solutions* was described by the *British Journal of General Practice* as "one of the most important texts of recent years," and shortlisted for an award by the British Medical Association.

Hari's TED Talks "Everything You Think You Know About Addiction Is Wrong" and "This Could Be Why You Are Depressed or Anxious" have been viewed more than 75 million times.

He has written over the past decade for some of the world's leading newspapers and magazines, including the *New York Times,* the *Los Angeles Times,* the *Guardian,* the *Spectator, Le Monde diplomatique,* the *Age* (Melbourne), and *Politico.* He has appeared on NPR's *All Things Considered,* HBO's *Real Time with Bill Maher, The Joe Rogan Experience,* the BBC's *Question Time,* and many other popular shows.

Hari was born in Glasgow, Scotland, and when he was a year old, his family moved to London, where he grew up. His father—a Swiss immigrant—was a bus driver, and his Scottish mother was a nurse and later worked in shelters for survivors of domestic violence. He studied social and political science at King's College, Cambridge, and graduated with a double first.

Hari was twice named National Newspaper Journalist of the Year by Amnesty International. He has also been named Cultural Commentator of the Year and Environmental Commentator of the Year at the Comment Awards.

He lives half the year in London and spends half the year traveling to research his books.

johannhari.com
Twitter: @johannhari101
Instagram: @johann.hari
facebook.com/JohannHari.Page

ABOUT THE TYPE

This book was set in Fairfield, the first typeface from the hand of the distinguished American artist and engraver Rudolph Ruzicka (1883–1978). Ruzicka was born in Bohemia (in the present-day Czech Republic) and came to America in 1894. He set up his own shop, devoted to wood engraving and printing, in New York in 1913 after a varied career working as a wood engraver, in photoengraving and banknote printing plants, and as an art director and freelance artist. He designed and illustrated many books, and was the creator of a considerable list of individual prints—wood engravings, line engravings on copper, and aquatints.

ALSO AVAILABLE FROM
BESTSELLING AUTHOR
JOHANN HARI

A radical new approach
to understanding—and
combatting—depression

"I am utterly convinced that the more
people who read this book, the better
off the world will be."
—NAOMI KLEIN

What if everything you thought
you knew about addiction was
wrong? A searing exposé of the
hidden truth about the War on
Drugs

**THE BOOK THAT INSPIRED THE FEATURE
FILM *THE UNITED STATES VS. BILLIE
HOLIDAY***

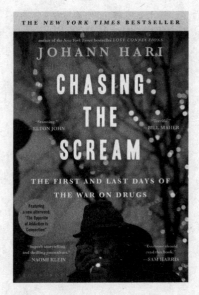